Zero-Sum Game

Zero-Sum Game

THE RISE OF THE WORLD'S LARGEST DERIVATIVES EXCHANGE

ERIKA S. OLSON

WILEY

John Wiley & Sons, Inc.

Published by John Wiley & Sons, Inc., Hoboken, New Jersey.

Published simultaneously in Canada.

For general information on our other products and services or for technical support, please contact our Customer Care Department within the United States at (800) 762-2974, outside the United States at (317) 572-3993 or fax (317) 572-4002.

Wiley also publishes its books in a variety of electronic formats. Some content that appears in print may not be available in electronic books. For more information about Wiley products, visit our web site at www.wiley.com.

Library of Congress Cataloging-in-Publication Data:

Olson, Erika S.
    Zero-sum game: the rise of the world's largest derivatives exchange/ Erika S. Olson.
        p.   cm.
    Includes index.
    ISBN 978-0-470-62420-3 (cloth); ISBN 978-0-470-93704-4 (ebk);
    ISBN 978-0-470-93706-8 (ebk); ISBN 978-0-470-93707-5 (ebk)
        1. CME Group. 2.   Derivative securities—United States.   I. Title.
    HG6046.047 2010
    332.64'273—dc22
                                                                    2010032272

Printed in the United States of America

10 9 8 7 6 5 4 3 2 1

For my husband, Dustin Weinberger

Contents

Preface

On the afternoon of October 6, 2006, in a conference room on the sixth floor of 141 W. Jackson, the Chicago Board of Trade's senior management team awaited CEO Bernie Dan's arrival. No one knew why we'd been brought together on such short notice. Once Bernie joined us, however, he wasted no time revealing the reason behind all the secrecy: Our crosstown rival, the Chicago Mercantile Exchange, had made an $8 billion offer for our company. Eleven days later, the firms would publicly announce their plans to form "CME Group"—a behemoth positioned to control 85 percent of the exchange-traded derivatives market in the United States.

I was one of only a few integration team members who had previous merger experience; I'd already been through three acquisitions by that point. Consequently, I knew that the fusion of two companies into one was a process rarely short on drama. Since Board of Trade and Merc employees, members, and traders had despised each other for over a century, I figured their attempt to combine forces would be particularly tumultuous. But I never could have foreseen the level of mayhem that would ensue between October 6 and the close of the deal nine months later.

Nor could I have anticipated how the general public—with help from the media—would come to consider *derivatives* a dirty word in the wake of the country's 2008 and 2009 economic meltdown. And I certainly never could have guessed how the very subjects of this book—CME Group and one of its fiercest competitors, IntercontinentalExchange—would find themselves at the center of the most profound financial regulation reform since the Great Depression.

When President Barack Obama signed the Dodd-Frank bill into law on July 21, 2010, one thing became abundantly clear: Capitol Hill approves of the way futures exchanges do business. The new legislation is poised to force a good percentage of the unwieldy and largely unregulated $615 trillion over-the-counter derivatives market—controlled almost exclusively by Wall Street banks—onto exchanges or through clearing houses in the coming years. The story you're about to read proves why that's probably a good thing.

When I set out to write this book, however, the financial crisis had not yet transpired, and futures exchanges had therefore not been identified as potential saviors. Back in 2006, my motivation for taking notes, saving articles, and sharing what I observed and learned during my year in the derivatives industry was twofold: (1) the multibillion-dollar bidding war that erupted between the Chicago Mercantile Exchange and IntercontinentalExchange for control of the Chicago Board of Trade was simply an incredible tale that needed to be told, and (2) I realized the realm of futures exchanges was sorely misunderstood, even by those in the broader financial services industry. Futures exchanges help provide price stability for goods and services people use day in and day out—cereal, cookies, cheeseburgers, electricity, fuel . . . the list goes on and on. They affect the lives of consumers across the globe much more directly than do any of the well-known banks, yet few understand how futures exchanges operate. That's most likely because until very recently, these companies were private, member-run institutions that didn't have much need or desire to explain their business to the outside world; in fact, they fought to remain a mysterious niche of the financial services industry for as long as they could.

If futures exchanges are enigmas to most people, then futures trading proves exponentially more confusing. Futures trading is a zero-sum game—for every winner, there must be a loser. It's not even remotely comparable to stock trading, but unfortunately the critical differences between the two are usually not explained in the news. In the equities market, there are a limited number of Company X shares. When lots of bids come in for Company X shares, the share price rises, and everyone holding Company X stock makes money (on paper). Futures contracts function nothing like this, and in the pages that follow, I'll describe how and why these instruments are used.

Even though I've been out of the industry for three years, I still find myself cringing every time I hear a so-called expert spouting the evils of speculation, or claiming that money flowing into commodities trading is the reason that prices of various products are increasing. These reports may provide great sound bites, succeed in riling up viewers, and embolden politicians to point fingers and make threats, but they leave out crucial information and fail to address the less sexy details of how futures markets work. I want to set the record straight through the story of the stranger-than-fiction battle for the Chicago Board of Trade.

ERIKA S. OLSON
September 2010

Cast of Characters

(Listed in alphabetical order by first name)

Chicago Board of Trade/CBOT
(Pronounced C.B.O.T. or See-Bot)

Bernie Dan, president and CEO

Bob Ray, senior vice president of business development

Bryan Durkin, chief operating officer

C.C. Odom II, board member

Charles "Chuck" Farra, director of international business development

Charlie Carey, chairman

Chris Malo, executive vice president of business development and marketing

Daniel "Grombacher" Grombacher, financial products economist

Dave Lehman, head of agricultural research and development, chief economist

David "Rod Stewart" Mitchell, marketing analyst

Franco Campione, manager of web site development

Fred Sturm, financial products economist

Gene Mueller, head of financial instrument research and development

Janella Kaczanko, human resources director

Julie Winkler, vice president of research and product development

Keith Rice, marketing analyst

Kevin O'Hara, chief strategy and administrative officer

Maria Gemskie, managing director of communications

Ted Doukas, director of education

Tom Hammond, managing director of trading operations
Tom McCabe, vice president of operations and quality assurance
William M. Farrow III, executive vice president of technology

Chicago Mercantile Exchange/The Merc/CME (Pronounced C.M.E.)

Anita Liskey, director of corporate branding and public relations
Chris Mead, director of product marketing
Craig Donohue, CEO
Leo Melamed, chairman emeritus
Phupinder "Gill" Gill, president and chief operating officer
Terry Duffy, chairman

IntercontinentalExchange/ICE

Chuck Vice, president and chief operating officer
David Goone, senior vice president and chief strategic officer
Jeff Sprecher, chairman and CEO
Kelly Loeffler, vice president of corporate communications and investor relations

Morgan Stanley (ICE's Banking Team)

Chris Lown, vice president in investment banking division
James von Moltke, managing director in financial institutions group, principal relationship manager
Steve Munger, co-chairman of mergers and acquisitions

Other Players

Bill Brodsky, CEO of Chicago Board Options Exchange (CBOE)
John Lothian, founder of the *John Lothian Newsletter* and broker at Price Futures Group
Will Vicars, joint chief investment officer of Caledonia Investments Pty Limited

There is no better, more interesting feud than the Hatfields and the McCoys. Our personal version is the CME and the Chicago Board of Trade. I think the merger of these two exchanges is destined to be a success. In my opinion, maybe someday they'll look at their struggles to make this merger happen and laugh.

—Rick Santelli, on-air editor, CNBC;
excerpted from *My Word Is My Bond:*
Voices from Inside the Chicago Board of Trade,
by Arlene Michlin Bronstein

Chapter 1

Welcome to the Jungle

July 11, 2006

"The floor" is a marvel of chaos, and one of very few places in this world that truly must be seen to be believed, especially at 1:14 P.M. every weekday. When the clock hits 1:14, an ear-piercing bell rings to remind everyone that only 60 seconds remain before the floor closes and all trading must stop. The bell sounds . . . a split-second passes . . . and then all hell breaks loose. What was already a loud buzz of traders shouting bids and offers at each other escalates into a deafening roar. The throbbing sea of colored jackets transforms into a pressure cooker of sporadic explosions—bodies jump, arms flail, hands frantically clap and wave, and every once in a while, a fist flies. Time seems suspended as brows bead with sweat, elbows jostle for position, and mouths open even wider in the final throes of trading ecstasy. And then suddenly— as quickly as it had begun—the mayhem ends. Shredded trading cards launch toward the sky as unfortunate souls pack up and try to convince themselves they'll do better tomorrow. Those who were successful might flash a quick smile as they head out, but otherwise their faces reveal no sign of what they just went through, except for perhaps a faint red glow.

I looked down at it all with awe. I had never laid eyes on a trading floor before—unless you count the scene from *Ferris Bueller's Day Off* where Ferris and Sloane contemplated marriage as Cameron mimicked traders not too far from where I now stood. For the first five years I lived in Chicago, I had neglected to visit the rowdiest 92,000 square feet in the city. For the next five years, however, I couldn't have seen the floor even if I tried. After the September 11 attacks, security was beefed up and the pits had been closed off to the public.

It was only because I was in the building for an interview that I got to witness the craziness in person. Merely watching the process from behind a glass window on the executive floor exhausted me, but I was hooked. I had to get this job.

The job in question was the managing director of marketing at the Chicago Board of Trade (also known as CBOT, sometimes pronounced "see bot"), the world's oldest futures and options exchange. If I succeeded in securing the role, I'd be leaving the financial powerhouse of JPMorgan Chase, where I'd spent the past three years after earning my MBA at Harvard Business School.

Preparation for my first meeting with Chris Malo, executive vice president of business development and marketing, had occupied the majority of my time for days. I had studied textbooks that explained futures markets, exchanges, and derivatives. I had subscribed to a daily industry newsletter compiled by John Lothian (a broker for Price Futures Group) and developed a list of questions based on the latest headlines. I had read annual reports, analysts' evaluations, magazine articles, message boards—anything I could find about the industry.

Moments into the interview, however, it became evident that those efforts might not have been enough. While Chris prefaced our meeting by saying that he was "probably the second-nicest, if not *the* nicest guy" at the exchange, he had perfected the art of the poker face. If I cracked a joke, there was no response. If I made what I thought was an insightful comment . . . nothing. While he was unfailingly polite, he stared straight ahead with no expression when he answered questions. His face was still friendly despite its lack of animation, though, and he had a thick head of wavy dark hair that complemented his tanned skin. He could have easily passed for a leading man from Hollywood's heyday— striking, fit, and impeccably dressed, although not quite as tall as the other men who passed by on the executive floor. I guessed him to be in his mid-forties, but I learned later that he had recently turned 50.

His office was spacious, probably 250 square feet. All of the furniture and cabinets were a rich, dark wood. There was a flat-screen TV tuned to CNBC on one of his two substantial desks, and framed pictures of his wife and college-age children were plentiful. Overall, he seemed organized—only one small pile of papers was visible in a tray beside his phone.

As my interview progressed, I attempted to show him that I was up on industry news by mentioning some of the things I'd read in Lothian's newsletter. I figured this would impress him, but my plan totally backfired. He could barely restrain himself from jumping out of his chair as he snapped, "You've been reading *Lothian*?"

Unbeknownst to me, John Lothian was one of just a handful of people in the world who could make my future boss's blood boil. Sensing that I was in dangerous territory, I changed tactics and posed what I considered to be a humorous question about CBOT's main competitor, the Chicago Mercantile Exchange, known colloquially as CME or "the Merc."

"So, is the Merc going to buy this place, or what?" I asked.

Chris finally broke out in a smile and chuckled. "There has certainly been speculation about that, but those rumors have been around for years—decades, even. I can't promise you that the Board of Trade isn't going to get bought out by *some* company, but quite frankly, I don't think we'd ever join up with the Merc." He seemed genuine. I would later learn that he really could not fathom a merger with CME at the time of my interview. This was probably because a year and a half prior, Bernie Dan, CBOT's CEO, had lured Chris away from Cargill Investor Services—where they'd worked together in the 1980s and 1990s—to help the exchange with its IPO and hone its business development and marketing operations. If anything, Chris, Bernie, and the rest of CBOT's executive team were probably hoping to get the exchange in position to make an acquisition—not be acquired.

Eventually, I ran out of questions. Chris and I shook hands, he made some parting comments, and as I headed back toward the elevators, I took one last look down at the trading floor. It was completely deserted.

July 20, 2006

I returned to CBOT's celebrated Art Deco building at the end of the LaSalle Street corridor nine days later to meet with the three senior managers who reported to Chris and would consequently be my peers, should I get the position. When I arrived at the reception desk, however, I learned that Bob Ray, senior vice president of business development, would have to reschedule as his mother had passed away.

My interviews with Julie Winkler, vice president of product development, and Maria Gemskie, managing director of communications, were still on. Julie headed the group of economists who created new futures contracts for the exchange; Maria's team trumpeted the success of those contracts to anyone who would listen.

A contract (also referred to as an exchange *product*) is not much more than a set of specifications pertaining to something that can be traded. For example, one Wheat contract represents 5,000 bushels of a designated type of soft red winter wheat. The twist—and the reason why futures contracts are called *futures* in the first place—is that the buyers and sellers of contracts agree to complete the physical exchange of goods in the future (on one of many predesignated dates), even though they're locking in their prices today.

Who would be interested in such an arrangement? Farmers and food manufacturers are two of the most obvious answers. Kraft Foods, for example, will have to continue buying wheat three months, six months, and a year from now in order to keep up with the ongoing demand for products like Wheat Thins, Ritz Crackers, Oreos, and Macaroni & Cheese. Grocery shoppers expect the prices of those goods to stay pretty much the same, week in and week out, and will find substitutes if things get too expensive. Therefore, Kraft wants to make sure it's always monitoring how much it costs to produce its most popular items. The company is motivated to lock in a price for wheat today so that it can manage the risk of wheat prices skyrocketing because of a freakish drought that might occur a few months from now. So Kraft has a brokerage firm buy Wheat futures on its behalf, and makes sure the settlement dates are spread out so the business is covered for a long time.

What about the wheat farmer? He likes this arrangement, too, because while Kraft is worried about the price of wheat going up over the next six months, the farmer is worried about it going down. What if the weather is perfect, resulting in bumper crops across the major soft red winter wheat–producing states? Such an event could result in an oversupply, and he'd be groveling to unload his product on the cheap. Unless, of course, he offsets a potential drop in the price he'll eventually get for his crop by selling futures contracts through a broker and locking in a price today.

Farmers and food manufacturers represent *hedgers*—parties who have a vested interest in a certain type of commodity and would therefore be adversely affected should the price of that commodity swing wildly. They use futures contracts to limit their exposure to price movements and even out business costs and revenues so that the prices for their end products, which line grocery store shelves across the world, remain relatively stable as well.

Then there are *speculators*. Speculators are people and firms who don't have any intention of ever actually producing or owning the products they're trading—they simply think they know which way prices will move, so they buy and sell various contracts accordingly and profit if their guesses turn out to be correct. Speculators have been around as long as futures markets have been around, and they play the critical role of providing liquidity in the market. If a farmer is looking to sell contracts at a certain price but there are no other hedgers who want to buy, chances are a speculator will be on hand, happy to take the other side of that trade.

Julie's team was responsible for providing both hedgers and speculators several moneymaking—and money-preserving—opportunities each year in the form of new future contracts. The economists she managed also regularly made subtle changes to products that had already launched. Julie had worked at the exchange since graduating college and knew almost everything there was to know about how CBOT operated. The executives asked for her opinion constantly, but it didn't seem to go to her head; she had a reputation for modesty, keeping to herself, and being extremely fair when called upon to settle disputes. Therefore, although Julie was only 32 years old, she was one of the most respected people in the company.

As our interview commenced, it became immediately clear that Julie was all business, all the time. Her sterile surroundings, run-of-the-mill black suit, translucent skin, and no-nonsense, pixie haircut couldn't have led to any other conclusion. Wilted tulips drooped in a vase on her desk, heightening the dreary atmosphere of her office, which was void of any personal effects and could have certainly been mistaken for a storage room.

She kicked off our meeting with several questions about the client research engagements I had spearheaded throughout my career. Her questions were direct and she had a formal air about her. It was as if she had taken a lesson from Chris; her expression remained blank no matter what I said. Finally, a homework assignment I'd given past focus group attendees piqued her interest. Her eyebrows arched as I described sending Polaroid cameras to research participants and instructing them to shoot pictures that captured their typical workday so that I could get a sense of how they interacted with various products and services.

A shocked expression crossed her face so suddenly that I snapped my mouth shut and looked over my shoulder in alarm. When she saw how I'd misinterpreted her look she quickly explained, "It's just that I would *never* give a Polaroid camera to any of our traders. The pictures we'd get back would be very, *very* disturbing."

I burst out laughing, probably louder and harder than I should have, but from that point on our talk was much more relaxed. When Julie saw that our hour together had ended, however, her serious demeanor returned and she offered me a stiff handshake goodbye.

Next was my talk with Maria. She'd been at the exchange for seven years and previously worked in Washington, D.C., as a congressman's communications director, so she was adept at handling all of the politics that ran rampant in both the company and the futures industry.

Born and raised on the northwest side of Chicago, Maria was the epitome of Midwestern friendliness. However, she looked like she'd just jetted in from California: long, straight blond hair accentuated her sun-kissed face. Demonstrating her comfort in sky-high heels and a designer suit that was perfectly tailored to her athletic frame, she wheeled her chair across the room and positioned it next to me after I entered her office. "It seems too formal when I sit over there," she proclaimed, waving her hand dismissively toward her usual spot behind a majestic wooden desk.

Maria's lavish, sizable office was the opposite of Julie's. It was decorated with pictures and memorabilia from trips around the world, all of which seemed to be for industry-related events. A full-size couch, several framed works of art, a TV tuned to CNBC, a variety of plants, and a multitude of boxes from Ann Taylor lined the perimeter of the room. There was no doubt that she was an absolute workaholic and essentially lived in her office on the sixth floor of CBOT's 141 W. Jackson building, in the heart of Chicago's Loop.

At the end of our meeting she asked suspiciously, "So, why do you want this job?" I later found out that the management team was shocked that not one, but two Harvard MBAs were jockeying for the marketing position. CBOT had been a publicly traded firm for less than a year, and its executives were struggling to break the company out of its "member-run" (read: old, white guys) stereotype. It was not a place that normally attracted recent business school graduates. I rattled off a list of serious reasons why I was interested in the exchange, and ended by saying that I also simply thought the Chicago Board of Trade seemed like a pretty cool place to work.

She beamed. "It *is* cool, isn't it?"

I had no idea I was talking to the person who loved the Chicago Board of Trade more than anyone else I would ever meet. In her mind, there were no truer words I could have spoken.

July 24, 2006

Finally, my rescheduled interview with Bob Ray arrived. Bob was tall, in his early fifties, and had a handsome, friendly face with twinkling eyes and a devilish grin that betrayed the fact he was constantly thinking up his next politically incorrect joke. He could have been actor Bill Murray's better-looking, higher-spirited brother. It was instantly obvious to me that Bob was always the life of the party—his sharp suit couldn't hide the fact that he emanated energy.

We met in his office, which was close to Julie's on the tenth floor, but about four times the size. Half of the room seemed to be set up for small group meetings—there was a circular table with four chairs surrounding it, in addition to two padded leather chairs across from Bob's desk. His personal space took up the far side of the room; he perched on a wheeled Aeron chair situated in the cradle of a large U-shaped desk. In that area also sat a small television—tuned to CNBC, of course—and on top of it was a strange glowing ball that signaled whether the stock market was up or down (and doubled as a funky decoration). A gigantic whiteboard displaying a rainbow of scribblings dominated one side of the room; the wall opposite the whiteboard showcased expansive windows, though the view they provided of a neighboring building was utterly unspectacular. A vodka bottle with handcuffs draped over its neck sat proudly on display near the window ledge, pictures of Bob in humorous poses at landmarks around the world hung on the wall behind his desk—Bob donning an oversized mouton ushanka in Red Square, Bob sporting his CBOT cap in front of Tiananmen Gate in the Forbidden City, Bob lunging at a Godzilla statue in Tokyo, and so on—and teetering stacks of magazines and papers were absolutely everywhere else.

At the beginning of our interview, I offered my condolences about his mother's passing, and he responded by launching into a few stories about his relatives. He was from a large Irish Catholic family, and quipped that it was always chaotic when they all came together, even under the recent circumstances. He went out of his way to make light of the situation, and I got the distinct feeling he had a tendency to do that in any situation.

After the obligatory small talk, he excitedly began to share his thoughts on how to promote both the exchange and its products. His voice was raspy and breathless as he explained that by and large, any person or company who wanted to trade futures at CBOT needed to enter their orders through a *futures commission merchant* (FCM), such as brokerage firms ADM Investor Services or MF Global, that had registered with the industry's main regulator, the Commodity Futures Trading Commission (CFTC). This was because even though CBOT created contracts and collected fees on each trade, it did not directly solicit orders from end customers. Therefore, the exchange's marketing strategy was to heavily publicize its contracts and constantly barrage the industry with press releases, in the hopes of influencing an end customer to take a new position in a contract or inspiring a current account to trade even more. The exchange also supplied its product materials—such as white papers, in-depth brochures, and contract specification sheets—to the various middlemen in the industry so that they could do the selling on CBOT's behalf. Bob's business development managers hoped their regular meetings with FCMs and end customers would result in a trading volume increase for the exchange. They were hungry for whiz-bang marketing materials so that they'd have something new to discuss on their rounds.

Next, Bob shared some of the unique tactics he had thought up—and was quite proud of—to battle rival exchange Eurex when it launched a direct attack on CBOT's U.S. Treasury futures business in 2004. A boycott of German beer somehow played a part in this nasty feud with the Frankfurt-based competitor. I had no idea what he was talking about.

It only got worse. He moved on to waxing poetic about "the bid-ask spread" and how the Germans had failed miserably in their attempt to steal market share from CBOT. Even though I couldn't follow what he was saying, I didn't have the heart to interrupt him—he was clearly having a ball reliving the firm's glorious triumph over its European enemy.

It turned out that I wasn't called upon to talk for the rest of the interview, anyway. When I did pipe in with a comment, Bob's attention went elsewhere. He would glance back at CNBC to catch the latest headlines or at his computer monitor to scan for new e-mails until I was done. He wasn't being rude, he just had extreme ADD. His tirade about things I didn't understand continued, and he talked faster and faster and got more and more animated—arms flying, fists pounding—as I desperately tried to catch terms that I vaguely recognized.

All of a sudden he stopped his rant mid-sentence.

"Hey, have you met Rod Stewart?"

Uh-oh. I must have *really* been misinterpreting the conversation. Before I had the chance to answer, he recanted, "No, I just call him that. The guy who looks like a young Rod Stewart with the funky hair, have you met him?"

I told him I hadn't yet been introduced to the person in question.

"Oh. Well, he and that other kid just walked by and looked in here. Probably trying to check out their potential new boss. I just realized I'm not sure I know their real names, for the love of Christ! HA!" He erupted into a hearty laugh and pounded his fist on the desk once more; he was the human version of the drummer Animal from *The Muppet Show*, but with more nicely groomed hair.

As quickly as he had stopped his earlier diatribe, he switched back into business mode, and that's when he saw our hour was up. Before I even left his office he was on to the next thing, whirling around in his chair to listen to all of the voice mails that must have accumulated— his phone had rung almost nonstop while we talked. It seemed unlikely he would remember my name if I came back.

■ ■ ■

By the end of that same day, I had an offer. Things moved much more quickly at the Board of Trade than they did in my division at JPMorgan. But then again, while my current employer had tens of thousands of employees, CBOT had fewer than 800, and a significant number of those were security guards, trading floor staff, or information technology operations resources. The entire strategic business team was quite small—probably fewer than 30 people—and managing directors at CBOT were only "two down" from the CEO, in the jargon of my co-workers at the bank.

I called Chris to accept the offer, and we set September 1 as my start date.

August 1, 2006

One month before I made 141 W. Jackson my second home, the team at CBOT celebrated a huge milestone: They finally launched side-by-side trading of their agricultural ("ag") contracts. This was the closest thing to a miracle that would ever happen at the exchange.

Side-by-side trading allowed clients to choose how they wanted their trades executed—either on the trading floor (often referred to as *open outcry*) or electronically (on the exchange's e-cbot platform).

Before going side-by-side, agricultural contracts could be traded via both methods, but at different, nonoverlapping hours. Meaning, prior to August 1, if Kraft needed to buy Wheat futures at 10:00 in the morning, its only option was to have a floor broker put in a bid on its behalf. If the urge to take a position in the agricultural market struck Kraft's risk management team after the floor closed, however, their only choice was to get their broker to enter the order on e-cbot. Each method had its pros and cons, along with its own fee structures. Trading online was much more desirable to the growing overseas client base (among other market participants) who didn't have a presence on the physical trading floor, yet wanted to bid on the ag markets around the clock.

What made the side-by-side launch of agricultural contracts historic, though, was that it signaled CBOT was taking its last step out of the dark ages to embrace electronic trading at the potential expense of open outcry and the floor traders. Many of the firm's board directors were (or had once been) traders in the agricultural pits, and almost all of CBOT's most influential members were ag traders. A *member* is a person or company that has complied with the exchange's membership requirements in order to have access to the trading floor and be eligible to trade certain products—and, most importantly, receive fee discounts. There were different types and levels of membership, which—for pit traders—were differentiated by specific jacket-badge colors. A *full* individual member, for example, had a yellow badge, could trade all of CBOT's products, and enjoyed the lowest possible fees in return for holding a certain amount of the exchange's stock and buying the most expensive type of *seat* (also called *trading rights*). With few exceptions, all financial exchanges—from the New York Stock Exchange to NASDAQ to the London Stock Exchange to CBOT and CME—offered memberships. Further, most exchanges listed the present value of their seats and allowed those seats to be leased, bought, sold, gifted, or transferred between family members.

It probably goes without saying that CBOT's members were powerful. Not only did their seats translate into Class B shares in the exchange—which granted special voting privileges and other benefits—but they also controlled about 80 percent of the publicly traded Class A shares following CBOT's 2005 IPO. The common stereotype of CBOT's members was that a good number of them were territorial and greedy, and showed little respect or compassion for the exchange's employees.

The members would be greatly affected by side-by-side trading, as many feared that launching agricultural trading online during the day—thereby ending the pits' order-execution monopoly—signaled the beginning of the end for the trading floor. And that's where generations of members had made their fortunes for decades. Interestingly, side-by-side trading already existed for most other types of futures contracts at the exchange (such as Treasury Notes and Federal Funds, among others). The agricultural markets were the only holdout, solely because most members earned their living in the pits, trading those specific contracts.

Why would the members ever allow the board of directors to bless the launch of side-by-side trading for Corn, Wheat, and Soybean futures, then? Perhaps it was getting too embarrassing to continue ignoring market trends. What the slow-to-change contingent of members lacked in business sense they made up for in pride, and they couldn't stand to be humiliated. The Chicago Mercantile Exchange, CBOT's nemesis since 1898, had surpassed CBOT to become the largest futures and options exchange in the country in 2001, mostly because its members embraced electronic trading earlier. This *killed* everyone at CBOT, because they despised CME. They despised CME with a passion that only more than 100 years of deep-seated institutional hatred could fuel. If CBOT's board of directors wanted the company's stock to rise, and if they wanted the value of their membership seats to increase, and if they wanted to hush the whispers that the company couldn't break free of its old-school reputation, and if—more than anything else—they wanted their counterparts at the Merc to stop laughing at them, they had no choice but to approve side-by-side agricultural trading. The fact was that electronic trading already constituted nearly 65 percent of total transaction volume at CBOT in 2005. It was eight months into 2006, and the pressure was on to move that percentage even higher.

Hence, the historic decision was made to step into the twenty-first century and launch side-by-side trading on August 1, 2006, for the Chicago Board of Trade's agricultural contracts.

September 1, 2006

Right before Labor Day weekend I finally began my tenure at CBOT and met the employees on my team: David Mitchell (a.k.a. "Rod Stewart") and Keith Rice, two 24-year-olds who had grown up together in Evergreen Park, a suburb 20 miles south of Chicago. Keith was uncontroversial in every sense of the word. He spoke quietly, dressed plainly, and kept an extremely low profile. David was a different story.

"It's fuckin' ridiculous, the things they ask us to do," he complained during our first meeting, as he ran his hands through his frosted, heavily styled hair. The short, two-toned clumps shooting out in all directions around his head were impossible to ignore, even if he hadn't kept playing with them. In addition to the funky hair, he had funky clothes: a pink-and-white vertically striped dress shirt, a purple-and-blue diagonally striped tie, and slim-fitting pinstriped gray pants. Somehow, it all worked for him. The nickname Bob had bestowed upon David was well deserved; he looked as though at any moment he might burst out wailing, "Young hearts, be freeeee, tonight!"

"Seriously, it's like they think we're fucking secretaries," he continued, explaining that in the months between my predecessor's departure and my arrival, Bob's team had taken advantage of him and Keith and had been relying on them to do all sorts of menial and tedious tasks.

His anger was justified, but I still found his tirade surprising. While most people are aware that those in the trading world tend to favor colorful language, it is difficult for an outsider to fathom exactly *how much* swearing goes on. It was not just the traders who cursed openly; the majority of the businesspeople working for the exchange talked the exact same way. In my last job, I knew of only one guy who had dared drop the f-bomb while on a conference call, and he became instantly infamous around his division because of it. At CBOT, however, the trading culture permeated everything, and there was no better example of this than young, dapper David swearing up a storm the first time he met me, his new boss.

I would have to worry about David's rant later, though, because my employee orientation—including a tour of the trading floor—loomed.

I wouldn't be looking down at the pits from the visitors' gallery, I would be right in the center of the chaos.

■ ■ ■

I had never experienced anything like the rush I felt while standing in the middle of CBOT's trading floor. It's hard to be surrounded by throngs of red-faced men screaming and yelling and gesticulating at each other wildly and scrawling things down and looking at their handheld devices and taking slips from runners and then starting the cycle over and over and over again and not get caught up in it . . . or marvel at how anyone knows what in the hell they're doing. The scene can only be described as complete mayhem—on the agricultural side of the floor, that is.

The Chicago Board of Trade's two trading areas, the agricultural floor and the financial floor, were located next to each other and traders could walk freely between them. It was impossible not to notice, however, that the adjacent floors had completely different vibes. On the agricultural side, waves of men (and a few women) in colored or patterned jackets pulsated rhythmically below a gigantic screen that beamed The Weather Channel, as split-second trading decisions were required upon any news of floods, droughts, extreme temperatures, or otherwise devastating acts of God. Bordering the weather screen were enormous electronic boards that spanned the perimeter of the room and displayed dozens of neon red and yellow columns of trading data. The agricultural floor appeared to be where all the action was, but that's probably because it was about half the size of the financial floor and consequently had to cram more people into less space. Its ceiling was lower by nearly 20 feet, too, which only served to make the room seem that much more compact and claustrophobic.

The financial floor, by contrast, was massive; the orientation tour guide said that a 747 could fit within its bounds. Unfortunately, online trading of financial futures took off shortly after this addition to the building was completed in 1997, so fewer and fewer traders were turning up in person to execute their orders. Our guide couldn't conceal his sadness as he recalled the days when this side of the cavernous structure was bustling with activity. Now it just seemed empty, even though a mammoth screen still broadcast CNBC overhead and certain pits remained busy. Each type of contract had a dedicated pit—an octagon-shaped area with a depressed center and steps running the length of each side that enabled a great number of traders (sometimes hundreds) to stand opposite each other and shout out bids and offers. There was a wheat pit, a soybean pit, a bond pit, and so on.

The new-hire orientation turned out to be quite interesting, even though it was hard not to be distracted by the activity surrounding our small group as we moved across the trading floor. Once our guide had led us to a relatively quiet area, he spent a few moments giving us the background of the 31-foot-high, 6,500-pound, brushed-aluminum statue positioned at the very top of the building. It was Ceres, the Roman goddess of agriculture. She had no face, and according to Chicago lore that was because back in 1930 when the building was constructed, her designer, John Storr, figured no nearby structure would ever be high enough from which to see his creation up close. At that time, 141 W. Jackson was 45 stories high and therefore the tallest building in the city. Oops. At least it was certain Ceres wasn't going anywhere—the CBOT building had been designated a National Historic Landmark in 1978. Since then it had also become a part of cinematic history, serving as a dramatic backdrop in movies such as *The Untouchables* and *Road to Perdition*. More recently it had been transformed into the headquarters for Wayne Enterprises in the 2005 film *Batman Begins*.

Next, the guide explained how the exchange served as a matchmaker of sorts for traders, and how it made much of its revenue by collecting a small fee on every trade. Judging from the wild ruckus on the ag side of the floor, CBOT was raking it in on that day.

The lecture was over, and our group was on the move again. I became acutely aware of the eyes that were staring at me intensely from every direction. The floor wasn't exactly a welcoming place for women. I'd been ogled by traders simply coming in and out of the building for my interviews months prior, but on the floor it was exponentially worse. If you were female and even remotely attractive, you would be the subject of not-so-discreet pointing, gawking, and maybe even a wink or two. Guys in their twenties and thirties nudged their friends to turn around and judge the latest round of women on the tour. They had no shame. At least the older fellows showed some dignity.

The orientation session came to an end right outside the always-active bond pit. As the group began to disperse, a hulking figure stopped his flurry of hand motions and whirled around to face us.

"HEEYYYYY!"

Some of the youngest new employees turned ashen.

"WHY DON'T YOU FUCKIN' FEED US ANIMALS?! YOU CAME TO STARE AT US, SO FEED US! WE LIKE PEANUTS! ANY OF YOU GOT ANY FUCKING PEANUTS?!"

He nearly doubled over with laughter as he stepped back into the pit, where he was met with howls and slaps on the back. Our very proper tour guide shook his head like a parent is prone to do when a child has done something naughty (but still kind of cute).

"They *are* quite a bunch of characters, aren't they? Welcome to the Chicago Board of Trade!"

Chapter 2

Into the Groove

Early September 2006

The tenth floor of 141 W. Jackson was, as Chris put it, "busting out at the seams." Piles of boxes were everywhere; old computer monitors and outdated CBOT brochures found their final resting places under counters or on top of shelves; and printers, fax machines, and copiers were pushed into any space that would hold them. Most salespeople and economists were forced to share so-called cube farms—small rectangular areas where four or five people worked with their backs to each other. A cubicle in a windowless corner at the end of the hallway, across from David and next to Keith, was the only spot left for me.

I'd been attempting to ignore the surrounding chatter and make my way through a list of department heads Chris wanted me to set up meetings with so that I could learn about the different operational and functional areas of the exchange. I was about to pick up the phone again when a voice behind me began, "Um, hello . . . I don't mean to interrupt . . . but I saw Chris taking you around the floor a few days ago and didn't get the pleasure of making your acquaintance."

Three feet away stood a man who had seemingly materialized out of thin air. Sharply pointed cowboy boots stuck out from beneath

17

his black, faded jeans. His red-and-white vertically striped shirt was partially hidden by a black vest. A bolo tie was kept in place around his neck by a Navajo-inspired metallic clasp, and a black cowboy hat topped off the whole unconventional ensemble. "Nice to meet you, I'm Dan Grombacher," he said while shooting a hand in my direction. However, before our handshake was even over, he started laughing and said, "No, of course I'm not Grombacher, I'm Fred Sturm."

Whoever he was, he must have noticed my smile drop and a look of extreme confusion cloud my face, because he quickly continued, "I'm sorry. So . . . how are you finding things so far?" As he asked this, he popped off his hat to reveal a bald head. He could have easily passed for R.E.M. frontman Michael Stipe. While I was still trying to figure out whether I should've understood the crack about his identity, he tossed his hat toward a cabinet, sat down in a nearby chair, and proceeded to kick his legs up onto my desk, exposing some seriously shiny spurs around the ankles of his boots. He clasped his hands behind his neck as he waited for my answer.

"Uh, it's great . . . I mean, I've only been here a few days, but it's really interesting so far. Very different from a big bank like JPMorgan—in a good way," I clarified, as he stared at me.

He didn't respond. He just kept staring, like he was sizing me up. It looked as though he might be preparing to say something, so I kept quiet. At least 10 seconds of silence passed. His eyes continued to drill into me and then suddenly shot upward when he finally stated, "This company used to be like the worst government bureaucracy you could ever imagine, crossed with a country club. And don't get me wrong, it's not perfect now—there are still a lot of 'Student body left! Student body right!' orders that come down from on high. But since Bernie took over, things have really turned around." His face rotated toward the ceiling and he held his eyes closed tightly, like he was in pain. Then, eyes still shut, he began massaging his brow with one of his hands. "This place was on its way to being a regional grain exchange. And Bernie really muscled it up, in all the right ways. There wasn't any Potemkin village stuff going on. He built value here, he *made* value."

I hadn't met our CEO yet, so I just nodded. At last, Fred's eyes reopened. "I have a good feeling about you," he declared, turning to face me. As I was still searching for a response, he bid me good night.

Next, he twirled his legs back down to the floor and stood up, dramatically fitted his cowboy hat over his head, and rounded the corner toward the elevator bank.

He vanished as quickly as he'd appeared. David poked his head around his cubicle wall with a big grin on his face, and Keith wore the exact same expression as he wheeled his chair over. "Fred rocks!" David cried.

"I didn't know what to do when he paused for so long—does he always do that?" I asked in a hushed whisper, in case the subject of our conversation chose to pop up again. Keith replied that he had been in meetings where a full minute had gone by while others waited for Fred to answer a question. "But that dude is so smart, seriously," he concluded. "Yeah . . . so are all of the other economists," added David.

Ah, so Fred was an economist. That explained a lot; quirky personalities were the norm in that profession. At CBOT, the economists served a critical function—they created and maintained all of the exchange's contracts. Two groups of economists reported up through Julie: those who focused on financial contracts, and those who worked on agricultural contracts. I understood what a contract was, but had no idea how new ones were dreamed up or what maintaining them involved.

That's probably why Chris suggested I meet with Gene Mueller, head of financial instrument research and development (the group in which Fred worked), as soon as possible. Gene cut an imposing figure—he looked like he belonged in a trading pit throwing elbows rather than behind a desk pushing papers. He usually wore beat-up khakis and a button-down shirt, sported some degree of facial hair on his chin, and always carried a mug of coffee in one hand. His voice was gravelly and rough. I was scared to death to talk to him.

My fear of Gene seemed somewhat unfounded once I saw his young daughter's stick-figure drawings hanging proudly on his office wall. But I still braced myself to be thoroughly confused when he started talking about how the economists did their thing at CBOT. Thankfully, he was unbelievably clear in his explanation of how new contracts were developed, and why. "We're not gonna launch anything that doesn't meet two basic criteria: It's gotta be able to serve a risk management need, and there's gotta be an economic need," he huffed, holding up two fingers of his right hand.

While the Chicago Board of Trade—and the Chicago Mercantile Exchange, for that matter—were both originally established as agricultural futures exchanges, products based on physical commodities like corn or butter had since come to represent only a fraction of revenues. This is because virtually anything that has, or can be assigned, any value whatsoever can be an underlying asset (often simply called *the underlying*) for a futures contract. There are contracts based on agricultural products—corn, wheat, soybeans, butter, sugar—which are what most people outside of the industry associate with futures trading, probably because of the Frozen Concentrated Orange Juice futures made famous in the movie *Trading Places*. Also fairly straightforward and more familiar after the Enron scandal are futures contracts issued on energy sources—crude oil, ethanol, natural gas, and so on. When newspaper headlines bemoan the skyrocketing cost of gas or, alternately, celebrate a drop in prices at the pump, their corresponding articles almost always reference the price of Light Sweet Crude Oil futures traded at the New York Mercantile Exchange, as gasoline is made from crude oil and their prices are inextricably linked.

But the *real* money is in financial futures: contracts based on interest rates, exchange rates, stock index values, and scores of other metrics. As may be obvious, there are many more types of businesses— multinational corporations, hedge funds, mortgage providers, mutual funds, and pension plans, to name a few—that need a buffer against fluctuations in interest rates, currency exchange rates, and the stock market than there are worrying about corn prices. So even though CBOT had started out and was still largely thought of by the public as an agricultural exchange, it collected only 20 percent of its clearing and exchange fee revenues from agricultural contracts in 2006.

Gene explained that because derivatives—the umbrella term for financial instruments like futures and options, which *derive* their values from their underlying assets—could be based on almost anything, the size of the worldwide derivatives market drastically eclipsed that of the global stock market. Securities markets are bound by the number of companies and entities that offer stocks or bonds, whereas derivatives markets are bound only by the imagination. And as I was finding out, people in the derivatives industry were nothing if not creative.

Gene then pulled a piece of paper from one of his desk drawers. "Look at that," he ordered. It was a list; "Date of Paris Hilton's Next Sex Tape" and "Length of Britney Spears' Marriage to Kevin Federline" were two of the items on it. "Those are ideas for binary option contracts," he explained. "Believe it or not, a lot of people would put good money on some of the ideas on there. But guess what? If we launch a binary option based on the length of Britney's marriage, it's not really serving any true economic or risk management need, now is it? It's just betting. We'd be no better than Vegas if we did stuff like that. So we FIRDsters just keep this list of ideas we brainstormed to ourselves."

"Wait a second," I said. "What are FIRDsters? And what are binary options?" I understood futures by this point, and even got the notion of options-on-futures: products that offered the right, but didn't represent an obligation, to purchase a specific futures contract by a certain point in time. However, I hadn't heard of binary options. Gene clarified, "Oh, yeah, sorry. A FIRDster is just what we call anyone in the financial instrument research and development group—I don't know who made it up, but we've been saying it for years." He went on to explain that a binary option, also termed an *exotic* or *all-or-nothing*, was a contract that had only two possible outcomes—either the event it was based on happened or it didn't. CBOT had recently launched Target Fed Funds Rate binary options that were based on interest rate adjustments the Federal Reserve might choose to make at specific intervals throughout the year. When binary options on a rate modification panned out the way an investor predicted, it would earn him $1,000 per option. Otherwise, the trader would bank nothing and be out only the cost of the option, which was always less than $1,000. "They're still essentially bets, but they do fulfill a risk management need for anyone with interest rate exposure—meaning pretty much any business—so, you know, we can justify it."

I asked how the group decided which contracts to launch out of all the ideas they came up with each year. Gene described a process that was not unlike the one product development groups in other industries follow. By talking with clients and keeping abreast of market trends, any given economist might think of a contract idea that, at first blush, seemed to have merit. Alternatively, a board member or a salesperson on Bob's team (or Bob himself) might propose a contract based on client feedback. The sponsoring economist would complete a write-up of the contract idea for internal review and subject it to the "red-face test"—meaning, if someone created a briefing that covered new contract specifications and corresponding target markets and potential trading volume, but was then embarrassed after others on the team took a look at it and gave their opinions, the idea was thrown out. "Do you know the Merc has contracts based on the fuckin' *weather*? Snowfall futures. Jesus Christ. We call 'em Snowflake futures. That idea wouldn't have gotten past red-face around here."

If an idea did pass the red-face test, however, then two economists would partner up and go around the country (and, more often than not, the world) to talk through the product concept with market participants. For example, before launching a futures contract based on the Dow Jones U.S. Real Estate Index—which was in turn based upon real estate investment trust (REIT) prices—members of Gene's team went out and spoke with property managers, REIT managers, and portfolio managers. These groups would want to protect their investments against downturns in the commercial real estate market and might therefore be interested in trading REIT-based futures. Gene called this part of the process the feasibility test. If there was interest in the contract, his team would usually tweak the product's specifications based on feedback they received.

The last step was to hold a meeting with what he called "the SWAT team." This was a cross-functional group of people from the exchange who would listen to a presentation by the economist who had created the contract. There would be a question-and-answer session at the end, and if everyone felt that they had enough information to make a decision, they would hold a go/no-go vote that would determine the contract's fate. And then it would go to the board for final approval.

The difference between the FIRDsters' process and the one most product development teams in other industries follow is that the FIRDsters were able to get things done much more quickly and cheaply. Normally, companies must make large investments in research, prototyping, and pilot launches before being able to offer their customer base a new product or service, whereas Gene's team was scouring established markets and looking for existing types of investments that people and companies might need to hedge. The trading system was already built, and it didn't take long or cost much to add a new product into the mix. Between Julie's two teams of economists, six or seven contracts would be introduced each year, and everyone crossed their fingers that after all of their hard work, at least one of them would resonate with traders.

Gene ended our meeting by repeating once again, "If it's not helping to manage some sort of risk, we're not gonna launch it."

■ ■ ■

Still processing everything Gene had said, I walked down the hall and almost ran into a man I didn't recognize. He was reading something over Keith's shoulder and exclaimed, "Holy Mary Mother of God, look at those chompers. She could open beer bottles with those fuckin' snaggle-teeth." I, too, peered over Keith's shoulder; a picture of actress Kirsten Dunst was the topic of discussion.

The mystery man turned to face me. "Hey. I'm Grombacher."

So *this* was who Fred was pretending to be the prior week. Now I understood the joke, kind of. He and Grombacher (I never heard anyone call him by his first name—ever—for the rest of my time at the exchange) couldn't have been more different. While Grombacher was also one of the FIRDsters, he was shorter and stockier than Fred, on top of being a much more conservative dresser. A thick head of strawberry blond hair made him look younger than he probably was, which I guessed to be between 39 and 42. I introduced myself and told him I'd been meaning to set up a time for he and I to talk. He replied in a rushed voice that accompanied a cocksure attitude. "Yeah, well, I'm gonna be in Asia for at least the next two weeks. The Japanese have been accumulating U.S. dollars like fuckin' rock stars for 20 years now, so they're all over our rate products. It'll be a while before I'm here again. Don't miss me too much, guys," he shot back at David and Keith as he sauntered away.

■ ■ ■

Back at my desk, I had barely sat down when the phone rang. It was the executive assistant for Bernie Dan, CEO of the exchange. "Bernie wants to finally meet you. Can you come down to six?" she asked.

"Do you mean right now?" I responded, starting to panic. "Yeah, if you're free, just come stop by."

In the elevator down to the executive floor, I recalled what the communications team had passed along to me about our CEO. They said Bernie prided himself on always being the first person to arrive at the office each day and was hypercompetitive—he even wanted our press releases to hit the wire before the Merc's. As Fred had alluded to, the majority of employees credited him with getting the exchange through the dark days leading up to its IPO, when the outside world thought CBOT was on its last legs.

Born in Oak Park, Illinois, at the end of 1960, Bernie formed his insatiable appetite for working hard—and making money—early. His father, the director of labor relations for a furniture company, was always able to put food on the table and clothes on the backs of his seven kids (Bernie was sixth to arrive), but the family "never did anything" and "didn't have a color TV like everybody else." So at the ripe age of nine, Bernie started helping his ten-years-older brother Michael with a job that involved venturing into bars in Chicago's roughest neighborhoods to refill cigarette and candy dispensers and retrieve coins from the machines in the process. They had attack-trained, unleashed German shepherds on either side of them as they made their rounds. Each night, Bernie would receive a small take of Michael's earnings, and from that point on, he "always wanted cash in his pocket." He found a way to fit multiple moneymaking gigs around his school schedule, and worked as much as he could every summer throughout his preteen and teenage years.

Bernie's father lost his job during Bernie's freshman year at Fenwick, a private Catholic high school, and wasn't sure how much longer he'd be able to afford his son's $1,500 tuition. This dire situation only motivated Bernie to work more—he slaved away at Parky's Hot Dogs from 3 to 11 P.M., five days a week. He was 15 years old and peeling 50 pounds of onions per shift, or spicing potatoes for the stand's famous french fries. He repainted the small restaurant inside and out, blacktopped its parking lot, and volunteered to do anything he could think of in order to work extra hours. His efforts paid off. He netted $4,000 that year—more than enough to cover his tuition and buy himself his first car, a used 1969 Delta 88.

It was a good thing Bernie continued his education at Fenwick, because he met his future wife, Jody, through a Blackfriars Guild (drama club) collaboration with Trinity High, an all-girls Catholic prep school. They both played courtroom reporters in a production of *You Can't Take It with You*. Bernie was smitten, and used some of his hard-earned cash to treat her to a dinner date. Little did she know it was the first time in his life he'd ever gone out to eat ". . . unless you count McDonald's." Even though Jody was one of eight kids, her family was well off. Her parents belonged to country clubs and had a house Bernie compared to a museum. He took it all in and made up his mind that he wanted to live like that one day.

After graduating from Fenwick, he traveled to Collegeville, Minnesota, to attend St. John's University. St. John's was home to the largest Benedictine monastery in the country, and as Bernie worked on his degree, he took a job in the refectory washing dishes in the mornings—in addition to stacking books at a book store in the evenings and selling rings for Jostens during big events like Homecoming and Parents' Weekend. He'd often tell classmates his future goal was "to pay more in taxes than most people make." They thought he was joking, but he wasn't. At the time of his graduation in 1983, however, the unemployment rate hovered around 10 percent, and Bernie had no delusions of grandeur. He'd pursued a bachelor of science degree in accounting solely because he figured it would arm him with a solid skill that could eventually lead to a job—which it did.

The newly created National Futures Association, which would serve as the futures industry's self-regulatory organization, was looking to hire its first class of auditors that year. Bernie landed one of the spots. After 18 months he moved on to a tax firm, but his heart wasn't in the accounting and control world. He began actively looking for something different, and in early 1985 joined brokerage firm Cargill Investor Services (CIS), which just so happened to be one of CBOT's largest customers. His boss? Chris Malo. A year later, Bernie jumped at the chance to go abroad after a co-worker turned down the opportunity. He was 26 years old, had been married for only five months, and suddenly found himself moving overseas and responsible for operations in the growing CIS London office, just when Prime Minister Margaret

Thatcher's "Big Bang" deregulation program went into effect for the United Kingdom's financial markets.

By 1988 Bernie was back in Chicago, but not for long. His next assignment was on the East Coast, where he was charged with "fixing" the New York office. He ended up staying there seven years until an even bigger opportunity came his way: opening the CIS Singapore office and spearheading the firm's efforts to become a member of the Singapore International Monetary Exchange (SIMEX). By this time he and Jody were raising four children, and they actually had to wait until their youngest turned six weeks old before they could head to Asia.

As fate would have it, while Bernie and his brood were in the air, rogue trader Nick Leeson was writing his infamous "I'm Sorry" note after realizing he'd blown up Barings Bank by making enormous speculative trades on SIMEX and other Asian exchanges. Leeson was fleeing Singapore just as the Dans were touching down. Cargill had sent a messenger to meet them as they disembarked. Bernie thought, "What could've happened in the last 20 hours?" as he was forced to leave Jody and the kids at a hotel and fly immediately to Japan. It turned out that Cargill had capital invested with Barings in Tokyo, and it was now Bernie's task to not only make sure his firm got its money back, but also determine whether they should still move forward with a SIMEX membership, in light of the unfolding Leeson fiasco.

Thanks to the Barings collapse and the beginnings of the Asian currency crisis, Bernie's role as the director of CIS Singapore turned into a much higher-profile position than he could have ever imagined. His track record had not escaped the firm's executive management team, and so in 1998, a year after he returned to the States, they chose him to succeed the retiring president and CEO. At 38, Bernie was at least a decade younger than the other managers in the running. He figured he landed the top spot because he "outworked everyone." He believed the other contenders were "way smarter . . . but effort was the big equalizer" that tipped the scales his way.

Once Bernie took over as CEO of CIS, he started volunteering on committees at the Board of Trade, since Cargill's two membership seats were always held in its chief executive's name. In 1999, CBOT's members were throwing around the idea of demutualizing—that is, transforming the member-owned exchange into a shareholder-owned company in order to eventually go public. But in 2000, when the Merc hired hotshot investment banker James McNulty away from Warburg Dillon Read to serve as president and CEO and oversee the exchange's demutualization and subsequent IPO, CBOT's directors knew they had no choice but to get moving. Bernie was asked to serve on the CEO search committee, which ended up finding an equally impressive leader: respected Chicago businessman David Vitale, a Harvard- and University of Chicago–educated executive who'd recently retired from a 30-year career at First Chicago NBD/Bank One. Though Bernie thought David was "smart off the charts," he recommended the board hire a strong "number two" from within the exchange world. To his surprise, six months later the board decided he was the best guy for the job. Bernie felt he'd gone as far as he could at CIS and was up for a new challenge, so in July 2001 he accepted the role as CBOT's executive vice president, overseeing everything at the exchange outside of the technology and audit divisions.

David knew the Board of Trade was in dire shape; it had been bleeding cash for over three years. The exchange lacked corporate discipline and needed a complete technology overhaul. So he brought in a fellow First Chicago alum, William M. Farrow III, as CBOT's executive vice president of technology. Prior to joining the exchange, William was the senior vice president of Bank One's e-business division and had earned a reputation—as well as a Smithsonian Award—for his innovative approaches to technological quandaries. William and Bernie worked with an outside consulting firm to complete an exhaustive assessment of the exchange's current state, and then created a business strategy and technology road map that would help turn the company around.

William and Bernie's plan enabled CBOT to make a remarkable comeback, and paved the way for its demutualization and IPO in 2005. The vision they'd laid out was still driving the company's strategy by the time I hired on. David Vitale's tenure as CEO, however, ended after 20 months. Conflict between the members and David was inevitable— he had always been viewed as an outsider and therefore a threat to the status quo. Things came to a head when the exchange's relationship with Eurex, the Frankfurt-based firm that powered CBOT's electronic trading platform and was consequently connected to all of its customers, turned fractious. David intended to pull the plug on the Eurex partnership, but CBOT had no plan B for its trading platform. Bernie grew concerned about the repercussions of such a bold move, and encouraged some of the company's directors to intervene. They did: The tenuous Eurex contract was left intact, David resigned, and Bernie assumed the role of CEO in November 2002.

■ ■ ■

The door to Bernie's large office was open, and he looked up from his laptop as I waited to be acknowledged. "Come on in!" He waved his hand and I took a seat across from him at his massive desk. Even though he was sitting down, I could tell he was a tall guy. He had short, reddish-brown hair, and a large smile that lightened his otherwise serious demeanor. While there were a few more TVs around than I had seen in other offices, and his space was clean and orderly. Pictures of his kids sat on a nearby bookshelf, but otherwise no personal effects were in view. "I'm sorry I didn't get to meet you earlier, I've been traveling," he apologized.

We proceeded to talk about everything from the history of the exchange to my previous job. He was extremely easy to have a conversation with, and liked to point out that he was "just an Irish kid from the West Side" who didn't have "a bunch of fancy degrees." He asked if I'd ever met Jamie Dimon, the notoriously hard-driving CEO of the firm I'd just left. I answered that I had, in fact, met Mr. Dimon. Three weeks after I'd joined Bank One (which later became JPMorgan Chase) in the summer of 2003, I had a short introductory meeting with him. He'd also gone to Harvard Business School, and asked me what I learned there. A response came out of my mouth before I really had time to think about it: "I learned that the people who talk the most are the biggest bullshitters." Jamie had laughed and agreed, "You know, I've got all these people e-mailing me and calling me every day, and they send me presentations and charts and graphs and all this stuff just so that they stay on my radar, and half of it is something I already read in the *Wall Street Journal* that morning. It's like, 'Tell me something I don't know. If you can't tell me something I don't know, shut up.'"

Bernie grinned and said that he, too, had met the man many considered to be one of the financial industry's sharpest minds. A few months prior, Dimon had hosted a dinner at his home in the Gold Coast—one of the city's most exclusive neighborhoods—for a subset of Chicago's business leaders. Henry Kissinger was the guest of honor and had signed a book for Bernie's mom that night. "I think she was more proud of me for meeting Kissinger than anything else I've ever done!" he exclaimed.

As we wrapped up our conversation, I asked if it would be okay for me to schedule a meeting with industry-newsletter-creator John Lothian in order to learn more about the exchange world. Chris, who had demonstrated he wasn't a big fan of Lothian's during my interview, had told me it was fine to reach out to him as long as I cleared it with Bernie first. "Sure, I don't care," Bernie said, seeming vaguely agitated. "But when you talk to him, can you try and figure out what he *is* exactly? I mean, is he a reporter, a blogger, a journalist, or what? I've told his people I will meet with him when he has something intelligent to say. So far it hasn't happened."

I thanked Bernie for taking the time to talk with me and headed back to the tenth floor, more curious than ever to find out what in the hell Lothian had done to make otherwise even-keeled men grow annoyed at the mere mention of his name.

Chapter 3

This Is How We Do It

Mid- to Late September 2006

"How ya doin', kid?" Bob shouted as I sat down across from him in his office. He kept talking as he swept papers into multiple piles on his desk. "Did you hear I had to get a bunch of fucking shots for my trip? I'm dreading it. All of us poor slobs going over there are going to get totally sick and puke our guts out, I know it."

People were constantly traveling for the exchange; Bob was heading to India with some of the economists, and Chris had already left on a three-week trip to Asia. Before he took off, Bob wanted to get me up to speed on his most prized contracts: CBOT's Precious Metals. In October 2004, CBOT launched Gold and Silver futures on its electronic trading platform, and ever since, Bob had been shouting the glory of these products to anyone who would listen. What was absolutely fascinating about "the metals story," as Bob termed it, would not be immediately apparent to those outside of the trading industry—it took me a few months to fully understand what the big deal was. In short, CBOT had broken the gentleman's agreement that existed between exchanges; in launching the metals complex, it had gone directly after another firm's contracts.

Metals had been traded via open outcry at the Commodity Exchange (COMEX) for decades, and became the territory of the New York Mercantile Exchange (NYMEX) in 1994 after the two companies merged. NYMEX members were so protective of their metals contracts that they refused to let them be traded electronically during the day—just as CBOT members had resisted allowing their cherished ag contracts to go side-by-side. Unlike CBOT members, however, NYMEX stalwarts didn't show any signs of budging.

Bob had played a big role in convincing CBOT's board to seize the opportunity to steal market share from NYMEX by launching Gold and Silver futures on the e-cbot platform. This move would require major cojones, because each type of futures contract is typically viewed as a monopoly of sorts; any given product only had one exchange it called home. If you wanted to trade corn, you're going through CBOT. If you wanted to trade cattle, the Merc's the place for you. Coffee was the domain of the New York Board of Trade (NYBOT), and so on. Unlike stocks, which can be bought on one exchange and sold on another, futures have to be bought and sold through the same institution, per exchange rules backed by federal law. Duplicate contracts rarely existed because no one thought it made sense to split a pool of bids and offers across more than one exchange. As the saying went among traders, "Liquidity attracts liquidity." Once a product was well established at a certain exchange, the story was over. *Similar* contracts existed across exchanges, however. For example, CBOT and CME both offered stock index futures, but CBOT's were based on the Dow Jones Industrial Average, whereas CME's were tied to the S&P 500.

CBOT's metals contracts were scandalous because they were almost exact replicas of NYMEX's Gold and Silver products—meaning, the underlying specifications were virtually identical. Metals traders would be in the rare position of having a choice between two exchanges that offered the same product. All that differed was the trade-execution method.

As Bob saw it, if NYMEX's board thought there wasn't a daytime electronic market for Gold and Silver futures, they shouldn't take offense to CBOT's move. Indeed, when asked about CBOT's apparent challenge to NYMEX's contracts, a NYMEX spokesperson stated, "We are not believers in side-by-side trading."

Within 14 months, however, CBOT had captured 15 percent of the Gold futures market. By the time I arrived at the exchange, that figure was nearing 50 percent, and Bob was absolutely beside himself with glee. Maria's team was cranking out multiple press releases per week, each touting some sort of new record that the metals contracts had broken. It wasn't discernible whether CBOT was actually stealing business from NYMEX; completely new traders might have entered the market, attracted by the ability to trade metals online during peak hours. CBOT may have simply grown the pie, as the saying goes. Bob didn't care why the trades were coming in—he was just utterly and completely obsessed with metals. Or perhaps for him it was really about beating NYMEX. He was definitely not one to shy away from a fight, as evidenced by his retelling of the battle against Eurex during my interview. Incidentally, Eurex was one of the only other exchanges to directly challenge an existing product when it targeted CBOT's Treasury contracts in early 2004, after CBOT finally ended the CBOT/ Eurex trading-platform partnership. But the German exchange had failed to establish a liquid market and eventually threw in the towel.

"I tell ya, the metals success can all be attributed to marketing," Bob beamed as he fondly recalled two years of ever-rising volumes. As he was prone to do, Bob had exaggerated just a tad. While the hard-hitting ads he'd created surely helped in some way, the success of the metals complex might have had more to do with the fact that CBOT had waived trading fees, enlisted the help of market makers to build liquidity, and, most importantly, offered the contracts electronically. NYMEX's CEO, James Newsome, had sorely underestimated the pent-up demand for electronic trading. When CBOT launched its competing contracts, Newsome made this somewhat naïve statement: "We are confident that the metals industry and trading community will continue to support our marketplace as the world's preeminent precious metals trading arena." Was he joking? The vast majority of traders cared about making as much money and paying as few fees as possible, and that's it. There was no loyalty.

Bob explained that for CBOT to win more market share in metals, it must continue to build open interest. While volume figures reflected the number of contracts that changed hands during a trading session, open interest revealed the number of contracts that hadn't expired or been fulfilled by delivery by the end of each day. In other words, the open interest level represented the number of outstanding contracts that would be closed out or settled at some point in the future. If open interest was growing, it meant more traders were entering the market for that product. Traders like to be where other traders are, so CBOT secured market makers for many of its contracts in order to boost volume, liquidity, and open interest. Market makers were usually brokerage firms for whom CBOT would waive fees in return for a commitment to put in both buy and sell orders. This arrangement ensured that anyone who wanted to trade would have his bid or offer met, within a logical price range. The hope was that volume would beget more volume, and then eventually the market-maker agreements would no longer be needed to encourage trading for that specific contract.

The higher the trading volume for metals, the smaller the *bid-ask spread*: the difference between the current buying price (bid) and selling price (ask or offer). If the bid for one Gold contract is $1,000 and the ask is $1,001, then the bid-ask spread is $1. An increasing number of bids and offers leads to a tight price range because—thanks to price displays both in the pits and online—everyone can see the details of the past several trades. This is what the industry calls *price transparency*. Yet unlike the price of a unique vase several bidders might fight over on eBay, a commodity contract's price is not driven higher simply because more traders enter the market. There is not a limited supply of Gold contracts. Whenever a buyer and seller agree on the future price of 100 troy ounces of gold, another Gold contract comes into existence. Higher trading volumes and open interest levels help the bid-ask spread to narrow, allowing market participants to zero in on the true value of a contract's underlying asset. This is a process the exchanges termed *price discovery*.

Bob wanted to launch a new set of metals advertisements to highlight the continuing success of the contract, and he was throwing out god-awful slogans left and right for me to consider. I told him we could reconvene to go over his ideas when he returned from India in early October. "*If* I return, you mean. If I die over there, then it was nice working with you," he said soberly.

■ ■ ■

In the second half of September, I finally got around to e-mailing John Lothian of the *John Lothian Newsletter* to see if he'd be willing to meet for lunch and help me learn more about the industry. His initial response explained that CBOT's management team had put him in "the virtual freezer" for the past several months, so he wasn't sure if speaking with him would be a help or a hindrance to me. When I assured him I'd cleared my request with Chris and Bernie, he wrote back again and indicated that because of his current "dysfunctional relationship" with CBOT, he would have to politely decline my invitation to meet so that I wouldn't get caught in the middle. *Very strange,* I thought.

So Lothian was out, but I still had other people within the exchange I needed to meet. I turned my attention to the agricultural group. Dave Lehman headed up the team of economists who managed the commodity-based contracts that were synonymous with the CBOT brand around the globe. Like Gene, he also reported to Julie. In the 1970s, Dave had worked on a large corporate farm in Iowa before moving east to pursue a master's in agricultural economics at the University of Maryland. While studying for a course that covered futures and options, Dave realized there was a career path that connected his farming background with his new degree. When he finished graduate school, he worked for three years in the Chicago office of the CFTC before joining CBOT in 1989. An impossibly nice guy who truly loved his job, Dave became somewhat of a celebrity in 2005 when almost all of the major news outlets interviewed him in the aftermath of Hurricane Katrina. He'd been asked to explain how flooding at the Port of New Orleans affected the delivery of several critical grains, such as corn, wheat, and soybeans, which are typically transported down the Mississippi River to the Big Easy from various points in the Midwest. The media loved him because he was handsome, well spoken, and personable. His hair was gray, but he had a youthful face and enjoyed going to rock concerts—during our first meeting, we discovered we both had tickets to an upcoming Eric Clapton show at the United Center.

Dave shared that the past few months had been particularly exciting for his team. "There's been a quicker transition to electronic trading than we expected after ags went side-by-side in August," he remarked. "That, combined with the large investments pension funds and hedge funds are making in commodities, has been a challenge to keep up with. The mix of our product users is changing drastically."

We then discussed the promise of the Ethanol contract that had launched in March 2005. "Biofuels are going to test our core products— Corn and Soybeans—which I'm sure is going to have contract maintenance implications," he speculated. I had yet to fully comprehend what "maintaining" contracts consisted of, so Dave explained that once any given futures contract launched, the economists followed its trading activity closely to see if the market was responding—if volume and open interest were growing. They would also monitor whether position limits or price limits were being hit, and check to see if prices in the cash market ended up converging with futures prices. For my benefit, he went through each maintenance concept separately.

As I'd already learned, volume and open interest showed whether the market was embracing the contract—the more trades completed and the more that were still outstanding, the better. I began to understand there was nothing worse for an economist than to see his contract wither on the vine once it launched. Similar to when a new television sitcom premieres, if a contract doesn't generate a lot of fans it's at risk of being pulled. Futures executives are more patient than studio heads, however; usually a new product has at least one year to prove its worth.

Another aspect of contract maintenance involved monitoring position and price limits. These limits were restrictions on the number of contracts any one person or entity could hold, and the amount a contract's price could fluctuate within one day, respectively. While the economists were aware when position or price limits were hit for any given contract, CBOT's Office of Investigations and Audits was the department responsible for closely reviewing trading data and keeping an eye out for suspicious trends. As the derivatives exchange industry is largely self-regulated, most exchanges dedicated an entire division to policing traders and handing out fines for bad behavior.

Position limits were instituted through the 1936 Commodity Exchange Act for a subset of agricultural contracts. The exchanges took it upon themselves to set position limits for other contracts as well, since these limits were necessary to prevent someone from cornering the market for a particular good. Limits for Corn futures, for example, were 600 contracts in the settlement month (the month the corn would be delivered if the trader didn't unwind his position first), 13,500 contracts in any other single month, and 22,000 contracts total across all months.

What most people outside of the industry didn't understand, and what the financial media often neglected to mention when running stories about the evils of speculation, was that position limits went a long way toward preventing market manipulation. This is because the limits are derived from estimates of physical supply levels for each commodity. If somebody had several thousand Corn positions set to expire in December 2006, the exchange would've instructed that trader to take his holdings down to 600 contracts by the time the delivery month arrived. Six hundred contracts represented 3 million bushels—just a fraction of the more than 10 billion bushels of corn produced in the United States each year. No single entity or individual could ever hoard enough corn through the purchase of Corn futures to affect the country's corn supply and in turn move the market price. There were exceptions to the position limit rules, but only for hedgers who could prove they needed to buy or sell a higher number of futures contracts in order to offset the risk inherent in a similarly sized transaction in the cash market.

It was easy to forget that market participants use futures to either hedge or speculate on price movements—not to actually buy or sell the underlying goods. In fact, only 2 percent of futures contracts based on commodities ever make it to their expiration dates and go through the delivery process. But the threat of delivery is necessary to ensure that prices of futures contracts end up converging with their cash market equivalents. Without the possibility of delivery, which leads to convergent prices, futures contracts would not serve as tools for price discovery and risk management.

The rationale behind position limits made sense to me. The need for price limits, however, wasn't immediately clear. "How can exchanges claim they provide a forum for price discovery if they restrict how much something like the price of a bushel of wheat can go up or down?" I asked. Dave began by clarifying that price limits were not rules that dictated overall price floors or ceilings for certain products. Rather, price limits were simply restrictions on how much the price of a contract could vary *within one day*. Only a select subset of ag contracts had price limits, and their purpose was to allow a cooling-off period whenever a high level of uncertainty existed in the markets. The Chernobyl nuclear power plant disaster in 1986 was such an example—no one knew how the catastrophe would end up affecting the world's supply of certain commodities. Once a contract hit one of its daily price limit levels, trading was suspended until the following day.

Because it was especially confusing, Dave skimmed over the last major aspect of contract maintenance: monitoring price convergence. "So let's take a really simple scenario. Let's say you bought one Wheat contract with an expiration in December 2006 for six dollars per bushel. If the markets are working correctly, then when December rolls around, the price you paid for your contract should be very close to the price you'd pay if you were to buy the same amount of wheat directly from a farmer, in what we call the cash or 'spot' market, that same month. Rarely, prices won't converge, and then we'll attempt to figure out why and make changes to the contract specifications if need be."

After my talks with both Gene and Dave, I had a whole new respect for the economists on Julie's team. However, I didn't envy the process they had to go through to create and then look after CBOT's contracts.

■ ■ ■

By the end of September, I had held introductory meetings with over 40 fellow employees. But I hadn't been able to catch Tom Hammond, our managing director of trading operations. He was one of those guys whose fun-loving personality and penchant for practical jokes might tempt people to write him off as a goofball . . . before they came to realize he was among a handful of people on the planet who understood exchange clearing operations inside and out.

One afternoon, I was at the copy machine outside of Bob's office when Tom walked by. His face looked sunburned; his thin, light-blond hair puffed out from all sides of his head; and his suit jacket remained unbuttoned to accommodate his belly. "So I know you've been trying to set up some time to meet with me," he acknowledged as he slowed his pace but kept walking down the hall. "Any chance you're free at 4:30 today?" I told him that time worked for me. "Great! Let's meet at the satellite office," he suggested as he continued on his way. "You know what? Make it 4:00 instead!" he grinned.

At 3:45 I set off to find him. Since I'd never heard about the other office location, I hoped I could catch him so that we could walk over together. As it turned out, Tom was already coming to find me, and we met once again in the hall near Bob's office.

"Oh, good. I didn't know where the satellite office was," I began.

"Nobody's taken you there yet? Are you kidding me? You've been here *a full month* and no one's shown you the satellite office?" he exclaimed, his face growing even more flushed. "We just go down ten floors and walk north about a hundred and fifty feet and it's right there. Let's go."

As we started toward the elevators, Bob sprang out of his office like a ninja and blocked our way.

"Uh-uh, Tom," he said sternly.

"What's going on?" I asked.

"The 'satellite office' is Ceres, Erika," Bob said, making quotation marks with his fingers. "You know, Ceres . . . the *bar* in the lobby?"

I felt like a total idiot.

"Oh, Jesus, Bob, why'd you have to ruin the surprise? We'll be fine. Come on," he said to me, and we were off. I glanced back at Bob as I rounded the corner; he was still standing there, shaking his head at us.

My mind started whirring as we rode down to the lobby. Was Tom the resident pervert or something?

Chicago was still holding out on the smoking ban that other large cities had put into effect, so as Tom and I made our way to the back room of the restaurant that doubled as a lounge, the air became thick with the smell of cigars and cigarettes. The crowded bar area, which was rumored to have once held the country's record for "most alcohol served per square foot," was packed.

Tom directed me to a darkly lit corner booth, which convinced me that I was indeed about to be hit on. "So here's the rule," he said in a serious tone as we settled in across from each other. "Anything but beer." I had been planning to get a beer, of course. "Okay, that's fine," I bluffed as the waitress approached. "Can I get a vodka and cranberry?" He ordered a Jack and Coke and the waitress disappeared into the thick haze. Within two minutes, our drinks were in front of us.

"I am seriously embarrassed and ashamed that no one has taken you to this most wonderful of satellite offices before now," he said with a wide smile as he raised his cocktail. "Welcome to the Chicago Board of Trade!" We clinked our glasses together and I took several large gulps, desperate to prove that I could hang with the guys. He glanced away as I nearly choked; when I caught my breath, I stared in bewilderment at my drink. The room was too poorly lit to be able to tell for sure, but my cocktail looked like it was perfectly transparent. As in, there was no color to it whatsoever. Tom was chatting away about his kids while grabbing handfuls of popcorn from a small basket the waitress had brought along with our drinks. Whatever concerns I had about him were long gone—he was engrossed in recounting soccer victories and seemingly oblivious to my inner turmoil. My new worry was that I wouldn't even be able to finish my first drink. If I didn't, I knew I would be the laughingstock of the exchange.

Only 10 minutes had passed when Tom signaled for and received his second Jack and Coke. A string of expletives flew through my mind. I was nearing the halfway mark on my drink, and getting there had been pure torture. Tom stopped talking and nodded at the small can of cranberry juice the waitress had left next to my glass. I picked it up and realized it hadn't even been opened. I looked back at Tom, but he had fallen over on his side of the booth, convulsing with laughter.

When he came up for air, tears were running down his cheeks. "Oh my god. That was the best. God bless ya," he cried as he wiped his face with the cuffs of his jacket. "Jesus Christ, you're a trouper."

"So you were aware I've been drinking straight vodka that tastes like shit?"

His face was neon pink and he was nodding his head, still reeling. He reached his hand across the table for me to shake. "Now you have been *officially* welcomed to the Chicago Board of Trade."

Early October 2006

Only Bernie and a few other executives knew that the first four business days of October would be the last four days of normalcy at the Chicago Board of Trade. Things were eerily quiet; people were either traveling or keeping to themselves at their desks as another harsh winter crept closer. Chris had become somewhat of a phantom boss—he was in his third week of visiting customers and partners in Asia and we rarely caught each other on the phone. In Chris's absence, Ted Doukas, CBOT's head of education, did everything he could to help me become fully functional. Hour after hour, day after day, he'd look at me with sympathetic brown eyes set beneath thick eyebrows on a strong, Greek face and explain industry jargon, technical terms, and company acronyms.

By my fifth week on the job, Ted could finally spend some time showing me what his own position entailed. Just as the exchange was perpetually sending out press releases and monitoring the actions of its competitors, it was also sponsoring presentations, courses, and seminars for both pit and electronic traders, as well as the brave souls who were thinking of entering the field. Ted managed these efforts, and could therefore be involved with anything from talking to large groups of foreign businessmen about the functions of the exchange and arranging floor tours for them with one of Bob's salespeople, to booking psychologists to speak with traders about the dangers of emotional decision making, to hosting professors from top universities who'd lecture about variables to consider when analyzing a specific market's volatility, to putting together trading simulations for industry conferences. Further, whenever the exchange launched a new contract, Ted would coordinate informational presentations with members of Julie's team, as well as handle the distribution of marketing material and signage on the trading floor.

As his job revolved around communicating to traders, Ted was always doling out fascinating insights like, "A real trader never, *ever* talks about how much money he's made, but he'll cry to anyone who will listen if he loses so much as a penny." He'd also seen some unbelievable things go down in the pits. On October 2, as he and I stood at the top of the ramp that led down to the agricultural floor and watched two men—inches from each other's face—start shouting as loud as was humanly possible, I felt compelled to ask if he'd ever witnessed anyone getting particularly rough.

"Oh, yeah," he replied, looking sideways at me, surprised I'd even posed the question. "A bunch of times. I've seen countless bouts of pushing and shoving, which sometimes results in a wave of movement across the pit—traders falling back on each other like dominos."

The heated exchange Ted and I observed ended with the men stomping off in different directions. We also turned away from the floor and headed toward the escalator so that Ted could begin setting up an afternoon trading seminar. But before I left him to his preparations, I told him I had to hear about the most ridiculous thing he'd ever seen go down during his time at the exchange. "I've got *two* good ones for you. I wasn't here for either of them; they're just legendary fights everyone knows about," he began. "One happened in the Treasury pit in the 1990s. Two guys started going at it; one of them totally lost his temper, and next thing you know, he chomped on the other guy's nose. There was blood streaming down both of their faces and they just kept trading. But the guy who did the biting was eventually brought before the disciplinary committee." I stared at Ted in disbelief.

"The other involved two guys who got into a fight, and somehow—I don't know if he was kicked or pushed down the steps into the pit or what—one of them ended up splayed out horizontally on the floor with a broken leg. This was right around closing time, so everyone just left him there and order-runners kept jumping over him until the final bell sounded. Apparently he didn't even try to get up because he knew no one was going to help him until business was done for the day. Talk about brutal. But sure enough, once the closing bell went off, someone got him to his feet and he was taken to the staff medic."

It was all so . . . barbaric. But the cold, hard truth was that everyone who visited the floor secretly hoped for something crazy to transpire in front of them so that they'd have a cool story to tell their friends.

Ted and I parted ways when the escalator brought us to the area that was still referred to as the Visitor Center, even though it had been closed to unannounced guests since the September 11 terrorist attacks. To satisfy the stream of curious tourists who continually asked the security guards if they could see the trading pits, Maria's team was spearheading the construction of a new, 700 square-foot, high-tech Visitor Center—complete with a floor cam—that would be open to the public and situated in the building's lobby. The original Visitor Center remained a resource for prearranged groups of a certain size. There, guests could look down on the chaos from observation decks, walk through an art and picture gallery, or settle into the theater, where a short video on the history of the company and the evolution of futures trading answered the majority of questions sightseers had been known to ask (and the staff had grown weary of answering over the years).

Nearly all tourists wanted to understand the meaning behind the bizarre signals the traders waved around. After CBOT was founded in the mid-1800s and market participants realized how loud it became when everyone shouted alongside one another in the same room, they created a system of communication known as *arb* (short for *arbitrage*) that supported their cries of bids and offers with arm, hand, and finger movements. If, when held in the air, a trader's palms faced inward, that meant that he was looking to buy. Palms facing outward indicated a seller. There were gestures shared across the floor for each of the 12 months (in order to specify contract delivery dates), quantities, and confirmations of trades, and then there were specific movements associated with individual products and therefore only usable in one pit. Though it looked like a bunch of insane people trying to fly or hitting themselves in the head over and over again, it worked. The walls of the Visitor Center had depictions of the more popular signals so that the activity below on the agricultural floor was remotely comprehensible.

Most sightseers came to CBOT in the hopes of catching a little trading floor excitement, and they might learn a few arb signals for the heck of it while they were there. However, few probably understood the extent to which the activity on the floor, the prices on the electronic boards around the building, and the decisions made by unseen, unheard futures traders at laptops across the globe affected their daily lives. For anyone to truly appreciate the global influence of Chicago's futures markets, a history lesson was required.

Before CBOT came to be in 1848, people gathered in open marketplaces and haggled with each other separately over the future purchase and delivery of corn, grain, hay, and other crop-based products. Inevitably, someone would end up getting a raw deal—either a farmer sold too low or a customer bought too high. They'd be none the wiser, however, unless they compared notes with a friend who'd made a similar transaction.

The Chicago Board of Trade's goal was to level the playing field; with the exchange came the public display of prices for everyone to observe. Sure, those prices might only be scribbled hastily on a chalkboard as the results of each negotiation were announced, but at least Farmer Joe now knew what Farmers Nick and Mike had gotten for their bushels of corn, and Grocer John could rest assured he was getting a fair bargain, too. In 1925, CBOT members founded an independent entity, the Board of Trade Clearing Corporation (BOTCC), to clear customers' trades. The existence of a financially sound clearing house constituted one of the biggest benefits of transacting through an exchange. If Farmer Mike and Grocer John made a deal directly, they'd each have to trust that the other would come through on his side of the agreement. If they conducted business at CBOT instead, that *counterparty credit risk*, as it came to be called, ceased to exist; the clearing house acted as a buyer to every seller and a seller to every buyer. If John fell upon hard times and couldn't pay what he owed, the clearing house would step in and do so.

For taking on the risk of any of its market participants defaulting—and to prevent such a thing from happening in the first place—clearing houses such as BOTCC required a deposit from each of them. This type of deposit is known as a *performance bond*, or *margin*. Exchanges set the margin levels for each contract, and additional margins were sometimes required by the clearing house and broker. The goal was to ensure customers were financially stable enough to trade and—barring wild swings in the markets—would remain viable for the duration of their contract terms. Margin amounts varied by the risk and volatility levels inherent in each product and market, but usually equated to somewhere between 2 and 10 percent of a contract's underlying value.

Fast-forward four decades to 1967: CBOT replaced its chalkboards with electronic boards and achieved drastically faster pricing updates.

In the 1970s, financial futures became available. Eventually, online data displays and Web-based trading came to complement the open outcry system, enabling futures based on everything from beans to bonds to be traded within fractions of a second by investors around the globe. The information age also meant that increasingly more data points were available to track. Traders needed to be constantly up on the news, because weather forecasts, government reports, sales projections, technological breakthroughs, and certain world events might each have an effect on how the market priced a given contract.

Once financial futures hit the scene and electronic trading became widespread, trading volumes at CBOT and its competitor CME skyrocketed. Pretty much every type of business imaginable now employs futures trading as part of its overall investment strategy. Farmers use futures as a type of insurance policy against problems that could adversely affect the prices they'll receive for their crops. Corn, Oat, Wheat, Cattle, Hog, Milk, and Butter contracts (among others) enable food manufacturers to keep the prices of their many mass-consumed products relatively stable. Treasury Note and Bond futures help mortgage companies hedge fluctuations in interest rates so that they can offer competitive financing options to home buyers. Utilities invest in energy contracts so that lower gas and electricity costs can be passed on to the public. Currency-based futures shield multinational companies from shifts in exchange rates. Stock index futures assist businesses in lessening their exposure to swings in the equity market. From pizza to hamburgers, building materials to jewelry, electricity rates to insurance rates—the prices of countless everyday products and services are stabilized by the contracts traded at futures exchanges.

The growth of derivatives exchanges also had an unexpected effect on foreign farmers in the form of *world benchmark pricing*. As CBOT's trading information went online, food producers from India to Brazil to Ukraine to Australia began to look to Chicago (and specifically, the exchange's web site) to understand how the world valued wheat, corn, and other agricultural products and get an idea of where prices might be headed. Even if a farmer's products would never be sold in the United States and his specific type of soybean wasn't the same as the underlying in CBOT's contract, he could use the exchange's current soybean price as a starting point to figure out how much he could expect to be paid locally for his own crops. For farmers in remote locations—or in cities and countries that lacked futures exchanges— CBOT's prices provided critical data points, without which the fair value for their products might be anyone's guess.

The rise of both futures exchanges and electronic trading had far-reaching implications for farmers, corporations, and the average consumer. The more I understood the global influence of CBOT's contracts, the happier I was to have joined the company. But little did I know that as I'd been absorbing everything I could about my new industry over the past month, CBOT's leaders had been holding secret meetings with their sworn enemies and crafting a deal that would throw the fate of everyone at the exchange into question . . . and change the landscape of the financial services industry forever.

Chapter 4

Don't Speak

October 6, 2006

An ominous voice mail message from Chris awaited my arrival at 141 W. Jackson. He sounded especially somber as he requested that I come to his office at noon. I called his extension and he picked up right away. "Is there anything I need to prepare for our meeting?" I asked. "Nope, see you then," he answered hurriedly and hung up.

When noon arrived, I found myself following several other department heads to the executive floor. No one spoke. The group's destination appeared to be one of the large conference rooms in the back hall, but I diverted from their course and popped my head into Chris's office. He told me to rejoin the herd.

Once in the conference room, I took a seat at the far end of its lengthy table. Tension was in the air, but it smacked more of nervous excitement than of dread. Chris eventually arrived and sat immediately to my right, but didn't make eye contact with me or breathe as much as a word. When Bernie strode in, the room fell deathly silent. He didn't say anything to anyone, either. Rather, he looked expectantly at the door. The final two people to enter were Bryan Durkin, our chief operating officer, and Kevin O'Hara, our chief strategy and administrative officer, who took the last open seat in the room—the one to my left.

Bernie was no longer the jovial fellow I'd felt so at ease with a few weeks prior. He was in full-on serious CEO mode. After conferencing in our Washington, D.C., liaison, he cleared his throat and explained that in mid-September, the Chicago Mercantile Exchange had approached CBOT with an offer to buy the company for $8 billion. Since that day, only a small group of executives had been involved in the deal negotiations, but they had now reached a point where they needed to inform a wider group of staff about the possible merger. An overwhelming amount of work had to be done before the date they'd targeted for a public announcement: October 17. "You can all do the math," he said. "We have 11 days."

Amid a smattering of murmurs, quiet gasps, and low whistles, he went on to state that everyone in the room had been selected for the merger planning team because of his or her area of expertise. "Right now, this exact same meeting is going on with your respective counterparts over at CME."

Bernie then turned the discussion over to Kevin, whose mission was to scare the living daylights out of the 30 people staring anxiously at him. Every time the accomplished lawyer opened his mouth, however, he was anything but intimidating. Blindfolded, one might mistake him for Keanu Reeves' brother; he had a surfer-dude drawl so full of inflections it was surprising when he'd fail to bust out a "Whoa!" or "No way!" in any given sentence. He bore no physical resemblance to the Hollywood actor, though. He was simply a guy in his forties with an undergraduate degree from the University of Chicago and a JD from Georgetown. Before joining CBOT in May, Kevin had spent seven years at Archipelago, the all-electronic exchange whose integration with the New York Stock Exchange was finalized at the same time the Big Board went public in early March 2006. He had jumped from one historic merger to another.

"Okay, so I'm about to give you guys what's come to be known as the 'Orange Jumpsuit Speech,'" Kevin began, tilting back to the point of concern in his chair and letting his hands swing casually at his sides. He went on to warn in his singsongy way that it was of utmost importance the deal be kept under wraps until October 17, meaning that we couldn't speak to anyone outside the room about what we would soon be working on. "What I'm saying is, you can't tell your friends, your family, your boyfriend, your girlfriend, your husband, or your wife about this. And don't talk about it among yourselves unless you are behind closed doors. Don't talk about it in the hall, in the restroom, in a cab, or over the phone—*only* in an office or conference room with a door, and only with people from either side of the merger team. If you are overheard saying something and that leads to someone trading on insider information—even if it's not you doing the trading—there are very serious consequences that will befall you personally, as in, going to jail and wearing an orange jumpsuit." He paused briefly and scanned the faces of everyone around the conference table for effect, and then explained all of the ways the authorities would be able to trace the leak, should someone attempt to profit off of the information or derail the deal. Bernie jumped in to reiterate that we better not tell a soul, not even our spouses, and that we had to clear our calendars for the next few weeks. "That goes for weekend plans, too. Forget about them right now."

Kevin ended with an overview of the Hart-Scott-Rodino antitrust act and a list of the types of information we could and could not share once we started working with the CME team. "You'll be e-mailed instructions about when and where you'll meet your counterparts. Oh, and we'll be using code names in all communications: 'Tiger' for CBOT and 'Cheetah' for the Merc." There were a few muffled snickers, and a handful of people rose to leave but then quickly plunked down again when Bernie raised his hand and boomed, "One more thing. One more thing I forgot to mention." Everyone settled back into their chairs and Bernie looked down at the table, as if trying to figure out how to phrase what he needed to tell us. Then his eyes traveled around the room as he proceeded in a much quieter tone, "Look, we all know that this news isn't gonna go over very well with some folks . . . especially a few members. In the recent past there have been threats of violence against our leadership team should we ever agree to merge with the Merc. For that reason, there's now a security guard stationed on this floor—you'll see him when you leave. He's gonna be there until this thing is completely over, so please be patient with him as he learns who you are and asks to see IDs. Thanks." With that, our CEO bolted out of the room before anyone had the chance to ask questions. Bryan and Kevin were at his heels.

Chris could barely contain himself; he dragged me into his office as everyone dispersed. "Honestly, we had NO idea about any of this when we hired you—they hadn't approached us yet. Hell, I only found out a few days ago. And to think that you asked about this exact scenario in your interview and I told you it wouldn't happen. . . . "

There was a knock on Chris's door, and he hollered that he'd be right out. I knew I wouldn't get much one-on-one time with him over the coming weeks, so I figured it was now or never to ask the burning question that had been on my mind from the moment Bernie broke the news.

"Does Bob know?"

Chris's face fell. "No, he doesn't. I'm going to call him later if the time difference works out. Bernie and I thought about asking him to cut his India trip short but then decided against it. There's really no reason he needs to physically be here at this point." I wondered if Chris was thinking what I was thinking: It would be hard for Bob to act normally and not give something away if he were in the office. Perhaps it was better he was thousands of miles from Chicago.

October 9, 2006

Chris, Maria, Julie, and I comprised the Tiger side of the merger communications team, along with CBOT's head of investor relations, a woman from Maria's group, and Janella Kaczanko, a human resources director. Some people, like Julie and Janella, were actually on more than one merger team, which made the task of scheduling covert rendezvous with our CME counterparts extremely difficult. While other groups met for the first time over the weekend, the communications team had its introductory meeting on Monday afternoon in the offices of Skadden, Arps, CME's law firm.

The second we entered our designated conference room at 333 W. Wacker, it became obvious we weren't going to have much control over our team's deliverables; we'd be lucky just to get a word in edgewise. Not only did CME's employees significantly outnumber us, but around the table were also lawyers from both Skadden, Arps and Mayer Brown (CBOT's legal advisory firm), investment bankers invited by both sides, and public relations experts CME had hired for the occasion. There was no telling who else might be dialed in to the conference line. While our team was tasked with creating 20 documents before the 17th—ranging from the press release to a script for the analyst call to an investor presentation to employee and member letters—did nearly 30 people need to be involved in the process? More importantly, how was the deal going to stay under wraps this way?

In addition to their army of attendees, CME came prepared with a truckload of documents. It was natural for the acquiring firm to take the lead in these situations, but it didn't help ease the tension in the room when it dawned on us that a substantial amount of work had already been done—without our input. "They *had* to have known about this before us," Maria grumbled under her breath.

As stacks of papers were passed around the large room, introductions began. Two people present that day, Anita Liskey and Chris Mead, would become the merger-planning counterparts for Maria and me, respectively. Chris immediately brought to mind the snarky character Chandler from the television series *Friends*—their voices were nearly identical and, like Chandler, Chris would frequently crack one-liners or make otherwise mood-lightening comments. He was fairly nondescript: brown hair, average height, average weight, and in his late thirties. He was the kind of person you'd pass on the street and never notice. Anita, however, might catch your attention. Despite often being in the spotlight as the head of CME's corporate communications division, she had a habit of wearing rather loud outfits that didn't reflect her senior position. She mostly kept mum during our first merger meeting, but her confident nature was apparent from the way she'd stride across the room during breaks or glare—through wide, heavily lined eyes—at those who made stupid comments.

Not that anyone from the Merc was ever conscious of making stupid comments. The Cheetahs all spoke with such assurance and such an air of arrogance it was easy to forget not one person from their side had been through a merger. When the meeting was over, Chris Mead caught Maria's eye and said quietly, "So let's talk about the real issues . . . like how we're going to control Leo."

Maria did her best not to draw attention to herself as she started laughing hysterically; she whipped on her coat and quickened her pace so that she could escape from the room unnoticed. On the way back to CBOT, she explained the joke.

The man Chris had been referring to was Leo Melamed, chairman emeritus of CME. Leo was infamous for having an extraordinarily high opinion of himself, and could usually be overheard making comments such as, "Wherever I sit will be the head of the table." But most people who knew him took his egotistical exaggerations in stride, probably because his political connections were enviable, both inside and outside of the Merc. On any given day, the likes of Hillary Clinton—who made a series of controversial Cattle futures trades in the 1970s that the White House asked Leo to review once she became First Lady—might ring his office. After the CME/CBOT merger was made public, Illinois Senator Barack Obama was one of the first to congratulate the young-at-heart businessman.

Although the saying in the industry was that Leo was "a legend in his own mind," there was no denying that his life story was absolutely incredible. In 1939, at age seven, he fled Poland and the horrors of World War II with his parents—who outsmarted the Gestapo and KGB in the process—and began a transcontinental journey that ended in Chicago in 1941. Just over 10 years later he was attending John Marshall Law School and answered a job ad for what he mistakenly assumed was a legal firm: Merrill Lynch, Pierce, Fenner & Beane. He inadvertently became a trading floor order-runner for Merrill at CME and found that he couldn't get enough of the place. Shortly thereafter, he bought his own membership seat, rose up through the ranks, and by 1969 was named chairman.

Three years later he tried to persuade the Merc's board to consider the idea of basing futures contracts on foreign currencies. This had been attempted in 1970 at the International Commercial Exchange in New York but was never commercially successful, presumably because the Bretton Woods system of monetary management—which set a fixed exchange rate between currencies—was still in effect. Until Leo pushed forward with his idea after President Nixon recalled Bretton Woods in 1971, the underlying assets of futures had always been commodities. Launching a contract derived from the value of a financial instrument was considered insane by almost everyone—except Milton Friedman. Friedman, the noted University of Chicago economist who would win a Nobel Prize in 1976, told Leo to go for it.

The rest, as they say, is history. Both CME and CBOT launched multiple financial futures contracts throughout the 1970s, and trading volumes skyrocketed. In 1981, the team at the Merc had another groundbreaking idea: cash-settled futures. Instead of having to physically exchange a contract's underlying asset once its expiration date rolled around, traders could now simply settle the transaction in cash. The first contract to use this new delivery mechanism was CME's Eurodollar (based on U.S. dollars earning interest in foreign accounts), and it opened up a whole world of possibilities. That's how futures contracts came to be developed for intangible indicators like stock indexes.

Leo wasn't done shaking things up, however. Inspired by a science fiction novel he'd written in which a supercomputer controlled civilization, Melamed next urged the CME board to invest in building an electronic trading system. For five years the exchange worked on the idea, and in 1992 launched Globex. By 2006, the system had been upgraded and enhanced countless times, and could process any trade within 30 milliseconds.

Leo, now in his seventies, continued to wield extraordinary influence over the Merc's day-to-day business, though some argued the level at which he was still involved with the exchange's management was inappropriate and distracting. As I had gathered from Chris's comment and would witness firsthand in the days and months to come, no one at CME ever seemed to be able to say no to Mr. Melamed.

October 12, 2006

The countdown to the deal announcement wore on, and the various merger subteams were constantly holding closed-door meetings on CBOT's sixth floor. It didn't take long for the new security guard to learn who was and wasn't allowed through. On this particular day, Bernie yelled for me from within his office as I passed by in the hallway. He had a favor to ask. "I'm kind of worried about how certain people are going to deal with the prospect of CME buying us. A lot of people have worked here their entire careers—I'm talking decades, since high school. This place is all they know. And we've always been so competitive with the Merc—many employees view them as the enemy. So if there's ever something you can say, you know, to help someone wrap their minds around this and remind them that it's not personal, please do."

On my way back to the tenth floor, I thought about how Bernie hadn't been exaggerating. The CME/CBOT rivalry put the Cubs/White Sox feud to shame, as far as Chicago-based grudge matches were concerned. The Merc was established in 1898, 50 years after CBOT, and had been hell-bent on giving its crosstown rival a run for its money ever since. Because of their founders' religions and the demographic makeup of their boards, CBOT became known as the Irish Catholic exchange, and CME—which until 1919 had been named the Chicago Butter and Egg Board—as the Jewish exchange. Each felt the other's culture was smug and arrogant. Each would have liked nothing better than to see the other fail.

Over the decades, this animosity manifested in strange ways. In the early 1970s, Leo, still new in his role as chairman, hired an agency to create advertisements for the Merc's Lumber contract. The end result? A photo of a two-by-four with the caption, "The Chicago Mercantile Exchange presents the board of trade." More recently, rumor had it that Mayor Daley had to physically separate quarreling leaders from the two exchanges when they started a shouting match in his office. And somewhere along the way, an annual boxing match was set up to pit CBOT and CME traders against each other in the ring so that—in the name of charity, thankfully—they could slug out their aggressions. It was a bloody, albeit black-tie event that the industry looked forward to each fall.

The culture clash between CBOT and CME only served to up the ante on their competition in the marketplace. For the first seven decades after CME was established, it trailed behind CBOT significantly in both size and stature. CBOT's Corn, Oats, Soybeans, and Wheat futures were so critical to grain merchants around the world that it really didn't have to put forth much effort to remain in its dominant position. However, the tide started turning with the advent of financial futures. Once the Merc developed currency contracts and CBOT subsequently launched Treasury bond products, the battle became one of creativity.

While CBOT's economists, board members, and staff may have come up with wonderful ideas—like the first options-on-futures contract—the older exchange simply couldn't keep up with CME's feverish clip of bringing innovative new products to market. In 1981, as CBOT's internal politics put a stranglehold on its business, the Merc was busy unveiling the Eurodollar contract, which would go on to become one of the most actively traded futures products in the world. The next year, it produced another huge hit, the S&P 500 Index contract. By the time CME launched the Globex trading platform in 1992, its archrival was the one playing catch-up.

After a century-long, uphill battle, CME was finally able to officially claim victory in 2001. Its trading volumes, led by the phenomenal success of the Eurodollar contract—which a few of CBOT's FIRDsters sourly deemed "a fluke"—surpassed CBOT's for the first time, meaning that the Merc was now the largest futures exchange in the United States. Merely one year later it became the country's first exchange to go public. CBOT, by contrast, took three additional years to go public and still another year to approve around-the-clock electronic trading of its agricultural contracts. Would CBOT's members ever admit, much less realize, how significantly they'd blown it?

Considering the exchanges' strained history, it was unlikely the CME/ CBOT merger would go off without a hitch. Everyone at the Merc had been waiting a long, long time to stick it to CBOT, and if Bernie was right, CBOT's employees were going to fight back.

October 15, 2006

Crunch time had arrived. With less than 48 hours to go before the deal announcement, the merger communications team was in a state of panic. We attempted to finalize our deliverables during a marathon meeting; by the time we adjourned, night had fallen. I walked a few blocks with Janella from HR just to get some fresh air before cabbing it home. "So I was at 141 earlier this morning and when I left for this meeting, I overheard the security guards whispering to each other," she began as we hurried across an intersection. "One of them said, 'Something's goin' on—all of the big dogs are in on a Sunday.' Sounds like Bernie and the other execs have been coming and going from the building a lot—people are starting to notice."

Later we would learn that a few traders were also at the exchange over the weekend and sensed something odd might be afoot when they saw a whole bunch of men in suits at the McDonald's next door. But it was Charlie Carey, CBOT's chairman, who almost blew the whole deal that night, thanks to a dinner meeting he held at the oldest chophouse in the city, Gene & Georgetti. Larry Dorf, a member and ex-director of CBOT, had been in the midst of a lavish meal at the landmark establishment when a waiter tipped him off that Charlie was in the adjoining room, enjoying a juicy hunk of meat with two other CBOT directors and one of the exchange's lawyers. Dorf knew it was extremely rare for the directors to get together on a Sunday, and could remember only two situations that ever warranted weekend meetings: the crash of 1987, and a soybean-market scandal a few years later. He decided to approach the table in question.

"Good evening, gentlemen."

"Hey, how ya doin'?" Charlie responded after looking up from his steak and realizing there was no way out of the situation.

"What are you guys doing here?" Larry asked pointedly.

"Nothin', just havin' dinner," Charlie stated nonchalantly and then fell quiet, hoping the uncomfortable silence would motivate Dorf to leave. His plan worked. If Larry had his suspicions, he must have kept mum, because the deal miraculously remained under wraps.

October 16, 2006

About 200 merger-related e-mails came through over the course of the day on Monday. It was impossible to keep track of all of the different versions of documents. In the evening, Maria, Janella, and I took a break and went down to Ceres in search of sustenance. Though the restaurant was closed, Maria persuaded the owner to make us sandwiches and let us stay to catch a few minutes of the shocking Bears comeback against the Arizona Cardinals.

Eventually there were only a few hours remaining before we'd have to return to the office for the big announcement, and Chris Malo insisted we go home. CME's board meeting was planned for 4 A.M., and CBOT's was scheduled to begin a half-hour later. If both boards voted the deal through, the press release would go to the wire shortly thereafter, and then hundreds of copies of the document were to be printed for distribution to traders on the floor. The latest rumor was that the boards *weren't* going to accept the deal—CBOT's board didn't think their exchange was being valued highly enough, and of course CME's board thought they were giving away the house. "They're playing chicken," Chris sighed.

October 17, 2006

As 6 A.M. neared I was back at my desk, scrolling through the latest e-mail updates. It seemed as though the deal was indeed going to happen, but there was major confusion about the timing of the announcement. In addition, the CBOT team would have to edit several documents that still hadn't been finalized by the lawyers, rather than wait to receive official versions later in the day. As I struggled to understand exactly what documents I needed to change, a voice behind me made me jump two feet in the air.

"Why, you're here early."

It was Fred, once again in black jeans and cowboy boots, but minus his rockin' hat. He pressed his hands together, waiting for an explanation. While all of the economists and many of the salespeople usually got to the office at the crack of dawn, I wasn't exactly known to be a morning person. I said the first thing that came to mind: "Maria asked if I could help out with the earnings call."

He continued staring at me for a good 10 seconds before giving me a quick nod and returning to his cube farm halfway down the hall. I resumed my editing.

About an hour later, the technology manager who'd been preparing to post information about the deal to both CBOT's web site and employee intranet called to see if we'd been given the go-ahead. "What's going on?" he asked.

"Ugh, I have no idea. I think we have to wait for final confirmation from Chris or Maria before we upload anything," I whispered, conscious that everyone on my side of the tenth floor could hear me. "I'll let you know as soon as I get word," I promised, and then went back to my documents.

Shortly after I hung up, my phone rang once more. It was the same IT manager I'd just spoken to. "Hi again," I began, but was quickly cut off.

"Somebody better figure out what we're supposed to do, because there's been a leak. They're reporting the merger on CNBC and Yahoo! Finance."

As TVs were positioned up and down the tenth-floor hallway, everyone around me would see the news at any moment. I braced myself for their reactions. There was no turning back now.

Chapter 5

Wanna Be Startin' Somethin'

October 17, 2006

News of the merger had indeed found its way onto CNBC and Yahoo! Finance before communications were sent out to the CBOT staff at approximately 7:15 A.M. Thankfully, regardless of how any given employee might have learned about the proposed buyout, the violent responses I anticipated did not transpire—at least not on my side of the tenth floor. One salesperson lamented that the announcement "kind of takes the wind out of our sails" in regard to customer events she'd been planning, but overall people acted more defeated than irate. Once everyone got over the shock of the news, however, it would only be a matter of time before anger and paranoia reared their ugly heads, and rumors about layoffs began swirling.

Bernie asked division leaders to join him on the executive floor that morning in order to gauge employee sentiment and prepare us to answer questions about the merger. Next, there was an all-employee town hall meeting held in The Standard Club's luxurious ballroom a few blocks down the street from CBOT's headquarters. As expected, attendees were most concerned with understanding when and how staffing decisions would be made. Bernie stated that a "reasonable man approach" would be taken to creating the combined exchange's organizational structure. I doubted that would be the case. The firm in the power position almost always chose to retain its own employees wherever there were redundant roles. And CBOT was certainly not in the power position.

After the meeting, I walked back to the office with Maria, who looked beyond exasperated. "Guess what kind of calls I'm getting from members?" she asked. "'What's going to happen to my parking space?' and 'I better get to keep my parking space!' and 'Will I get a parking space over at the Merc?'" she spat. "Can you freakin' believe *that's* what they're worried about?"

■ ■ ■

While those in Chicago were fretting over parking spaces—or celebrating the merger that was poised to cement the city's status as the risk management capital of the world—700 miles away in New York City, James von Moltke's wheels were turning. Von Moltke, grandson of Helmuth James Graf von Moltke, a founding member of the Kreisau Circle resistance group against Adolf Hitler during World War II, stared out of the window of his midtown Manhattan office and replayed one of the day's phone calls in his head. James was the principal relationship manager for Morgan Stanley's exchange clients, and was therefore not surprised when Jeff Sprecher, CEO of the six-year-old, all-electronic IntercontinentalExchange (ICE), rang him shortly after CME and CBOT made their big announcement. Morgan Stanley was one of the original founders of ICE, and so the investment bank had a particularly strong relationship with Sprecher. That morning, James and Jeff had the same knee-jerk reaction to the CME/CBOT deal: It drastically undervalued the Board of Trade, might not meet regulatory approval, and was clearly a takeover masquerading as a merger.

As the day drew to a close, von Moltke received a second call from ICE's Atlanta-based CEO. "So, I've been thinking about things, and I'm wondering if there's a better strategic outcome for both CBOT and the industry than for CBOT to get rolled up into a giant monopoly. I'm wondering if I could possibly stick my nose in," Jeff stated.

As it turned out, James and his team had spent the past several hours running numbers to calculate whether ICE could make an interloping offer. "It's funny you mention that," von Moltke replied. "We were asking ourselves the same question over here. We thought, 'Who could challenge this deal?' The quick math we've done demonstrates that it is not outside the realm of the possible for ICE to get involved. In fact, ICE would be one of the only exchanges in the world capable of doing it."

That was all Jeff needed to hear. He'd thought about the possibility of joining forces with CBOT before, and always had a vision of how the industry's consolidation might unfold, but the Merc's announcement had forced his hand. The problem was that ICE was presently consumed with finalizing its purchase of the New York Board of Trade (NYBOT). "Do you think we can get NYBOT done and then turn around and do something with this?" Jeff asked. "I really believe it would be a much better outcome for the industry."

James agreed that if ICE was going to launch a competitive offer for CBOT, it absolutely had to have the NYBOT transaction completed first. He assured Jeff that his team at Morgan Stanley would start working on a CBOT proposal in the meantime.

October 18, 2006

The morning after the announcement I picked up a few newspapers to save as mementos, now that all of them had headlines about the $8 billion merger splashed across their front pages. There were also stories on everything from how Bernie stood to make nearly $20 million from the deal, to how cafes near the CME headquarters already feared bankruptcy (as the combined trading floor would be housed at CBOT), to how the merged exchange's full name—CME Group, a CME/Chicago Board of Trade Company—was a bit of a "deep-dish mouthful." Unsurprisingly, absolutely no research was done in picking the new, convoluted company name or its associated logo; a few of the Merc's most influential members, including Leo, had simply given their blessing. The focus of the vast majority of newspaper articles, however, was the 23-year friendship between the two exchanges' chairmen: CME's Terry Duffy and CBOT's Charlie Carey.

It was definitely Terry and Charlie's day to shine. That afternoon, Charlie received a standing ovation as he ascended the small stage that had been erected near the soybean pit in order for him and Bernie to discuss the terms of the deal with CBOT's members.

Our stocky chairman had become a member of the exchange in 1978 and could still be found trading grains on the floor from time to time. CBOT was in his blood: His grandfather had joined the exchange as a messenger in 1903, worked his way up the ranks, and was eventually elected president—a precursor to the chairman role— in under 30 years' time. Charlie's father had been a soybean trader, and throughout his career the Carey family experienced a roller coaster of booms and busts, depending on how the market was doing. Charlie's uncle Bernard was also a trader, and in the mid-1960s became the second in the Carey clan to hold the position of chairman.

Like his familial predecessors, Charlie started out as a grain trader, but when a dry spell hit those markets in the early 1980s, he moved over to the Merc to try his hand at Hog futures. That's where he met Terry Duffy, who got a job as an order-runner at the Merc after learning about futures from the summering traders he served while tending bar in upscale Lake Geneva, Wisconsin. Terry soon started trading as well, and over the course of two decades took on increasing levels of responsibility and involvement at CME, culminating in his election to the chairmanship. He and Charlie shared a career path— and much more.

They were both born on Chicago's South Side, they were both Irish-American (and fiercely proud of it), and they were both strongly tied to Windy City politics. Charlie's grandfather, in addition to serving as CBOT's chairman, later became the sheriff of Cook County. Terry's grandfather had been a city alderman and the president of the Cook County board. Growing up, the two men became familiar with the Chicago machine, and now their positions at CME and CBOT kept them in close communication with Illinois' various representatives, as well as the multitude of agricultural and industry committees in Washington, D.C. Over the years, the duo's political connections—and, when it came to Duffy, aspirations, as many believed his ultimate goal was to run for some sort of office—helped rank them among the Midwest's who's who. Case in point: Chicago Mayor Richard M. Daley, yet another South Side Irishman raised around politics—his father, Richard J. Daley, a.k.a. "The Boss," had reigned as mayor from 1955 to 1976—invited them both to President George W. Bush's sixtieth birthday bash in July 2006.

While CME and CBOT always had an intense—and at points, vicious—rivalry, throughout the years the exchanges' various leaders had been able to look past their differences and see the value in combining forces. The Merc had, in fact, courted CBOT several times over the decades—the most recent being right before CBOT had its IPO in 2005. Yet CBOT's executives always felt the Merc's offers were too low. Once CBOT established a market value for itself after going public, however, its board began exploring various strategic alliances and Charlie decided to broach the subject again. Near the end of 2005, he got his chance. Terry invited him to lunch at Gene & Georgetti in order to discuss extending the exchanges' common clearing arrangement. "What about goin' for the whole enchilada instead?" Charlie countered. "Will you think about it and get back to me?"

Terry said he would, and by the springtime the two men had arranged an informal luncheon at another popular steakhouse, Sullivan's, for some of the most influential members and traders from each exchange. The invitees weren't aware of any merger talk; Charlie and Terry simply wanted to see if everyone could get along—if it was possible for the two cultures to coexist. The meal came and went without incident, but since "there was nothing on the line," Charlie felt he might've hit a dead end.

Fast-forward to August 22, 2006. The two friends, each accompanied by his respective company's attorneys, were at Gene & Georgetti yet again, this time for dinner. "You know, we're still open to a combination," Charlie reminded Terry. But if the Merc's team was interested, Charlie didn't have that impression by the time he left the restaurant. After all, he and Terry had been musing about a CME and CBOT merger since the days they'd meet after work at Raoul's Mexican joint in 1983, so "this was just another one of those dinners" in his mind. That all changed, however, once he and Terry resumed discussions a few weeks later. This time it was just the two of them at The Clubhouse, an upscale restaurant in the western suburb of Oak Brook. Over dinner, Terry made the Merc's intentions known: They did in fact want to move forward with merger negotiations and had been debating the idea internally for quite some time.

The following evening, Charlie was in the midst of grilling hamburgers on his backyard deck when his cell phone rang. It was Terry. "I want to talk," he stated.

In shorts and a T-shirt, holding his phone to his ear with one hand and flipping burgers with the other, Charlie replied coolly, "Okay, but you guys better be serious this time." He took care not to burn the meat for his wife and kids' dinner as he awaited Terry's response.

"We're serious."

"Are you gonna try to lowball us like before? We'll just reject it," Charlie warned. Terry reiterated that the Merc's board was serious. Charlie said he'd call CBOT's outside legal counsel, who happened to be his cousin, Peter. That weekend, Charlie and Peter met Merc CEO Craig Donohue and attorney Jerry Salzman at Terry's house, and—over bagels, lox, and countless cups of coffee—hammered out the non-financial details of the deal, like the fate of the trading floor and who'd be chairman. Then Charlie brought Bernie into the loop, and the lawyers and bankers took over. By the evening of Sunday, September 10, Charlie felt cautiously optimistic enough to enjoy a cigar in his office. The reality sank in to him that this time, it just might work out between the exchanges. Now, five and a half weeks later, he and Bernie faced CBOT's members, who stood to make millions off of the deal.

Though most floor traders revered and trusted Charlie because he was "one of them," the same couldn't necessarily be said for Bernie. That's probably why he wasn't quite as chipper as he'd been at the staff meetings the day prior. He proceeded robotically through a PowerPoint presentation full of charts, graphs, and statistics that were meant to sell the members on the merger, as their votes could make or break everything. When it was time for questions, he looked as if he were physically steeling himself for what the burly men in the crowd were about to throw his way. His stance widened ever so slightly and he squared his shoulders before raising his head up from his notes.

The first question was from a member who wanted to know what would become of his CBOE exercise right privilege (ERP) if the Board of Trade merged with the Merc. The ERP was a unique type of trading right that CBOT's full members acquired in 1973 when the neighboring Chicago Board Options Exchange (CBOE) spun off from CBOT. In CBOT members' minds, holding an ERP meant that they also owned equity in the Options Exchange. But many CBOE members disagreed. Their view was that the ERP did not entitle its holders to an ownership stake in the exchange—it simply gave people the right to trade there. This disagreement didn't reach a boiling point, however, until exchanges around the world started going public. Once that trend kicked in, it became clear that whoever could prove they had an equity stake in the Options Exchange could make a lot of money in its eventual IPO.

To make the issue even messier, in the summer of 2006, when Charlie thought the Merc wasn't interested in joining forces, CBOT and CBOE had entered into merger negotiations that ended up falling apart. CBOE's CEO, Bill Brodsky, had approached the Board of Trade and said, "Let's solve the exercise right issue by doing something even more bold. Let's put Humpty Dumpty back together again—let's bring the two exchanges together again. Then the CBOT and CBOE will be bigger than the Merc."

After completing due diligence, CBOT's leadership team felt there weren't enough synergies between CBOE's equity-based business and its own futures markets. They made an offer that Brodsky deemed "grossly insufficient," which spurred him to break off negotiations. The next thing he knew, late on August 22—the same night Charlie and Terry were having dinner at Gene & Georgetti—CBOT's board filed a lawsuit against the Options Exchange in an attempt to enforce its interpretation of its members' exercise right privileges. Relations between the two exchanges hit rock bottom in the ensuing two months.

That's why the guy who asked Bernie about the status of the exercise right issue had good reason to worry. Even though CBOE and CBOT disagreed on what holding an ERP actually entitled someone to, it was definitely clear that a CBOT member must own 27,338 shares of CBOT stock—which equated to full member status—in order to keep his ERP in the first place. When CBOT's stock ceased to exist after the merger with CME, what would that mean for the exercise rights?

Bernie saw this question coming from a mile away. In fact, because he knew a good chunk of the member base would forever be critical of anything he said or did, he always prepared a response to every imaginable question before he met with them. He felt some members were out to "embarrass and destroy the credibility" of the business staff, and he'd seen enough others "get decimated." In regard to the ERP issue, Bernie explained that under the terms of the merger deal, CBOT members would get .3006 shares of CME Group stock for every share of CBOT stock they owned. So it was simply a matter of multiplying .3006 by the 27,338 CBOT shares required to keep one's ERP. The resulting number would represent how many CME Group shares a member would need to hold on to in order to ensure his ERP remained in play. The guy who'd asked the question attempted to figure the numbers out loud and got it totally wrong. Bernie cut off the confused fellow by revealing the answer—out to four decimal points: "8,217.8028 shares of CME Group stock are necessary to keep your ERP." From where I was standing, I heard other traders grumble in disapproval of their colleague's inability to do the calculation. "This is fucking embarrassing."

Next came a pointed question from one of the most notoriously grumpy older members. Chris Malo had told me this man absolutely loathed both him and Bernie. The fiery septuagenarian was dressed in his usual garb of suspenders and bow tie, with a cane in his hand and thick glasses perched on his nose, covering quite deranged-looking eyes. "Who's going to be overseeing the floor consolidation? How are the pits going to be combined?" he croaked in a venomous, hoarse voice. Up on the platform, a resigned look crossed Bernie's face that signaled he knew no matter what he said, it wasn't going to satisfy this particular individual. "None of those things have been decided yet. I would assume that a committee will be formed and that there will be representatives from the floor involved," he stated diplomatically. The elderly man turned in disgust from Bernie's direction and faced the rest of the pit as he muttered, "Yeah, well, we just better make sure that HE doesn't have anything to do with it, 'cause he'll screw it up."

I glanced at Chris, who was standing next to me at the side of the pit and staring after the old codger with a bemused look on his face. He met my eyes briefly, shot me a quick "I told you so" smile, and winked.

The next several questions confirmed the stereotype of members as extremely greedy men who would never be satisfied. Charlie, looking every bit "the pit bull in a suit" that *Forbes* magazine would deem him 15 months later, started fielding complaints about why the Merc wasn't coughing up more dough. Bernie tried to keep from blowing his lid and agitatedly shifted his weight from one leg to the other. Then Dennis Flynn, a *particularly* stout trader—and former offensive tackle at Illinois—bellowed out a comment that made me reconsider my attitude about the seemingly thankless lot. "You know, I'm hearing a lot of complainin' today about why the conversion rate's not higher and this or that, but all I know is that I bought my seat for $400,000 in 1993— and now it's worth over $4.5 million. So Charlie, I for one want to pick you up and carry you around on my shoulders for getting this deal done." There was a brief pause and then someone else from the crowd shouted, "And you're about the only one who could do it, too!"

Applause, hoots, and hollers erupted across the cavernous room, and Charlie took that as his cue to quickly adjourn the meeting on a high note. Perhaps the rational, appreciative traders represented a bigger contingent of the member base than I'd assumed.

October 19 to November 13, 2006

With the exception of a jubilant Mayor Daley ringing the opening bell on Halloween—"I was in London . . . but all anybody could talk about was Chicago!" he shouted triumphantly as he recalled where he was when he heard the news—the month following the big October 17 announcement was fairly uneventful. Across town, CME hired a consulting firm to help plan out everything that needed to be done before CME and CBOT members and shareholders would vote on the merger in April. Meanwhile, all but a few people on the integration team were off the hook until mid-November, when we'd reconvene to begin hashing out the particulars of exactly how the two exchanges were going to mesh into one. Those of us at CBOT who'd been so harried working on the announcement were thankful to have our lives back for a while.

Bob wasted no time in returning his attention to our metals contracts, which were continuing to hold their own against NYMEX. Now, however, there was one huge hiccup: Prior to finalizing its purchase offer for CBOT, CME had signed a deal to host electronic trading of NYMEX's metals futures on the Globex platform, beginning in the fourth quarter. The old-boy network at the New York exchange could no longer ignore the beating their business had taken in the two years since CBOT launched its Silver and Gold online-only contracts. What's more, the small, Atlanta-based IntercontinentalExchange had debuted an electronic version of NYMEX's extremely successful West Texas Intermediate Crude Oil futures in February 2006, and proceeded to snag 25 percent of the market. The message was clear: The punches were going to keep coming for NYMEX unless it allowed its pit-traded contracts to go side-by-side. The quickest way to do that was to partner with CME and leverage Globex.

My guess was that Bob had assumed CME would simply drop the NYMEX metals complex once the CBOT merger closed, but statements trickling out of the Merc seemed to indicate otherwise. The one we saw the most was, "NYMEX is an important and valuable partner to the CME, and we will do nothing that upsets that alliance." As far as Bob was concerned, those were fighting words.

That's why he wanted to make our metals complex the star of CBOT's exhibit space at FIA Expo. FIA Expo, one of the industry's largest conferences, took place annually in Chicago and was organized by the Futures Industry Association (FIA). I would be vacationing in New Zealand when the event kicked off in late November, but my talk of going on a *Lord of the Rings* filming location tour was apparently just the inspiration Bob needed to dream up a show-stopping display.

"Okay, picture this," he began to the small group who had camped out in his office to throw around ideas for the conference. "Imagine we have a replica of a trading pit, and we get some poor slob to dress up as Gollum or Frodo or something and stand in the middle of it, and we could have a big sign over him that says, 'LORD OF THE PIT HOLDS THE ONE RING,' and he could be standing there with a huge GOLD ring. And then we could have flat-screens showing real-time data for Gold and Silver and kiosks with our brochures all around—wouldn't that be great?"

Everyone chimed in at once.

"You'd be perfect, Bob, if you weren't so goddamn tall—no one'd buy you as a hobbit."

"But maybe if he crouched down he'd pass for Gollum."

"Yeah, he could sit there all night crying, 'My precioussss . . .' over and over, stroking the gold ring," I said, actually starting to warm to the idea. But Bob's eyes were wide and he was staring off into the distance, and I knew we were about to hear the stream-of-consciousness flow of other ideas that were ricocheting around in his brain.

"Or you know what?" he continued excitedly, ignoring the suggestion that he play Gollum. "We could do an Austin Powers/*Goldmember* theme and have people painted in gold—and then we could have some of those go-go girls like in the movie walking around with trays of drinks. We have to have *good* tchotchkes, too—not our usual crap that looks like it was made by a family of refugees. And we could serve *Gold*schläger shots, and all of those beers that have 'Gold' in their names, and mixed drinks made with gold and silver rum . . ." He trailed off and was surely running through every movie, song, TV show, and pop culture reference he could think of that could somehow be related to metals. By the end of the meeting I thoroughly regretted the timing of my trip.

November 14, 2006

The merger work officially kicked off in style with cocktails and dinner at the Ritz-Carlton. "So, does CME put its employees up in the Ritz or the Four Seasons when they travel, too? Because I'm not really a Holiday Inn type of gal," Maria said not-so-jokingly to Anita as we took in the lavish décor, waterfalls, and intimidating chandeliers positioned throughout the hotel. Pretty much everyone who had been involved in the 11-day announcement-preparation marathon would also be working on the integration planning effort. Bob, Julie, Maria, and I were each heading up functional subteams with our

CME counterparts; all in all, approximately 70 people were present from both exchanges, representing every division from technology to accounting to human resources.

During dinner, I sat next to Price Pritchett, a world-renowned authority on company integrations whom CME had brought in to speak to the group in order to set expectations about the coming weeks. Merger consultants had also met with the CME and CBOT teams separately in the days leading up to the formal start of the integration planning. In those sessions, we had been urged to "take off our CBOT hats" and "try to think like members of an objective third party" when the time came to discuss with our CME equivalents how our respective areas should be organized and managed once the two exchanges combined.

As the dessert course began, Price went to the front of the room to address the group and share insights from the countless mergers and acquisitions he had helped firms navigate. He brought up a fascinating study on optimism and the power of positive thinking, a study conducted over the course of 50 years—with nuns. Not too long after he mentioned the nuns, a blast of gasps and nervous giggles rang out from Bob's table. I could only imagine what Bob had said to cause such a reaction. Price chose to take all of the goofing around he observed as a good sign. "This group is already much further along in terms of being comfortable with each other than what I usually witness at the start of an integration process. I think that bodes well for what lies ahead."

His prediction didn't end up being entirely accurate, but everyone believed him that night because nothing short of a kumbaya session was going down in the dining room—most likely because drinks had been flowing freely for nearly two hours. At the same time Price was wrapping up his speech, the head of CBOT's IT department returned from the restroom. He had missed the part about how wonderful it was that we were all getting along so well, and jumped about three feet in the air when his CME counterpart leapt from his seat and almost knocked him to the ground with a huge bear hug while shouting, "I LOVE YOU, MAN!"

Price decided to end his spiel before things got any rowdier, but we still had one more speech to go. Phupinder Gill, CME's president and COO—who, in an effort to avoid the slaughtering of his first name, just went by "Gill"—rose to say a few words. I hadn't been introduced to Gill yet, but had heard from several people that he was funny, smart, and well liked at CME—and that it was nearly impossible to keep him from swearing. The room finally fell quiet as he stepped up to the microphone.

"Let me start out by saying that I believe this integration process will be both good and bad, like your mother-in-law driving over a cliff . . . in your brand-new convertible." He paused to let that gem sink in and bowed his head as guffaws rolled through the crowd. "Seriously, though, I think what we've learned from the merger consultants this week, and again here tonight, is that the CME team has to be more sensitive, and the CBOT team has to be more sensitive. Oh . . . wait, fuck. I screwed that up." More laughter. "The CBOT team has to be LESS sensitive. Shit, you all get what I'm saying. Anyway, thanks to everyone for all of the hard work so far, and enjoy the rest of your night."

November 15, 2006

The next morning the fun and games came to a screeching halt as everyone on the integration team piled into an enormous conference room above the Merc's lobby for an all-day meeting that would serve as the beginning of the high-level planning phase. Floor-to-ceiling windows offered a sweeping view of the always-bustling Wacker Drive, but not many of us were tempted to gaze outside on this dark and gloomy day. Instead, our attention was focused on CME's chairman, Terry Duffy, and CEO, Craig Donohue, who gave us a short pep talk before turning things over to the merger consultants. The consultants informed us that this initial phase of work would last about two months, and during that time our goal was to simply identify everything that needed to be done to successfully combine each functional area of the two exchanges. There would be a big three-day meeting in early January to wrap everything up before moving on to the next phase. At that meeting, we would present our final high-level plans to executives from both exchanges and hope we didn't get ripped apart.

It was also expected that at some point during the next few months, the Department of Justice (DOJ) would carry out its antitrust investigation by requesting documents—and interviewing several people—from each exchange.

Since today was one of the only days all 70-plus team members would be in the same room, we were instructed to first work with our counterparts to list out all of the projects we could think of for which we would eventually need to create detailed plans, and then cross-reference our lists with other groups to ensure everyone knew who was responsible for what. On the marketing front, our list would inevitably include tasks such as "Decommission the CBOT.com and CME.com web sites/Build CMEGroup.com" and "Integrate and then purge customer and prospect databases for duplicate entries." While those projects were complicated, my counterpart Chris Mead and I had it pretty easy when compared to some of the other teams. Formidable undertakings like moving CBOT's electronic-trading customers onto CME's Globex platform, creating the schematic for the combined trading floor, and developing one intricate set of trading rules filled their to-do lists.

For the first half of the day, Chris and I began forming our plan for the marketing division alongside the communications team—made up of Anita, Maria, and one member of each of their staffs—as so many of our projects were intertwined with theirs. Things did not go smoothly. The Merc employees were hung up on the future organizational structure of our division, even though we were instructed not to worry about such details just yet. The situation turned awkward quickly.

After a break for lunch, the consultants told us to join up with other groups that had cross-dependencies with our teams, so Bob, Julie, and their respective CME counterparts came over to our table. From the looks on their faces, they could sense the tension that had carried over from our earlier session. For once, Bob didn't blurt out what he was thinking. Instead, he leaned back in his chair, crossed his arms, and scanned the table while his co-lead spoke about projects on which we'd all have to collaborate. By the time we adjourned for the evening, the mood in the big conference room had become quite somber.

Late November 2006

While I was in New Zealand, FIA Expo was in full swing at the Hyatt Regency Chicago. The second evening of the conference, CME and CBOT jointly hosted a reception at the chic River East Arts Center. Attendees discussed the latest industry gossip and toasted the future of CME Group. Not one of them was aware that earlier in the day, in a private dining room at a steakhouse on the edge of the Chicago River, Jeff Sprecher and James von Moltke met to discuss the possibility of a very different merger.

Shortly after Jeff and James had spoken about the CME/CBOT announcement in mid-October, Jeff put in a call to an antitrust expert at Sullivan & Cromwell, one of the world's most prestigious law firms.

"Do you think the Merc deal is going to make it through the DOJ investigation?" Jeff asked. Although CME Group would control approximately 85 percent of all exchange-traded futures in the United States, and 100 percent of certain product categories like Treasuries, the fact that each contract already enjoyed monopoly status premerger made the CME/CBOT situation fundamentally different from a normal antitrust case.

"It's not going to be easy, but ultimately, they may be able to do it," the attorney replied.

"What if the Department of Justice saw in front of them a better way for the market to unfold—would that influence them?" Jeff continued.

"Legally? No. Legally, they will only look at the facts of that merger and not anything extraneous. But I will tell you that the decision makers are only human. And it is very hard for humans *not* to pay attention to extraneous materials."

"That's exactly what I needed to know," Jeff said. He thanked the lawyer and hung up, convinced that if he could show the DOJ team there was another option for CBOT—an option that would not result in a firm with an 85 percent share of the market—they just might be emboldened enough to stop the CME deal from progressing.

The first step was to ensure ICE could even present such an option in the first place. The lunch break during the FIA conference gave Jeff the opportunity to finally sit down and talk things over with von Moltke. At Smith & Wollensky, nestled beneath Chicago's famous Marina City "corn cob" towers, the two men were joined by Chris Lown, a vice president in Morgan Stanley's investment banking division; Chuck Vice, ICE's president and COO; and David Goone, ICE's senior vice president and chief strategic officer.

The group went over an analysis the Morgan Stanley team had put together that explored the feasibility of ICE launching a competitive bid for CBOT. The Atlanta exchange was still a few months away from closing its merger with NYBOT, but the bankers' presentation gave Jeff reason to believe that by early 2007, he might have a real shot at making a play for the world's oldest futures exchange. And he was quite positive that no one would see him coming.

Chapter 6

Dirty Laundry

Mid-December 2006

A month into the merger preparations, I was invited to meet with some of the Merc's top executives, seeing as how I was one of the few people from the CBOT side they didn't already know. I figured I'd be in for a treat when my time with Gill arrived.

"I am *so* sorry I'm late, Erika—those fuckhead consultants have been driving me nuts all day," he bellowed after swinging open the door to his corner office on CME's posh executive floor. "It's very nice to meet you, come on in," he added as I took in his impressive view of the Loop. While I'd been in the same room as Gill several times since the kickoff dinner at the Ritz, we'd never talked to each other directly until now.

Born in Malaysia and a citizen of Singapore, the Merc's 46-year-old president and chief operating officer did not look like most men at the exchange—as in, he wasn't white. He had brown skin, jet-black hair, bushy eyebrows, a self-described "mutt" accent (a mix of Singaporean and British), and a wide, genuine smile. Though Craig Donohue, Terry Duffy, and limelight-seeking personalities like past-chairman Leo Melamed were the faces most often associated with CME, those

74

intimately familiar with the company knew that it would have a hard time running without Gill. In fact, even Leo thought of Gill as "the single most important exchange official."

After earning both a BA in finance and an MBA from Washington State University, Gill landed a job at CBOT's spin-off, the Chicago Board Options Exchange (CBOE), in 1987. He began his tenure on Black Monday. Within a year, he'd left CBOE for CME because he found the futures exchange to be "a much better place to work." Gill spent the vast majority of the subsequent 18 years in CME Clearing, the division that formed the very heart of exchange operations by serving as the buyer to every seller and the seller to every buyer, in order to reduce customers' counterparty credit risk. In 2006, CME's clearing house—which had never seen a member default in over a century—settled 2.1 billion transactions.

Gill had played a prominent role in the 2003 agreement that set up the *common clearing link* (CCL) between CBOT and the Merc. Before the CCL, the Board of Trade Clearing Corporation (BOTCC) cleared CBOT's customers' trades. But once BOTCC also started working with Board of Trade rival Eurex—the German competitor Bob despised—CBOT's leadership let their sentiments about BOTCC's disloyalty be known by moving their clearing business to the Merc. In retrospect, many pointed to the CCL as the first step toward the eventual merger of the two companies. The agreement made CME Clearing the clearing house for all CBOT trades, and the two exchanges estimated that it saved their customers over $1.5 billion in administrative and operating costs. Because of the CCL, traders and trading firms would have one set of trade-processing interfaces, and would only be required to fund one margin account instead of maintaining two separate ones for business done at the Merc versus CBOT. Further, if customers' positions across CBOT and CME contracts offset each other, their single margin requirement would be decreased accordingly. The CCL deal and others like it, such as the CME/NYMEX clearing agreement, were responsible for 8 percent of the Merc's revenue in 2006.

After the common clearing link was fully functional, Gill stepped outside of the clearing division at the beginning of 2004 to assume his current title of president and COO of the entire exchange. Since his background was almost exclusively operational and technical, I figured he probably didn't have much interest in marketing. It turned out that—in great contrast to the conversation I'd have days later with Craig Donohue—most of my introductory meeting with Gill wasn't spent talking shop, anyway. Instead, he treated me to several stories about CME holiday parties past (probably because the company's latest year-end shindig was just a few days away). As I listened, I realized I already felt like I'd known Gill for a very long time. He carried himself without a hint of pretension—the kind of person it's nearly impossible not to like. "Last year I had flown all day and most of the evening from Asia and touched down in Chicago pretty late," he shared. "I took a limo directly from the airport to our party in order to catch the very end of it. Doing so was against my better judgment—I was *really* tired. I should've listened to my gut. By the time I got there, some people were drunk out of their minds and falling all over the place and I had no choice but to play chauffeur because cabs were scarce. I had to pile a ton of people into the limo and have my driver take them home—including destinations in the suburbs. I don't think I got in bed until 3 A.M., and my wife said, 'Where were you?' and I told her, 'Don't ask.' I guess I was glad I could do it, but this year I won't put myself in that position. I'm not going to stay late!"

Somehow we got around to talking about the people I worked the most closely with at CBOT, and inevitably the conversation turned to Bob. "Bob probably thinks I'm *insane*," Gill began, head in hands. "This one time we were at a conference together—I think it might've been the first time we ever met—and we were sitting next to each other and there was some speaker who was just blathering on forever. This guy wouldn't shut up. I remember leaning over and whispering, 'This is like when you try to stop pissing midstream—drip . . . drip . . . drip . . . ' and Bob just stared at me blankly and said, 'You're *weeeiiiirrd*.' I realized later that he probably had no fucking idea what I was talking about, see, because I am not circumcised!"

Wow. What to say to that? I laughed along with Gill as he shook his head and gazed off into the distance for a few seconds, most likely remembering the look on Bob's face back at the conference in question. I loved how he was totally uncensored. In that way, at least, he was very much like Bob. By the time we wrapped up our meeting, I'd decided that Gill was my favorite person at CME. This wouldn't have surprised the rest of the Merc's leadership team. They were, in fact, acutely aware of the effect Gill had on people—his effortless charm was the exchange's secret weapon. And in seven months, the outcome of the CME/CBOT merger vote would depend on it.

■ ■ ■

Eventually, lawyers from the Department of Justice came to rifle through the offices of anyone they felt might have materials relevant to their antitrust investigation. While the deal couldn't close until the DOJ indicated it was not going to block the CME/CBOT union (the agency never gave an outright blessing to any merger), no one at either company had seemed too concerned about the investigation during the preceding eight weeks. The executives' argument to the Feds was that even though CME Group would end up with 85 percent of the country's exchange-traded futures market, it was the "exchange-traded" qualifier that made that figure acceptable. Merc CEO Craig Donohue got especially fired up when talking about how his firm was *not* a monopoly because it had to compete with players in the unregulated over-the-counter (OTC) derivatives industry.

Contracts traded on futures exchanges are standardized—one Soybean contract means the same thing to everyone—whereas the OTC market deals in customized derivatives transactions negotiated privately between two parties. One of those parties is usually an investment bank, often referred to in this context as a *dealer*. No central clearing house currently exists in the OTC market, meaning that the companies entering into derivatives deals with each other have to be confident in their trading partners' financial stability. Customers also have to simply trust that their dealers aren't taking advantage of them, as there is no comparative price data available for these private transactions. What makes the OTC market attractive, however, is that approximately 33 percent of the time, dealers require absolutely no up-front margin payment or collateral to make a trade. When a deposit is deemed necessary, it still usually isn't at the level required by an exchange.

Perhaps the biggest difference between the exchange-traded and OTC derivatives markets is that every day—sometimes twice a day—exchanges zero out traders' positions in a process called *marking-to-market.* Here's a simple example: Through an exchange, a food manufacturer buys a futures contract whose total underlying value is $50,000; this contract requires a $2,000 (or 4 percent) margin deposit. Over the first day's trading session, the market decides that the contract's value should be $200 higher. This earns the food company $200, and its margin account now stands at $2,200, but whoever *sold* the contract just lost $200. The following day the price goes down $300. At the closing bell, the food manufacturer's account will go from $2,200 to $1,900, but the seller's account will have increased by that same amount. This process continues daily until the settlement date of the contract, and it's why futures trading is a zero-sum game—it's not like the stock market where all holders of a rising stock make money. For a futures contract to even exist in the first place, there must be someone to represent both sides of the trade, and therefore one side's losses will cancel out the other's earnings. With frequent marking-to-market, everyone trading through an exchange always knows where their accounts stand, and the clearing house can keep a lid on unbridled losses.

In the OTC market, daily marked-to-market accounting does not transpire, and the value of the underlying asset can often become a bit of a mystery as time goes by. Since there's no public market displaying OTC contract values like there is at an exchange, customers and dealers might have different ideas about what their positions are worth as weeks and months pass. This also means that their debt can accumulate to large amounts, unchecked. The lack of price transparency and marked-to-market positions has been known to lead to rather inventive accounting tricks—which might not be so worrisome if the notional value (the underlying or face value) of the OTC market wasn't approximately $415 trillion in 2006, or about seven times the entire world economy. This was what CBOT and CME were trying to convince the DOJ they were competing against.

The antitrust team wasn't concerned with the tribulations of the OTC market, however. They were solely focused on the proposed merger at hand. And they had no intention of rushing their analysis. Rather, the DOJ attorneys had recently opened a second-stage competition review for the CME/CBOT case, prompting the exchanges' executives to warn constituents that this new development could push back the merger's anticipated mid-2007 close date. While Craig,

Bernie, Charlie, and Terry never publicly wavered in their conviction that the Feds would eventually approve their deal, merger analysts expressed cause for concern. Such second requests from the Justice Department typically indicated that a serious antitrust review was at hand. Under the Bush administration, out of the thousands of merger deals that originated between 2002 and 2005, there'd been only 82 second requests initiated by the DOJ—one-third the number during Clinton's final four years in office. That meant the proposed formation of CME Group was among a relatively small number of cases the DOJ determined to be worth analyzing further. Not exactly the kind of attention the exchanges' executives were looking for.

Two members of the DOJ team took a number of documents from my filing cabinet, but that was nothing compared to what was turned over from those who had worked at the exchange for a decade or longer. Box after box of files from Bob, Julie, and all of the economists' offices had been wheeled away on dollies. The federal lawyers would be back in early January to collect everyone's laptops in order to download our e-mails and electronic files. The notion that *all* of our e-mails were going to be read by complete strangers made many people uneasy. But there was no getting around it.

December 27, 2006

Right before the year came to a close, I had my one-on-one meeting with the Merc's CEO, Craig Donohue. Craig had assumed his role on January 1, 2004, after Leo staged a boardroom coup to oust CEO James McNulty and Chairman Scott Gordon at the end of their respective terms. McNulty and Gordon had begun to question Leo's extensive involvement in day-to-day operations, as well the board's prior commitment to compensate him as both a director and a special policy advisor. When the ex-chairman caught wind of their concerns, he leveraged his five decades of political influence within the company to vote his dissenters out of their positions. The story told to the media, however, was that McNulty had infuriated floor traders by making several organizational changes and negotiating a pay package worth more than $60 million after the company's IPO. But since

CME's stock fell nearly 7 percent on the day McNulty's impending departure was announced, Wall Street obviously felt he'd done a fantastic job transitioning the Merc from a committee-laden, member-run club to the first publicly traded U.S. exchange. Alas, he and Gordon had crossed Leo, and Leo could not abide such disloyalty. So Craig, a corporate lawyer by trade who'd proven to be indispensable during the firm's demutualization process, took the reins from McNulty, and Terry Duffy assumed the chairmanship after Gordon.

Craig hailed from Des Plaines, Illinois, a middle-class suburb about 21 miles northwest of Chicago. He had planned to become a pharmacist like his stepfather—until their family drugstore proved no match for the larger competitors that descended upon their town. Thankfully, Craig's love of learning offered him many other paths. He went on to earn not one, not two, not three, but four degrees: a BA from Drake University, an LLM in financial services regulation from the Illinois Institute of Technology's Chicago-Kent College of Law, a JD from John Marshall Law School, and an MBA from Northwestern's Kellogg Graduate School of Management. After a short stint at the law offices of McBride, Baker & Coles, he joined CME in 1989 and worked his way through the organization with positions in the legal affairs, market regulation, strategic planning, and business development groups. Craig's background didn't exactly make him a hit with traders, though—many found him to be snobby. But there was something to be said for the fact that he spoke the language of financial analysts and industry reporters. While he wasn't thought to have political aspirations like Terry Duffy, he probably would have made a good senator or congressman because he was known for staying cool under pressure and being able to talk circles around anyone in a debate. He was also a complete workaholic, only taking breaks once in a blue moon to enjoy a game of platform tennis—a winter sport that's a combination of tennis and racquetball, played on a raised, heated, and partially enclosed court, and usually only offered through the most exclusive of country clubs.

Craig came to the reception area to meet me, looking like he'd just stepped out of a Ralph Lauren ad with his wispy blond hair, blue eyes, and outfit consisting of a sweater, button-down, khakis, and penny loafers. I'd never seen his Bentley convertible, but I could definitely imagine him driving it. Part of CME's fourth-floor executive suite was under construction and jackhammering had commenced right outside Craig's office, so he suggested we go into a conference room. I could hear the loud hum of various power tools as we walked down the hall; they almost drowned Craig out when he asked if it was okay for him to eat his lunch while we talked. He was toting a grilled chicken sandwich in a Styrofoam container. "I'm trying to be healthier," he explained as we settled in around a table. I had to inwardly chuckle—he already had a very slight frame and appeared to be in better shape than the vast majority of our meat- and pizza-loving city's other inhabitants.

He didn't get far with his sandwich before one of his assistants found us in the conference room. "I'm sorry to interrupt, but Gill's on the phone," she said. "Tell him I'll call him back," he replied and continued munching away. "I'm trying to figure out what to get Gill for Christmas," he shared once his secretary was gone. "I'm fresh out of ideas. He's so hard to buy for; he has everything. I need to figure it out quickly because I'm leaving for a ski trip tomorrow and want to get something ordered." He finished his sandwich, wiped his hands on a napkin, and closed up the container.

He turned to face me a bit more directly and it was evident the small-talk portion of our time together was over. I figured I had about five more minutes with him, so I wanted to get at least one question in. I told him I didn't understand why the media was trying to make higher trading fees seem like a foregone conclusion once CBOT and CME combined. "If each contract is already essentially a monopoly, why hasn't anybody been hollering about this issue *before* the merger announcement? Both exchanges have proven they won't raise trading fees simply because they can."

"Exactly!" he agreed, banging his hand on the conference table in frustration. He then went on to say that since it was such a complicated industry, not all of the journalists who covered the space truly understood how futures worked. "There's still a lot of education that needs to be done," he sighed. "Throughout our merger road show so far, there haven't been many questions from people who *get it*."

Craig then proceeded to talk at length about marketing. It was clearly his passion. He told me to hang tight as he ran out of the room in order to grab some of the exchange's old ads from his office. They were horrible, and he knew it. The focus of the first one was a freighter drifting aimlessly at sea; another had a sad-looking man pushing a rack of clothes down the street in what I could only assume was Manhattan's Garment District. Neither had much copy, so I agreed with him that it was hard to understand what the spots had to do with a futures exchange. "On top of that, they're *so* depressing," he grumbled as he stacked them back together and then pushed them off to the side. "But our new campaign, well, that's a different story. When people see Ken Griffin, they're going to pay attention."

He was referring to a set of five advertisements the Merc had launched in early September. Ken Griffin, founder and CEO of one of the world's largest and most successful hedge funds, Chicago-based Citadel Investment Group, was featured in a full-page piece. Sporting a perfectly tailored suit and eye-catching red tie, Griffin confidently crossed a gaping sidewalk fissure and remarked, "Risk is what you make of it." It was a big score for the Merc that the fairly press-shy billionaire had shown his support for the exchange and its products in such a public way.

Craig then divulged that his hope for the brand campaign was that it would disassociate CME from the stereotype of the futures industry. "There was an FBI raid here in the 1980s, you know. It was a huge scandal and people haven't forgotten about it. Many folks are under the impression that this place is just a bunch of shady traders with eighth-grade educations and slicked-back hair, driving nice cars and waving pinky rings."

Operations Sourmash and Hedgeclipper—code names for the dual two-year-long investigations at CBOT and the Merc—comprised, at the time, the most ambitious financial sting the FBI had ever launched. After four undercover agents were set up to live like successful traders—multihundred-thousand-dollar seats on either exchange, apartments at the ritzy Presidential Towers, luxury cars and watches, and memberships at the swanky East Bank Club—they worked their way into the inner circles on the trading floors at both exchanges, taped conversations, and gathered evidence of fraudulent trading activity. On the night of January 18, 1989, while almost all of CME's leaders were in Washington celebrating President George H. W. Bush's upcoming inauguration, federal agents fanned out across the Windy City and its suburbs and starting rapping on the doors of traders' homes—and handing out subpoenas. The end result of the sting? Forty-six indictments.

The exchanges had thousands of traders between them; those charged with any wrongdoing made up a minuscule portion of the customer base. As former CBOT Chairman Pat Arbor put it, "In the Catholic religion there were twelve apostles. The Lord himself had a doubter, a denier, and a traitor. Three out of twelve—a 25 percent failure rate for the Lord himself . . . I think we did pretty well."

While the FBI was never able to pin a dollar amount to the crimes, the media storm surrounding the sting had succeeded in shaking the exchanges. It shook them so much that two decades later, the management team and boards of both CBOT and the Merc still remained hyper-vigilant and excessively paranoid about how the press portrayed their businesses and industry. Craig hoped CME's new advertisements would help any remaining doubters see his firm in a different light.

"With this branding campaign, I want to show our clients that we can do everything for them that Goldman can do," he explained determinedly. "Do you know how much money goes through this place on a daily basis? More than the GDPs of entire countries. If it costs ten million in advertising to change our old image, so be it. That's such a tiny piece of our revenue in the whole scheme of things."

It didn't feel like it, but by the time we wrapped up our conversation, nearly two hours had passed. In the final minutes of our talk we discussed the intense internal and external politics at the Merc. Though I never brought up any specific complaints, it was like Craig could read my mind and sensed my frustration with how the merger work had been going. Before he left me at the reception area, he smiled and said, "I'm sure you've probably experienced a bit of arrogance from some employees here." I smiled uneasily back at him, but didn't respond. "It's just that we've accomplished a lot in the last few years, and people are very proud of that."

I bit my tongue, shook his hand, and thanked him for his time.

Mid- to Late January 2007

The end of the high-level planning phase finally arrived. Executives from both exchanges had made a conference room in the Sears Tower their home for three days as team after team paraded in front of them to present their plans. Once everyone had finished, we all reconvened at the country's tallest building so the consultants could officially close out the phase and give us a quick overview of what the upcoming detailed planning process would entail.

The lead merger consultant, whom we all referred to as "Shaggy" behind his back because of his resemblance to a certain *Scooby-Doo* character, addressed the large group. "The structure of the functional teams will change a bit—they will each report to one person who we will pick to be the accountable executive, or AE."

"What's an accountable executive?" interrupted Kim Taylor, head of the Merc's clearing division, before realizing how her question could be misinterpreted.

"Yeah, what *is* an accountable executive?" someone shouted, and of course everyone in the room had to snicker.

Shaggy attempted to settle us down before explaining that the accountable executive would be the one ultimately responsible for ensuring his or her group's detailed planning deliverables were not only completed on time, but also thorough enough to leave no doubt as to precisely how the two exchanges would integrate.

Next came news that no one wanted to hear. Since the high-level planning presentations had concluded much earlier in the day than expected, the management team decided to cancel the happy hour that had been meant to serve as a thank-you to everyone for their work over the preceding three months. If there was one thing I'd learned, it was that you do not promise an opportunity for free drinks to those in the trading industry and then renege.

CBOT's executives understood this, which is why I received a phone call from our COO Bryan Durkin's assistant shortly after I returned to 141 W. Jackson. "Bryan is inviting the team leads from CBOT to Martini Bar because your other event was canceled," she stated. "CBOT people only?" I asked. "Yes," she confirmed. I was in.

■ ■ ■

"This is the kind of place you come to if you're having an affair and don't want to be caught," Bernie cracked as we all gathered around tables in the narrow, dimly lit, and off-the-beaten-path bar behind the exchange. It did in fact feel like we were sneaking around—there'd been so much talk of trying to lessen the "us versus them" rivalry between Merc and CBOT employees that Bernie and Bryan must have been aware that the consultants would've frowned upon a CBOT-only event for merger team members.

Once he'd unwound a bit, Bryan—who had been leading the integration efforts for our exchange since it was clear Bernie wouldn't be staying on after the deal closed—let his true feelings be known. "I just thought it was really shitty not to have something for you guys."

As a few CME employees had observed during the kickoff dinner in November, Bryan brought to mind the fashion designer and *Project Runway* judge Tim Gunn. They shared a similar voice, wardrobe, and silver head of hair, as well as an overall set of mannerisms. Unlike Gunn, however, Bryan was married with children. I now understood that when my boss Chris had referred to himself as "the second-nicest guy at the exchange" during my interview, the person he considered *the* nicest guy was Bryan. Few would disagree.

Bryan had been at CBOT since 1982, knew the company inside and out, and was promoted from senior vice president of exchange operations to executive vice president and chief operating officer in 2003. As others saw it, Bernie had plucked Bryan from obscurity and created the COO position just for him after recognizing his potential during the exhaustive review of exchange operations he'd undertaken with William Farrow. In return, Bryan was fiercely loyal.

Although much of Bryan's career had been spent in audit or technology-focused roles, he had a personal interest in and passion for organizational behavior. When I'd had my introductory meeting with him prior to the merger-planning kickoff, he was very curious to hear about my past experiences on the acquiree end of three different buyouts. He wanted to know what I'd seen go wrong in those integrations, so that he could help CME and CBOT avoid the same mistakes.

Now he stood with a drink in his hand, animatedly retelling one of his favorite stories. In June, he, Bob, Maria, and Julie had been in London for the International Derivatives Week conference. They were staying at the Ritz-Carlton, and one evening Maria just so happened to share an elevator ride—alone—with none other than Joan Rivers. The two women struck up a conversation and complimented each other on their respective handbags. Maria retired for the night, but not before notifying the others about her encounter. A few hours later, the rest of the CBOT group was in the lobby bar and Bob pointed toward the hotel's outdoor sitting area. "Hey, I think Joan Rivers is out there!" he whispered excitedly. Bryan told his co-workers that his mother was one of Joan's biggest fans. Bob came up with the idea to send over a bottle of champagne to the brash comedienne, so they did—and received an autographed napkin for Bryan's mom shortly thereafter.

They all had such a great time reliving the experience—cutting each other off and interrupting to pepper in details—that I found myself wishing I had joined the exchange years earlier. The group had a blast wherever they went, and that night was no exception. Before we adjourned to seek out cabs well after midnight, I had persuaded most of the men—even my Ceres hazer Tom—to order girly-pink pomegranate martinis. They'd curse me for it in the morning when they tried desperately to tame their raging hangovers.

■ ■ ■

During the lull between the high-level and detailed planning phases of integration work, Chris Malo attempted to resume our weekly business development division meetings. One afternoon as we were convening in a small, windowless conference room, Bob slammed the *Wall Street Journal's* "Money & Investing" section down on the table for all to see. The front page featured an extremely unflattering cartoon of Charlie Carey. Our chairman was depicted in an ill-fitting suit, attempting to barricade a door that the neighboring CBOE's CEO, Bill Brodsky, was trying to push his way through. "They made Charlie look like a fucking pig, seriously," Bob stated, loosening his tie. Maria winced. "This is not good," she conceded. The article detailed the ongoing legal battle between the two exchanges over the CBOE exercise rights—the same issue I'd learned about when Bernie and Charlie had addressed floor traders and members right after the CME merger plans were announced.

The situation had turned so hostile that when a CBOE executive sat next to Charlie at a recent charity event, Charlie warned him that if anyone saw them together, "your members might shoot you." Most people figured Charlie was joking. Others weren't so sure. "Charlie's not going to be happy about this," Maria said, stating the obvious and staring at the cartoon in dismay. She made a note to have a word with her *Journal* contact.

■ ■ ■

After spending the first half of January 24 at CME in merger meetings, I returned to the office only to sense tension in the air as I walked down the tenth-floor hallway and past the rest of the business development team. Various salespeople were crowded around each other in small groups, reading something and taking turns commenting. I asked what was going on.

"A press release came out listing the executive management of the combined firm," one of them said.

I quickened my pace and pulled up the *John Lothian Newsletter* once I reached my laptop, knowing it would contain all of the day's industry news—along with Lothian's pithy commentary. Sure enough, the press release was there, and it was embarrassingly silly. CME Group was going to have the exact same senior leadership team as did CME—with only one exception. Bryan Durkin, our esteemed chief operating officer, had made the cut and was the only CBOT name on the 10-person list. Lothian couldn't help but make a remark of his own: "Congratulations to Bryan Durkin of the CBOT for being the only senior CBOT executive to survive the '*merger*.'"

The next headline in the newsletter belonged to an article from the *Financial Times*: "CME Details CBOT Takeover." Under that one, Lothian commented: "Headline writer gets it right."

Ouch. I went back to the press release again, this time reading it more closely. My heart sank as I found Chris Malo's name—it stated that he, William Farrow, Kevin O'Hara, and Glen Johnson, CBOT's CFO, would "continue in their current roles until the close of the merger." I moved on to an article from *Crain's Chicago Business* about the same subject. ". . . The CME said Wednesday it has made room for just one CBOT senior executive on its post-merger management team. . . . The personnel moves underscore the fact that the deal leaves CME management largely intact."

I peered down the hall at my co-workers, and overheard a member of the ag group say glumly, "It doesn't look good for rest of us, does it?"

Chapter 7

Under Pressure

Late January to Late February 2007

After CME Group's future executive slate was announced, there wasn't much to deter CBOT employees from obsessing about the impending organizational decisions that would affect the remaining levels of staff. Bernie held another town hall meeting in order to congratulate his troops on making 2006 a record-breaking year for the exchange—which of course triggered some sniping about "working ourselves out of a job"—but all anyone wanted to hear from him was the latest merger scoop.

He reiterated that one of the main drivers behind CME's bid to buy CBOT was the wave of global consolidation that had hit the industry. Several exchanges around the world were demutualizing or making plans to go public, and merger mania quite naturally followed. In March 2006, the New York Stock Exchange (NYSE) had completed its integration with former rival Archipelago, and then by year's end had won a bidding war against Germany's Deutsche Börse for Euronext, a successful Paris-based exchange (not to be confused with Bob's enemies at Eurex). The NYSE had pursued Euronext in the first place because its main competitor, NASDAQ, had been busy buying up shares in the London Stock Exchange. Atlanta's IntercontinentalExchange (ICE) had completed its purchase of the New York Board of Trade (NYBOT) just two weeks before Bernie's town hall meeting. In short, the leading exchanges were in an all-out scramble to gobble up as many other smaller securities and derivatives marketplaces as they could. If CBOT didn't join forces with the Merc, there would inevitably be another suitor stepping in to take our old foe's place. Our CEO didn't have to tell us that keeping the exchange's headquarters in Chicago—as opposed to some foreign city—would be a preferable situation for any employee who still found himself with a job after the deal closed.

There weren't many details about the staffing process that the executives at either exchange were allowed to share, so Bernie's answers to the questions people had about the stability of their employment were not very meaningful. However, he went out of his way to claim that "the CME staff is just as uncertain," which prompted a member of the merger team seated next to me to mutter, "Yeah, I can barely get them to do anything over there, they're just so *nervous*."

One rumor that had everyone up in arms was that the Merc planned to offer certain people positions that paid less than their current roles, and if those positions were refused, then the employees in question would no longer be eligible for severance packages because, technically, a job offer had been extended. I knew the CME leadership would never try to pull such a scam—they wouldn't have wanted the bad press in the local media, at the very least. But Bob, who'd recently returned from a trip to Asia with a nasty case of pneumonia, was having a ball fanning the flames of paranoia. In between his coughs and gasps for air he managed to wheeze, "Hell, I think they're going to make me either a janitor or a cafeteria chef. I'll be wearing a hair net and slingin' egg salad sandwiches!"

■ ■ ■

As the winter wore on, those of us at CBOT found ourselves in an odd position: Our focus was supposed to be "running the business," but we were extremely restricted in what kind of projects we could undertake. Bob's staff had to scale back their traveling, and couldn't commit to any industry conferences or customer events that were more than a few months away. The IT team needed to keep the trading systems and various data feeds up and running, but had to halt plans for technology upgrades or, in some cases, much-needed overhauls. The service group couldn't offer insight to customers about how the merger would affect their network connections to the trading platform, because those answers simply weren't available yet. In short, everyone was expected to keep their heads down, not rock the boat, and await further instructions. It was a complete one-eighty from the constant buzz of activity that the usually stretched-thin people on my hall had grown accustomed to. Without that daily adrenaline rush at the office, the atmosphere turned downright depressing. I didn't know whether to laugh or cry when I walked by an ag salesman's desk twice in the span of an hour and noticed he hadn't budged from the odd position in which he'd slumped in his chair. Upon closer inspection, I could see that he had nodded off, and even heard him snoring ever so softly.

■ ■ ■

Although our detailed planning responsibilities weren't particularly enjoyable, those of us on the CBOT side of the integration team tried to remain upbeat when talking to other employees who weren't involved with the merger efforts. But as soon as we were all together in one of our biweekly briefings (where only CBOT team leads were present), our collective frustration bubbled over. Even Bryan Durkin, who led the sessions, finally lost his cool when describing how he'd been unable to quickly resolve a technical glitch the week prior. "I couldn't get *anybody* around here to take my phone call—in *any* of your areas that I rely on. And that's because everybody was over at the Merc in merger meetings. I know we're asking people to do a number of things at once . . . but whenever you're over there, you gotta make sure you have your right hand over *here* to help us run this business. I totally understand and appreciate and compliment what all of you are trying to do with the detailed planning work, but I can't help but believe we're forgetting about our business."

That was just the start of his diatribe. He grew louder and more agitated and shifted around in his seat as he took a moment to look at every single person sitting around the long conference table. "We made the order of our priorities very clear to the Merc: one, giving the DOJ whatever they need; two, running this business; and three, the detailed planning work for the merger. They have to have a little more consideration for the fact that we've got to keep CBOT running. They have twice as many employees, so they're able to be in meetings all day, every day."

A technology manager jumped in. "They don't do a very good job of, uh, ever wanting to come over here, either." That broke the tension and everyone laughed, even though another IT staff member came to the Merc's defense. "In all fairness, a lot of it is the weather. Five meetings a day when it's four degrees below outside? There are more of them and so logistically it just makes sense that we go over there."

But Bryan wasn't going to abandon his point. He repeated his concern about the continual absence of so many critical members of CBOT's management. The senior project manager who worked most closely with the consultants and the Merc team had no choice but to offer to do something about the situation. "I'll definitely take this up with them. They're a bit process-heavy."

That comment inspired a chorus of, "Please tell them that we need to stop having *so many meetings!*"

The poor project manager handled it the best he could. "I agree. I wholeheartedly agree. There's a difference in our cultures—it's ingrained in the way they run their projects. *They meet.* And they bring 58,000 people to every meeting. And they've got PowerPoints up the ying-yang. I mean, a meeting like this one we're having right now would never be held over there without at least two premeetings to put together a deck about everything there is to discuss. I'm *trying* to get them to change. Now I'm the one venting. Sorry," he added hastily, seeming a bit embarrassed.

When we'd all aired our gripes, the briefing returned to its normal agenda. Bryan went around the room and asked the heads of each functional area if they were running into any roadblocks with their detailed planning efforts. The updates from the various trading-floor-related teams were the most fascinating. There were many issues those groups had to work through before they'd be able to consolidate the trading floors in our building—issues that might seem silly at first blush, but were deadly serious to the men and women who'd spent years in the pits at either exchange. Take jacket colors, for instance. At the Merc, gold coats were required for clerks, and red coats, while not mandatory, were given at no charge to members. At the CBOT, both clerks and members could wear whatever kind of jacket they wanted. At the Merc, there were X-ray stations one must pass through before being allowed on the floor, and over 70 surveillance cameras that kept track of activity on the inside. CBOT had standard keycard-activated turnstiles outside the pits, no X-ray machines, and no security cameras. CBOT allowed *dual trading*—where brokers could fill orders for both their customers and themselves on the same day—but the Merc prohibited this practice. CME fined traders frequently and publicly when they didn't follow the rules. CBOT fined its traders as well, but kept its list of transgressions private. These were but a few of the reasons why thousands of anxious traders were waiting to see whose guidelines would prevail when the floors merged together at 141 W. Jackson after the deal closed.

A woman from the member services division brought yet another interesting conundrum before the group. "You know how we retire certain acronyms?" she began.

"Yeah . . . " Bryan answered hesitantly. Every floor trader wore a jacket badge displaying a unique acronym that typically reflected his initials, name, or other obvious association. The buyer's acronym, the seller's acronym, and trade quantity and price information were recorded—and then keyed into the clearing system—for every pit transaction. Plaques of retired acronyms hung in the fifth-floor art gallery. They were kind of like the exchange industry's equivalent of retired sports-jersey numbers.

"Well, did you know there are more than 600 overlapping acronyms between current CBOT and CME traders?" the member services representative asked. "Given that overlap, do you think we might be able to . . . um . . . "

"*Un*retire the retired acronyms?" someone at the far end of the table offered. There was a smattering of snorts and gasps, as well as grumblings of, "Just like Michael Jordan."

"Yes, do you think we could unretire them—is that even a possibility?"

Bryan looked grim. "This could be big," he said, almost to himself. There was no denying that putting retired acronyms back into the mix would rile up the exchanges' most political constituents, which is exactly what the executives of both firms wanted to avoid before members and stockholders were asked to vote yea or nay on the merger.

"So should we even contemplate it?" the woman continued. "Or should we just say, 'These have been retired' and—"

"It's only the living ones that are an issue, really," Chris Malo interjected, eliciting snickers. Bryan, however, did not want to discuss the topic any further and indicated that he would circle back with member services at a later point. But the woman who brought up the issue threw out one more idea. "We're actually kinda thinking of having an auction whenever two guys have the same acronym—to see who wants it the most."

"That's what they do with personalized license plates in the UK! You want it, you pay for it. Supply and demand," Chris said, slapping his hand on the table. There were jokes about Acronym Auctions becoming a new revenue stream—and traders fighting over call letters like "ASS"—until Bryan forced the conversation to move on by asking to hear the latest from the head of the trading floor consolidation effort.

Tom McCabe, CBOT's vice president of operations who'd been at the exchange for over 20 years, cleared his throat. He and his counterpart at the Merc had been tasked with figuring out how the two sides of CBOT's trading floor would be able to accommodate all of CME's pits, brokers, clerks, and traders after the deal closed. In previous update meetings, Bryan had stressed the importance of keeping details about the trading floor consolidation particularly well guarded, as the executives already had their hands full with members calling and demanding to see "the blueprints"—which didn't even exist. No one had any intention of announcing the pit consolidation (or, in some cases, pit retirement) plans until after the merger vote so as to avoid pissing off, and subsequently receiving "Against" ballots from, the influential members.

"As it turns out, there are not going to be significant changes to the exterior of the pits. There will be interior pit changes, but the exterior layout of the trading pits will remain, as of right now, largely the same—which is huge," Tom stated.

"This is quite different from what we thought originally," Bryan remarked, seeming pleased to have possibly avoided a firestorm of controversy.

"There are two or three spots that are going to be an issue and we're going to need to work through them," Tom continued. "We've got to consider trader perception. And we're also making significant assumptions about the pit population. We're looking at what we have today and assuming we'll have 70 percent of that a year from now. If those assumptions are off, we're gonna have a much harder time."

"So is it fair to assume that our ag floor will remain the same?" Bryan asked.

"I think our current ag floor will remain pretty much the same," Tom affirmed.

"And by pretty much . . . you mean 'exactly.'"

"We're not touching the ag floor," Tom reiterated cautiously. "Some people say it's staying 'pretty much the same'; some people say it's saying 'exactly the same.'" He shrugged while others gave him a ribbing, but I don't think anyone blamed him for wanting to choose his words carefully.

Next, a member of the technology group asked if we could be less guarded about the plans for the trading floor now that we knew not much was changing.

"The fact of the matter is you've crossed the line if you're going outside these walls with any information," Bryan replied harshly. "There are bigmouths on the wider operations team and I'm sure they would love to tell their crony friends that they know what's going to happen to certain pits."

Either we were all drained from hearing about other teams' issues, or none of the rest of us had anything to report to Bryan, because the remainder of the roundtable updates went by quickly. I had a feeling, though, that this wouldn't be our last epic bitch session.

■ ■ ■

The following week, Bob was uncharacteristically glum as Chris Malo got the business development group meeting under way. The first item to discuss was the metals situation. Craig Donohue had continued to make statements to analysts that hinted at the Merc's intention to stick with NYMEX's metals contracts as opposed to CBOT's Gold and Silver suite after the merger closed.

"It seems to me that they already know what they're going to do," Maria lamented.

"Yeah, I sure didn't like Craig's answer to the metals question on their analyst call," Chris added.

"It was tapioca," Bob agreed.

"Well, our metals will still be trading on e-cbot when the merger closes," Chris said defiantly, referring to the fact that no immediate changes would take effect when the deal was voted through, no matter what CME decided to do about the situation. Chris's words didn't make anyone feel better, though. None of us wanted to consider the possibility of losing the metals complex. But while CBOT's ability to capture 50 percent of the metals market in two years was nothing short of incredible and gave employees something to rally around, the fact remained that the Merc's deal with the New York Mercantile Exchange covered both its metals *and* energy contracts. Even if the Merc's management felt CBOT's Gold and Silver futures were superior, they would be loath to relinquish the trading-fee revenue associated with NYMEX's high-volume Light Sweet Crude Oil contract. Then there was the matter of the 10-year agreement the Merc and NYMEX had signed. Any way you sliced it, things didn't look good for Bob's cherished metals products.

Chris closed the meeting with a quick update on personnel issues. Key employees had started to resign, and those remaining were growing increasingly nervous. The head of the ag economists, Dave, shared that one of his team members who had just moved to the United States for the firm was worried about the possibility of having to turn around and leave the country. The news Chris shared about the staffing process didn't help matters. He'd heard that the Merc intended to make many organizational decisions without even interviewing CBOT employees first. To add insult to injury, CME had released a list of 24 staff promotions in early February.

When the meeting was over, Maria and I asked Chris if he'd stick around for a few minutes so that we could get his take on a quandary we'd found ourselves in. My CME counterpart, Chris Mead, had asked Ted, the head of CBOT's education division—and the one who always told me great trader stories—to create the education strategy for CME Group going forward. He wanted Ted to detail out exactly how the combined exchange should make use of available channels to train its vastly different customer segments around the world.

Maria and I thought that picking Ted's brain to such an extent was clearly a violation of the information-sharing guidelines laid out by the lawyers. If the DOJ didn't approve the deal—or if it did, but then shareholders or members voted it down—CBOT and CME would remain separate entities . . . and the Merc would be in possession of a competitive strategy devised by one of our senior managers. Chris Malo confirmed our suspicions that it was time to escalate the matter to the CBOT's senior project manager.

This particular project manager must've already been banging his head against the wall when we left him a voice mail about the situation. An e-mail came through that same day from his counterpart at the Merc that attempted to address the concerns the CBOT team had about the crush of meetings. The irony was that attached to the e-mail was a "Best Practices for Holding Meetings" document. No advice was given on how to cut down on the number meetings—just how to have *better* meetings. It was hopeless.

■ ■ ■

After remaining mum about the CME/CBOT merger for four months, the Futures Industry Association (FIA) finally took a thinly veiled stance against the proposed transaction in the last half of February. The FIA was a D.C.-based lobby organization that represented the brokers and investment banks—collectively known as futures commission merchants (FCMs)—responsible for 80 percent of the volume transacted on U.S.-based derivatives exchanges. The most damning part of their official statement read:

> FIA acknowledges that the merger could have short-term cost
> savings and operational efficiencies. . . . In FIA's view, however,
> the CME-CBOT merger would concentrate significant market
> power in the new CME Group, substantially lessen competition

among U.S. futures exchanges, and raise even higher the barriers to entry for new competitors.

The association's jabs only served to motivate the leadership teams at CME and CBOT, who worked feverishly behind the scenes to secure a date for their respective shareholder and membership votes. On February 26, they announced the big day: April 4, 2007.

Early March 2007

The first half of March dissolved in a flurry of activity. Still fuming from the FIA's statement—and FIA President John Damgard's subsequent comment that members of his organization believed "fees can go up willy-nilly" if CME and CBOT combined—the exchanges' executives struck back. Craig Donohue retorted that the FIA "generally has bad arguments and weak facts."

He didn't have positive things to say about a subset of FIA's members—Wall Street investment banks—either. He accused those firms, which were also CME clients, of beefing up their profits through over-the-counter (OTC) derivatives trading and speaking out against the formation of CME Group solely because they feared the combined exchange might take away a chunk of their OTC business. "We have a lot of support from our largest customers," maintained Craig, explaining that hedge fund managers, for example, were all for the merger. CBOT's chairman echoed Craig's comments. "We understand where opponents are coming from: It's the profit motive, not the greater good," Charlie said in an interview with the *Financial Times*.

While Craig and Charlie dealt with the media, Bernie had his hands full trying to calm hundreds of freaked-out CBOT employees. Much to his chagrin, a March 6 *Wall Street Journal* article that encouraged those going through mergers to consider a "cut and run" approach was making the rounds in every division. Quotes such as "Acquirers tend to favor their fellow staffers over unknown quantities employed by a target" crystallized a truth that several of my fellow co-workers were reluctant to accept. Less than a week later, Bernie sent out a firm-wide e-mail that was meant to reduce uncertainty about the upcoming staffing process, but instead only heightened tensions. He explained that we all had two weeks to fill out one-page skill assessment forms that would be reviewed by hiring managers at the Merc. Some people would eventually have interviews and some wouldn't, but the lack of an interview invite did not mean that you'd definitely be laid off. In fact, no *employment actions*—the politically correct term for both dismissals and job offers—were likely to occur before the merger closed, as the DOJ's investigation limited such moves.

Shortly after Bernie's two-and-a-half-page message hit the servers, Chris Malo held a meeting with his staff to answer questions. He got an earful.

"Are we supposed to say what we're working on in this one-pager? Isn't that still confidential?"

"Will we have a job description for what we're interviewing for, or will it just be a general interview?"

"At what point are they going to tell us the organizational structure and where we would fit so that we can determine if we would even *want* to take a role that's offered?"

"I don't think it's legal for them to see our performance plans. Our HR policy is only to confirm employment when called for a reference."

"Yeah, our goals for the entire year are in our performance plans!"

Julie cut in and attempted to ease concerns. "These one-pagers are about your skills. If someone at the Merc asks to see your performance plan, which is a different document entirely, we will know about it. By and large, that is not going to be the case."

Her words failed to satisfy many, and mumbling continued about how this process "couldn't be legal." Bob set everyone straight.

"It absolutely *is* legal. Here's the thing: We're being *bought*, okay? This is not even remotely comparable to someone quitting, going to a competitor, and then calling HR for a reference. We're going to be one and the same with CME!"

Chris could sense that Bob was on the verge of completely losing it and making the situation worse, so he held his hand up and stated calmly, "Look everyone, if you get an interview, you can supplement this one-pager with your resume or any other materials you want. You should treat it like you would any interview."

That was the wrong thing to say. Chris had forgotten that the bulk of people in the room had *only* worked for the exchange, or had been there so many years that they probably couldn't remember the last time they had to prepare for an interview. He was scaring them to death; I could see it in their faces.

FIRDster Fred had looked especially contemplative since the discussion began. Finally, he spoke. "Are CME employees going through this same process?" He clasped his hands in mid-air, and his fingers drummed repeatedly as he waited for an answer.

Chris and Julie exchanged quick glances before Julie responded. "No. Clearly the hiring managers are at CME and they know their own staff, so Merc employees will not need to fill out one-pagers or be interviewed. But that in no way means they are all 'safe.'"

She didn't fool anyone.

■ ■ ■

As the realities of working for a company on the acquiree end of a merger were sinking in to CBOT employees, ICE was moving full steam ahead with its attempt to upend the proposed union between the Chicago exchanges. Over the three months that had transpired since their Smith & Wollensky lunch meeting, the Morgan Stanley bankers had vetted the idea of an ICE counteroffer with their executive management. The transaction had been thoroughly considered and was given an initial green light, but now that only days remained before Jeff Sprecher intended to make his big move, the bank wanted to talk through its remaining reservations about the deal. Although ICE was a strong firm that had already accomplished a lot in its short lifetime— and had enjoyed a 328 percent rise in its stock price since the end of 2005—it was still considered a niche player in the exchange industry. Its trading volumes were a fraction of the levels the Chicago exchanges enjoyed, and its market cap was only half the Merc's. Morgan Stanley's leadership knew ICE could never emerge victorious from a bidding war with CME.

"What is the strategy to win against the Merc's proposal?" asked Steve Munger, co-chairman of Morgan Stanley's M&A department. "You realize they can easily outbid you, right?"

"*If* it turns into a bidding war, you're correct—we won't win and we'll be out in a day," Jeff replied. "But I know these guys. I think we can outmaneuver them." He then proceeded to share a few of the ideas he'd come up with to do just that.

Munger still wasn't convinced. "You can't go into an M&A deal with public companies on the assumption that your competitor will make mistakes. If that is what you're thinking, you need to be very cautious about moving forward with this."

"I'm telling you, I know these guys and have studied them—they will not want to raise their bid," Jeff repeated. He reminded the bankers that the Merc had made lowball offers for not only CBOT, but also ICE, in the past. CME was a company of traders, after all. "They will not get into a bidding war easily. That will be the last weapon they'll draw. If they do, we'll lose, but there's a lot that could go on before that happens."

"It's very likely their advisers are going to tell them to come back with a higher offer immediately—within twenty-four hours after you enter the picture," Munger countered.

"I don't care what their advisers tell them to do. They won't do it. I'm sure of this," Jeff insisted. There was no changing his mind.

Anyone who knew Jeff Sprecher also knew he had a way of seeing around corners—of anticipating what was going to happen before it happened. So Steve Munger and the rest of the Morgan Stanley team were inclined to support their client's bold vision. The deciding factor for Munger, however, revolved around the proposed timing of ICE's bid. CME and CBOT had scheduled their member and shareholder votes for April 4. Exactly three weeks earlier, FIA Boca—one of the industry's most high-profile conferences—was set to commence. Jeff believed that if they could pull everything together in time to announce ICE's proposal for CBOT at FIA Boca, they'd have the perfect opportunity to not only garner support within the industry, but also use the media coverage of the event to their advantage. Munger thought it was absolutely critical for ICE to make its move in such a way that it would leave CME and CBOT no choice but to delay their early April merger votes. That would buy ICE more time to strengthen its position and, if nothing else, allow the CBOT board some breathing room to consider ICE as a viable partner, especially if the DOJ ended up blocking the CME/CBOT deal.

So James von Moltke and Chris Lown at Morgan Stanley took the lead in finalizing ICE's interloping bid for CBOT. Jeff Sprecher had waited patiently in the wings while CME and CBOT moved ahead with their integration plans, but now he intended to blow those plans to hell—in the most public way possible.

Chapter 8

ICE ICE Baby

March 14, 2007

When FIA Boca kicked off, the heads of CBOT and CME knew they would have to face their opposition in person. Not only was the event sponsored by the FIA, but 800 of the top executives in the derivatives space—in addition to members of Congress and representatives from key regulatory bodies—would also be descending upon Palm Beach County for four days in order to network, browse exhibits, discuss the state of the industry, and, of course, drink and play golf. CME leaders planned to host a forum on the first afternoon and had lined up traders, industry commentators, and former regulators to endorse their proposed merger.

They timed a press release to hit the wire that same morning. It boasted that the combined exchange would be able to move all of CBOT's contracts onto CME's Globex trading platform and consolidate the trading floors over at 141 W. Jackson three to six months sooner than they'd stated in the original merger announcement. "Both organizations are working very hard to ensure that CME Group will be in a position to deliver at least $125 million in annual expense synergies as soon as possible after the close of our historic merger. Our valued customers, who will also realize annual savings of approximately $70 million, will benefit greatly from our accelerated integration timeline," Craig declared.

That evening at the Old Homestead Steakhouse located within the Boca Raton Resort, Craig, Charlie, Terry, and Leo were joined by senior managers and board members from both companies, a couple of high-volume trading customers, a handful of the exchanges' top shareholders, and a few industry analysts to honor the CME and CBOT engagement. Everyone was in high spirits as they talked about the deal and the outlook for the industry; the last thing on their minds was a possible threat to the merger. After their meal, the group retired to Bar Luna in the resort's lobby, where—surrounded by mahogany paneling and hand-cut Venetian glass mirrors—Terry bought rounds of shots for those still standing, and the celebration raged on until 3 A.M.

At the same time, in the same hotel, and specifically in Jeff Sprecher's suite, 20 people were working furiously on ICE's surprise bid for CBOT, which they planned to announce at the crack of dawn the following morning. Like CME, ICE had developed an all-stock offer, so the team had been anxiously tracking CME, CBOT, and ICE's share prices for several weeks, hoping their firm's position would be strong when the Boca conference commenced. The timing did indeed work out in their favor: ICE's bid stood a full *billion* dollars higher than the Merc's, which currently valued CBOT at $8.9 billion.

After Jeff received one last all-clear from his board late that evening, his team of company executives, Morgan Stanley bankers, and public relations specialists had precious little time to finalize everything. They needed to take another look over the letter that would be sent to CBOT's board, make copies of the press release to distribute to the conference's media attendees, and put the finishing touches on the script for Jeff's as-of-yet-unannounced analyst call. ICE's PR firm had been coordinating with CNBC all week, and their plan was for anchor David Faber to break the news during the *Squawk Box* program. Now it was just a matter of keeping things under wraps a short while longer.

To that end, Kelly Loeffler, ICE's vice president of investor relations and corporate communications (and, since 2004, Jeff's wife), decided it was better to be safe than sorry. She stuffed towels underneath the doors of the suite after discovering that Jean-François Théodore, CEO of Euronext, was in the next room. Team members took care to keep their voices low as they attempted to tie everything up. The suite had taken on somewhat of a war room appearance, with pizza boxes and food remnants strewn around the floor. Banker Chris Lown was one of the only people who got a bit of fresh air that night, as he made multiple trips to the local Kinko's between midnight and 4 A.M. He was also one of the only people on the ICE team who spied the Merc guys enjoying themselves at the hotel bar well into the wee hours of the morning. They weren't going to know what hit them.

March 15, 2007

No one who'd been working in Jeff Sprecher's suite got more than two hours of sleep before they needed to reconvene for ICE's big moment. At 5 A.M., Kelly and some of the Morgan Stanley bankers stood nervously in the resort's business center and ran off a few last photocopies. They worried someone would spot them and grow suspicious because they were all wearing suits, but the reality was that everyone else attending the relatively relaxed conference was still asleep.

Around 6:30 A.M., Chris Lown tipped two bellmen $50 each to deliver sealed envelopes containing Jeff's letter to the CBOT board, and the details of ICE's proposal, to both Bernie Dan and Charlie Carey. The bellmen had strict instructions to wait until 6:45 A.M. to knock on the men's doors. CNBC would be breaking the news 30 minutes later.

Shortly after the envelopes reached their destinations, Jeff intended to call Charlie, Bernie, CFTC Chairman Reuben Jeffery III (who was scheduled to address conference attendees later that morning), CBOT board member Jackie Clegg (Connecticut Senator Chris Dodd's wife), and a short list of other key individuals. Jeff also planned to contact Bill Brodsky, CEO of the Chicago Board Options Exchange (CBOE). Jeff had an idea about how to potentially solve the CBOE exercise right issue that had long plagued CBOT and CBOE, but knew he couldn't discuss it with Bill until after ICE had publicly announced its proposal. That's why some of the Morgan Stanley bankers were caught off guard when Bill stepped into the elevator with them mere minutes before ICE's plan went into action. Bill found it odd that they "looked like they'd seen a ghost" when he joined them, but didn't think much more of it. The bankers observed that the CBOE executive was headed to breakfast at one of the hotel's restaurants, so they reported his whereabouts back to Jeff.

And then the clock ticked to 6:45 A.M. It was go time.

■ ■ ■

Ever the early riser, Bernie—who had not taken part in the drinking festivities the night before—was the first to receive the news. He'd been in the shower when the bellman banged on his door, but a few minutes later when he was getting ready for the day, he saw an envelope lying near his room's entrance. He picked it up, opened it, and began to read its contents.

■ ■ ■

Charlie was standing in his robe, shaving, when his assigned bellman came knocking. "Hey, just slide whatever it is under the door," Charlie yelled. But the bellman was anxious to carry out his mission in person. Charlie assumed he'd been invited to one of the conference's many cocktail parties or dinner events, and went to open the door.

The envelope, of course, did not contain a party invitation. Once Charlie read Jeff's letter, he couldn't believe his eyes. *Uh-oh. Oh, brother,* he thought. He scanned the document again. And again. In the middle of his third review, the phone rang. It was Jeff.

"I know you just received my letter," Jeff began. "And I know I'm dropping a lot on you guys. But I think the combination of ICE and CBOT could be strong."

Charlie's mind was spinning. "You gotta do what you gotta do," he grunted, before reminding Jeff that CBOT still had an agreement with the Merc it had to honor. After hanging up, Charlie turned on the TV and was astounded to see the news splashed across CBNC. He immediately called his cousin Peter, who served as CBOT's outside legal counsel.

"Jesus Christ, whadda we do with this?" Charlie cried. "It's all over the goddamned TV!" Peter, who was also at the conference, told Charlie to hang tight, and gave him high-level instructions on what he could and could not say about this turn of events. He suggested pulling together as many board members as they could and arranging a private room in which they could all meet and review ICE's offer together.

Right as the Carey cousins ended their conversation, Bernie called Charlie. He'd just hung up with Jeff.

"Did you get the news?" Bernie asked.

"Yeah."

"Look, we've got to get going with the lawyers. We gotta make sure we respond to this. It's gonna be all over Boca today. We just have to manage ourselves."

"Understood."

Bernie did his best to stay as unemotional as possible when he talked to Charlie, since he knew the chairman must have been reeling. In his own mind, Bernie considered the significant amount of work that lay ahead. He wanted to talk to CBOT's legal team at Mayer Brown as soon as possible in order to understand what his obligations were and how the exchange should go about handling this unexpected situation. He called Maria and told her to cancel all of his plans—including the press breakfast CBOT had intended to host that morning.

Meanwhile, Charlie rang Terry Duffy and informed him that they'd have to scrap their afternoon golf game. Since it was still early, Terry was in his room and hadn't yet heard about ICE's party-crashing move. "I can't really say anything else right now—you better talk to your attorneys," Charlie advised his friend.

■ ■ ■

After Jeff Sprecher finished his short number of calls, he headed down to the lobby level to find Bill Brodsky. Bill and another gentleman were in the middle of breakfast when Jeff approached their table and asked if he could have a few moments with the CBOE executive. He led Bill out of earshot before saying, "I just made an offer to buy the Board of Trade."

Bill stared at him blankly, looking slightly taken aback.

Jeff continued, "I just want you to know that you're in my thoughts and that this is gonna work out well for you. One way or the other, I'm gonna get you a 'Get Out of Jail Free' card."

As the news sunk in, Bill—who'd spent more than 10 years as president and CEO of the Merc before taking over at CBOE—started laughing. "Wow," was the only response he could muster.

"I can't talk about things now, but I will make an appointment and come to your office when this all settles down so I can tell you what I have in mind," Jeff concluded, before shaking Bill's hand and heading back to his suite. He wanted to catch as much of CNBC's report as he could before holding an impromptu analyst call at 8:30.

■ ■ ■

Those of us not in Boca and not watching TV were clued in to ICE's counteroffer thanks to a special report John Lothian sent out before we reached the office. No one could get over the fact that such a young company had bested the Merc's deal by a billion dollars. ICE's all-stock transaction valued CBOT at approximately $9.9 billion—11 percent higher than CME's offer. My co-workers and I speculated whether ICE had a spy within our company, as some of the nonfinancial details laid out in Jeff's letter revolved around issues our members, traders, and fellow employees were particularly emotional about. Four such points were:

1. If CBOT shareholders accepted ICE's offer, they would own approximately 51.5 percent of the combined company—compared to 31 percent of a CME/CBOT amalgamation.
2. The corporate headquarters of the merged entity would be 141 W. Jackson, and the Chicago Board of Trade name would not only be kept—as opposed to "subsumed under a larger organization," as Jeff put it—but also leveraged to create a new brand identity for ICE-owned futures exchanges in New York, London, and Dublin.
3. ICE intended to "protect and grow" the CBOT metals complex.
4. Together, ICE and CBOT would have a 33 percent share of the U.S. exchange-traded futures market, versus a CME/CBOT share of 85 percent. In the ICE management team's view, this equated to an absence of antitrust concerns with their deal.

Jeff made a particularly stinging observation near the end of his letter. "While the CME transaction represents a sale of the company, our proposal is truly a merger that is intended to preserve the culture and heritage of the Chicago Board of Trade." His words had their intended effect. Immediately, e-mails between employees began to fly.

"This looks like a better deal, doesn't it?"

"It's almost like ICE knew the sore spots in the deal with CME."

"How could they justify not taking this offer?"

"This is just like *Barbarians at the Gate*!"

I e-mailed Maria to ask her what the buzz was down in Boca. She responded right away. "This is so crazy. Our stock is up, CME's is down." The media was quick to predict a bidding war.

I knew Maria was going to be swamped fielding questions from reporters, so I resisted the urge to call her and instead wrote back a short message that ended, "By the way, this is exactly why we shouldn't be sharing so much information with CME."

Others were thinking the same thing. When I got into the office I called Janella to get her take on the news. "It will be war between us and the Merc if the deal fizzles," she muttered, and then told me she'd been talking with another team lead who indicated he had no intention of continuing with any merger work until we heard from Bernie. "He said, 'Wouldn't it be so great to give the Merc guys the finger about this whole thing?'"

CBOT employees weren't the only ones impressed with ICE's strategy. "This is the industry upstart making an aggressive move for the granddaddy of all futures exchanges," London Business School professor Bruce Weber told *Bloomberg*. "It's a very bold move." Anyone who was familiar with our new suitor, however, shouldn't have been surprised. Jeff Sprecher was no stranger to bold moves.

■ ■ ■

Born in 1955 in New Albany, Indiana, and raised in Madison, Wisconsin, Jeff got his first glimpse of the spoils of entrepreneurship by watching his grandfather—an engineer by trade—build and run a successful concrete factory in a small Midwestern town. While Jeff's father, an insurance broker, and mother, a medical technologist, provided Jeff and his two younger sisters with a comfortable middle-class upbringing, his grandfather did exceptionally well financially.

However, it was not his grandfather's wealth that made an impression on Jeff; it was the adoration the townspeople and factory employees showered upon the accomplished businessman. Locals were extremely appreciative that Jeff's grandfather had financed and built much of the infrastructure in their quaint city. Every time Jeff was with his grandfather, who lived until the end of Jeff's high school years, he saw people stop him on the street in order to have a quick chat or shake his hand.

Witnessing the impact his grandfather's company made on so many lives sparked a passion for business within the future mogul. In his preteen years, Jeff began reading *Forbes*, and particularly liked the magazine's final page, the quote-filled "Thoughts on the Business of Life." He also started working as soon as he was able—first managing a paper route, and then washing cars at a dealership during both the school year and summer breaks.

Jeff stuck close to home to pursue his degree in chemical engineering at the University of Wisconsin–Madison, and as his graduation neared, air conditioning manufacturer Trane came courting. They were looking for "engineers with social skills" to join the sales staff of their newly formed industrial equipment division, and the dean of the College of Engineering indicated that Jeff—a member of the popular Sigma Alpha Epsilon fraternity—was the only one who fit the bill. But Jeff was considering other career paths, and told the Trane representative he wasn't interested.

The Trane rep wouldn't give up. He relentlessly called Jeff over a period of months, and finally offered to fly him—in the company's private jet—to their headquarters in La Crosse, Wisconsin. Jeff conceded. Once he was in La Crosse, Trane's management set him up in a huge hotel suite, wined and dined him, and promised that if he joined the firm and worked hard, he'd be able to earn $100,000 within a short amount of time. To Jeff, that was an eye-popping, almost inconceivable figure— over eight times the average starting salaries of some of his fellow engineers. He replied that if he could eventually move out west, he would accept the offer. Trane's executives agreed, and lived up to their promise three years later. Jeff worked short stints in Wisconsin and completed a two-year management-training program in Philadelphia, and was then tasked with opening the company's Los Angeles sales office in 1981. By that time, he was indeed making over $100,000.

Jeff was responsible for selling a Trane product portfolio that included steam turbines used for electric power generation, so over the next few years, he'd soon met all of the major players in the power industry. He'd also learned about California's burgeoning deregulation movement from an executive he'd been introduced to through his evening classes in the MBA program at Pepperdine. This businessman had an idea for a company that would build and manage power plants across the country, and wanted Jeff to join him in launching it. Jeff loved his job at Trane and was earning more money than he knew what to do with, but found this new opportunity too interesting to pass up.

To make the power plant business a reality, the first issue to tackle was funding. Jeff happened to know of a guy who could help: a Beverly Hills-based junk bond whiz named Michael Milken. The go-go 1980s were in full swing, and Milken's team at Drexel Burnham Lambert had no problem pulling together the financing to get the company off the ground. So in 1983, Jeff bid adieu to Trane, and Western Power Group (WPG) was born.

For 14 of the next 17 years, Jeff led WPG, which was similar to a real estate development company in that its management team would oversee the build-out of power plants and then bring together groups of investors to purchase ownership interests. Jeff was personally invested in many of the sites as well. By the mid-1990s, the Golden State was ratcheting up its deregulation plans, and Jeff was asked to serve on an advisory committee, composed of individuals from both the private and public sectors, to help determine the best design for a proposed energy marketplace. Unfortunately, the California government seemed to be leaning toward a structure that Jeff feared might leave smaller, independent power plants like his own Western Power Group with no chance to compete.

Jeff believed strongly that energy commodities should be traded through a free-market-based system, and wanted to prove it. He knew of only one power exchange in the world that might be able to help him—Nord Pool in Oslo, Norway. So he called Nord Pool, explained what the state of California was trying to achieve, and was invited out to Scandinavia to meet with the company's management team. As personal computers were becoming more prevalent by this time, Jeff figured he would find an electronic trading system upon his arrival at

Nord Pool's offices. Instead, he was met with a room containing several telephones sitting across one long table and large whiteboards on the opposing walls. Utility managers and power plant owners would call Nord Pool and relay their energy orders over the phone, and then Nord Pool employees would hang up, turn around and record the data by hand on the whiteboards.

"I'm shocked—I thought everything would be done on a computer," Jeff told his host. The Nord Pool executive shared that the company did have plans to build a computer-based system, and had recently partnered with Options Mäklare (OM), Sweden's first options exchange, for the job.

Jeff was unfamiliar with OM, so his Nord Pool contact made an introduction. Before long, Jeff flew to Stockholm. There, he met with Magnus Böcker, an OM executive who showed Jeff how his small exchange was on the forefront of developing innovative trading-platform technologies. Jeff explained the kind of energy-trading system he wanted to build, and Magnus offered OM's assistance. So Jeff packed up and moved to Sweden for four months to help guide the process. When the platform was completed, he bought the U.S. rights to the technology, and then headed back home.

Jeff was eager to show the California government that electronic, free-market-based energy trading was a realistic possibility. To get his point across, he rented a tent, a truck, and a generator, purchased two computer workstations and a refrigerator-size DEC VAX system on which to run OM's software, and set up shop on the lawn of the state capitol in Sacramento. He and an OM employee started a mock trading session under the tent, while one of Jeff's attorneys ran into the capitol building and encouraged lawmakers to come take a look.

Shortly thereafter, Jeff received a call from one of Magnus's direct reports at OM. "So . . . the California government loved everything about the system. Except for you," he explained. "They're really interested in it."

"Well, that's too bad, because I own the rights," Jeff replied. But the Golden State was willing to pay quite a large sum for the technology, and the OM team begged their American friend to reconsider. They proposed a trade-off. They'd identified another company that had established an electronic energy-trading platform: a small firm called the Continental Power Exchange (CPEX) in Atlanta. CPEX's customers used its hard-wired system to put in bids and offers for electricity—not electricity futures, but actual electricity in the spot market. OM had been planning to buy CPEX, but if Jeff released the Swedes from their exclusive licensing arrangement with him, they vowed to back out of the CPEX deal and let Jeff consider purchasing the company instead. All Jeff cared about was ensuring that a fair and transparent trading system was in existence for his Western Power Group business to eventually utilize, so he agreed to look into CPEX.

The more Jeff learned about the small shop, the more he understood why OM had been interested. He called the CFO of MidAmerican Energy, the firm that owned CPEX, and told him he was interested in making a deal. The CFO responded that if Jeff could be at the MidAmerican offices in Des Moines, Iowa, by the following afternoon to talk things over, he'd consider it. The only way Jeff could get there from Los Angeles was a *six-legged* Southwest flight, so he booked it. Miraculously, all of his connections were on time, and he made it to his meeting without a hitch. (Years later, Southwest Airlines co-founder Herb Kelleher would jokingly take credit for Jeff's subsequent career success.)

It turned out that MidAmerican wanted Jeff to manage CPEX, not buy it. That hadn't been Jeff's intention; he had planned to remain at WPG and simply wanted to purchase CPEX in order to ensure that a free-market energy-trading company continued to exist in the world. But following tough negotiations with MidAmerican, he agreed to not only buy the firm, but also take over as its CEO, in return for giving MidAmerican an option to buy back a percentage of the company from him in the future, should it prove successful.

In 1997, after cashing out of his stake in WPG and taking the helm of CPEX—which was losing $1 million per month—Jeff focused on figuring out how he could apply the same kind of open and transparent trading that took place at futures exchanges to the energy market. He had to move quickly, because the California government ended up altering the OM software they'd purchased. They intended to employ a pricing algorithm that Jeff—and others on the original advisory committee—felt did not offer price transparency, was prone to manipulation, and favored larger participants. Yet, despite warnings and filed statements opposing its plans, California launched the Power Exchange (PX) in March 1998. Jeff was concerned that other states would begin to replicate California's model. To prevent that from happening, he needed to produce a strong alternative.

In Atlanta, two of CPEX's executives, Chuck Vice and Edwin Marcial, had been hard at work on a next-generation trading platform that would allow customers to put in bids and offers over the Internet, versus the network-based system their company had originally been built around. Jeff knew, however, that even if they had the best platform in the world, it wouldn't matter unless there was a critical mass of market participants using it. So he began the process of going to visit 107 of the biggest firms in the industry—those who supplied various types of energy, and those who had asset management arms that invested in energy. Every week, for months on end, he and Chuck flew to the offices of heavy hitters such as Goldman Sachs, Morgan Stanley, Deutsche Bank, British Petroleum, and Royal Dutch Shell, as well as dozens of other power and gas companies across the United States. Although Jeff owned 100 percent of CPEX by this point, he knew he had no choice but to give up most of the company in order to secure order-flow commitments from the major players.

His plan worked. In total, 13 banks and energy firms split about 80 percent of Jeff's equity among themselves in exchange for a promise to provide liquidity on his trading system; smaller gas and power companies divvied up another 15 percent. Jeff's enthusiasm for and deep knowledge of the energy industry probably played a large role in convincing Goldman and the other firms to go into business with him. But there was also another huge reason why these competitors put aside their differences and joined Jeff's marketplace: It gave them a fighting chance against the formidable Enron, which had launched EnronOnline in November 1999. Energy industry players were starting to grow wary of Enron's puzzling business model, and Jeff offered a more straightforward option.

In May 2000, CPEX officially morphed into Intercontinental-Exchange and—based on feedback from its founding firms—planned to host over-the-counter and spot-market trading for oil, natural gas, and metals. In its first year of operation, ICE was something of a hybrid between the long-standing *voice broker* system for OTC trading (i.e., calling an investment bank to place an order) and a traditional derivatives exchange. Through ICE, over-the-counter trading was still conducted bilaterally—privately between two parties—but ICE's online trading execution was much more efficient than the over-the-phone alternative. Market participants now had the ability to trade some of the most common OTC products—the kind of transactions made so often between parties that they could pretty much be considered standardized—over the Internet. And though ICE did not provide clearing services at that point, it did offer a unique pretrade credit risk management tool that gave its customers insight into the stability of their potential trading partners. In addition, ICE listed data on recent trades, supplying clients the price transparency they lacked in voice-brokered OTC transactions. The only other major Web-based competitor, EnronOnline, forced all parties to trade directly with Enron and did not provide pricing information.

No one would've guessed that 19 months after ICE opened its doors, Enron would be bankrupt—and, as it were, found to be responsible for much of the western U.S. energy crisis of 2000 and 2001. It had manipulated electricity prices on the California Power Exchange, just as Jeff and others had warned might happen when PX was being developed in the mid-1990s. Enron's death was a boon to ICE's volumes; energy traders simply transferred their OTC orders from Enron to the industry's new kid on the block. Around this same time, ICE purchased the International Petroleum Exchange (IPE) in London and officially entered the exchange-traded futures business. IPE was home to the extremely successful Brent Crude futures contract that had been traded solely via open outcry for over two decades and served as a world benchmark for oil prices. Even more importantly, IPE had access to a clearing house that ICE would be able to leverage for its other businesses.

By April 2005, Jeff and his team had transformed IPE into a completely electronic marketplace and turned their focus toward taking ICE public in November. Ten months after their IPO, they bought the New York Board of Trade. That deal closed in January 2007, bringing soft commodities like Coffee, Cocoa, and Sugar—and, of course, the infamous Frozen Concentrated Orange Juice futures featured in *Trading Places*—into ICE's product portfolio.

Now Jeff hoped to continue his winning streak by throwing his hat in the ring for CBOT.

■ ■ ■

By 8:30 A.M. on March 15, CBOT and CME's management teams were well into hashing out their next steps in separate conference rooms at the Boca Raton Resort, but they took a break to dial in to Jeff Sprecher's call with industry analysts. It was pretty obvious Jeff hoped CBOT's influential members were also on the line. He laid his commitment to Chicago's storied institution on thick, repeating more than once that ICE intended to "preserve the proud heritage of CBOT" and "carry its legacy forward." He also pointed out that CBOT shareholders "should be concerned" that they were expected to vote on the CME/CBOT merger before they even knew whether the DOJ was going to ask for certain concessions from the combined exchange or, worse, seek to block the deal. And he certainly didn't mince words when he stated, "We simply do not believe that the CBOT should proceed with a transaction that undervalues the CBOT, shortchanges its shareholders, disadvantages its customers, and reduces competition and innovation in our industry."

Nothing, however, compared to the calculated remarks he made before opening the floor to analysts' questions: "I have in my office a copy of a hardcover book that the CBOT presented on its 150-year anniversary. It details how the company was formed by concerned Chicago businessmen; how it survived the Great Chicago Fire; adapted through the invention of the telegraph, the telephone, the television, and now the Internet; and navigated through the Great Depression and every modern war. I ask the members of CBOT that may be listening here today—are you prepared to vote on April 4 to write the final chapter to this book? Or will you work with my colleagues at ICE to build your next 150-year history?"

BOOM.

No matter what was going through CBOT members' minds after Jeff's impassioned plea, steam was no doubt billowing out of Craig Donohue and Terry Duffy's ears. They were absolutely going to have to come up with another $1 billion, but the harder part might be massaging the thousands of egos—upon which the entire deal depended—that had just been assaulted.

Yet four and a half hours later, the only peep out of the Merc was this terse statement: "We are confident that the CME/CBOT merger will create a strong combination and provide significant and unique benefits for shareholders and customers of both companies. We are working toward the successful completion of our transaction." CBOT's release was slightly longer, but mostly just repeated the details of ICE's "unsolicited, nonbinding" offer. The most amusing part was a statement explaining that the powers that be at the exchange would "review the proposal as soon as practicable." Like they had more important things to do than closely inspect a $9.9 billion deal for the company.

At 141 W. Jackson, productivity was at a standstill as everyone floated from group to group to gossip and share thoughts on what might happen next. Since John Thain, CEO of the New York Stock Exchange, had been quoted the prior week as saying, "If you look at the mix of our business, I'd like the derivatives piece to be bigger because derivatives are both growing faster and have better margins," lots of my co-workers figured the Big Board would enter the bidding war next. Others agreed. "It's clear the Board of Trade gets bought by someone, and the NYSE, the ICE, the Merc, and Eurex are all potential suitors," Wendell Kapustiak, a managing director at Merrill Lynch, told *Crain's Chicago Business*.

Eurex? What would Bob do if he had to answer to the Germans?

Chapter 9

War

March 19–21, 2007

Once everyone who'd been in Boca returned to the office, I cornered Julie Winkler and Chris Malo to get their takes on the previous week's drama. "Did you hear the CME guys had gone out drinking the night before ICE's announcement? Shots—the whole nine yards," Julie relayed. "When I saw them the next morning, they all looked so pale— they were hating life." By that evening, though, CME's management had bounced back into fighting form. Chris reported that Terry Duffy had been overheard grumbling about "those motherfuckers" at ICE during dinner. "The whole thing was so perfectly orchestrated," Chris marveled, his voice fading out as he relived March 15 in his head. Julie picked up where he'd left off. "People were coming up to us the rest of the conference asking, 'What's it like to be the prettiest girl at the ball?'"

Bernie and Bryan held a merger team meeting at the beginning of the week and instructed us to "stay the course." But since analysts, reporters, and the approximately 150,000 Illinois residents whose jobs were connected to the Chicago exchanges had spent the weekend comparing and contrasting the pros and cons of the two offers, it was admittedly hard to remain focused. ICE took out a full-page ad touting its proposal in both the *Wall Street Journal* and the *Chicago Tribune*, while CME announced that it would be hosting an analyst call and a presentation to CBOT members in a few days' time.

One of the biggest concerns that had surfaced about the prospect of an ICE/CBOT merger was whether ICE's trading and clearing platforms could handle CBOT's transaction volume. ICE would presumably be leveraging the clearing house of its latest acquisition, the New York Board of Trade, and in the first quarter of 2007 that system had processed 1.3 million contracts per day. CBOT's volumes, which were cleared through CME thanks to the common clearing link (CCL) arrangement, were at 4.1 million contracts per day—over three times what ICE was used to seeing. But in an interview with *Futures* magazine, Jeff downplayed this risk by pointing out that the clearing agreement between CME and CBOT wasn't due to expire for two years, which would give his team more than enough time to beef up their system. "Look," he added, "I built a $10 billion business with the platform that I started myself with my own checkbook; these things can scale. . . . For people to raise issues as if this were going to happen tomorrow is just not the case."

Another matter some found troubling was that if the CME and CBOT common clearing link were to dissolve, its nearly $1.8 billion in customer savings would also disappear. Jeff's counterargument was that an ICE/CBOT scenario offered customers a competitive marketplace, which was priceless. "What is the value of having two derivatives exchanges compete?" he questioned. "What is the value of just saving the Gold contract and having two Gold contracts? While it is easy to throw out the $1.8 billion because it *sounds* like a big number, I think the reality is that it is a very small number in the scheme of the derivatives business, and it is a very high price to pay to create a virtual monopoly in derivatives in the U.S." An executive at a large futures commission merchant, who granted an anonymous interview to *FOWeek* magazine, presented a similar sentiment. "What's $1.8 billion in savings given the overall business they do? It's nothing. With ICE and CBOT, and then CME and NYMEX, you'd have two true-blue competitors with no gray areas. Both would have the ability to compete and I think that's a better business model for the industry."

Jeff had wanted to hear concerns about his proposal firsthand in a meeting ICE had planned with CBOT's members in Chicago the week after FIA Boca—but then that meeting was canceled. CBOT's board had asked Jeff to hold off on talking to the exchange's members until their two executive teams had a chance to sit down together, and Jeff complied. But that sit-down had yet to occur, even though on March 20, CBOT released a statement indicating that its board had authorized due diligence discussions with ICE. Considering ICE's significantly higher offer for the company, Jeff "found it odd that the red carpet hadn't been rolled out."

In the meantime, pressure was mounting for CME to break its silence. The media picked up on a note Banc of America Securities analyst Chris Allen had written to investors, which declared that the Merc could afford to raise its bid a full 45 percent (from $158.42 to $230 per CBOT share) without diluting its own earnings per share, whereas ICE could probably only manage to increase its present offer of $179.46 per CBOT share to $215. Next, CBOT sent another press release to the wire, indicating that its April 4 shareholder and member meetings—the meetings where everyone was supposed to vote on the CME/CBOT merger—had been "postponed." No new date was given. But during the integration planning session at the Merc the following day—even though no one from their side ever uttered the word "ICE" or could even bring themselves to acknowledge that a counteroffer had been made—the lead project manager announced that the target for CME Group's first day of operations was now May 30 instead of April 17.

Finally, the Merc came out swinging. Craig Donohue told reporters that ICE's proposal was "significantly inferior," claimed its synergy estimates of $240 million were "significantly exaggerated" and that overall, an ICE/CBOT combination "poses significant execution and integration risks that could adversely affect customers and shareholders." Jeff Sprecher's response? "The CME rhetoric will not fool CBOT shareholders." CBOT shareholders' response? Elation. This war of words between their suitors had pushed CBOT's market value to a record-high $10.5 billion, and ICE's offer stood to put an extra $1 million in every full member's bank account. Bidding war fever had reached such a pitch in the industry that the U.S. Futures Exchange—which had been formed from the leftover scraps of the Eurex division that had tried to challenge CBOT's Treasury contracts in 2004—announced plans to launch binary options based on the ongoing battle for CBOT.

Beginning in late April, traders could use the binaries to bet on whether they thought CME or ICE would ultimately prevail; if a third party entered the fray, or if all deals fizzled, there would be no payouts. As I'd learned in my first weeks at CBOT, those in the futures industry were nothing if not enterprising.

March 22, 2007

The anti-ICE statements CME made earlier in the week were just an appetizer for what was to come. At 7:30 A.M., the Merc had a call with analysts and attempted to lambaste ICE's offer. The entire CME executive team was on hand to present chart- and graph-filled PowerPoint slides they'd been slaving over since the morning of March 15. Craig began by laying out how CBOT members should be concerned that they'd be getting a "weaker currency" if they went with ICE and its proposed stock-for-stock transaction. He reiterated that in terms of average daily trading volume, CME was the biggest futures exchange and CBOT was in position number 3, whereas ICE was way down the list in slot number 10. Further, in the one and a half years since ICE had gone public (versus CME's four), its stock was 30 percent more volatile than the Merc's. "Unlike CBOT and CME, which have steadily built their businesses and franchises for more than a century, ICE is six years old," he pointed out, before going on to say that ICE's business was heavily concentrated in the energy markets, and therefore "brings very little" to CBOT and its shareholders.

Then it was CFO Jamie Parisi's turn to tear apart ICE's projected synergy numbers. He presented a detailed argument for why the Atlanta exchange was not being realistic in its approach to estimating cost savings, and ended with saying that he believed synergies from an ICE/CBOT combo would be 55 to 75 percent lower than what Jeff Sprecher had outlined the week prior. Kim Taylor, president of CME Clearing, was next at bat, and did an excellent job of reminding listeners about the Merc's operational strength. "We have a 109-year history of running a clearing house without a clearing member default," she stated proudly, before listing out all of the crises the firm had withstood, from the crash of 1987 to the recent bankruptcy of its largest brokerage client, Refco. She also threw out a dizzying array of statistics comparing the Merc's volumes and open-interest values to ICE's. Her point was that CME dwarfed ICE no matter how the data was sliced, so why would CBOT want to go with the smaller new guy?

Finally, Gill talked about the execution and integration risks he felt were inherent in an ICE/CBOT merger. However, there was no mention of the CCL agreement's two-years-away 2009 end date when he asserted that ICE would have to plan for a "several-fold overnight ramp-up in trading" in order to accommodate CBOT's volumes. He also reminded listeners that the Merc had invested $360 million in system upgrades over the past five years, compared to ICE's $100 million, and was connected to nearly twice the number of countries as its opponent. Finally, Craig took the floor once again at the end of the call's prepared segment to summarize what his leadership team had conveyed: "CBOT shareholders are being offered a 'minnow trying to swallow the whale' alternative."

■ ■ ■

While the Merc's analyst call was successful in casting serious doubt on ICE's ability to smoothly integrate CBOT's business, ICE was still offering $1 billion dollars more for the country's oldest futures exchange. My fellow CBOT employees knew this was a fact our members would not abide, and so we eagerly awaited the Merc's afternoon meeting with CBOT's shareholders. I ordered Keith and David to stop whatever they were working on and dial in from their desks.

The meeting was held a few blocks away from CBOT at the W Hotel. Two hundred fifty members gathered to hear what the Merc team had to say for themselves, and another 600 people were dialed in to the conference line. Terry Duffy kicked things off by telling the crowd that at the end of the presentation, everyone would have the opportunity to ask questions and "get straight answers." He then proceeded to remind his audience why the Merc team felt the ICE's offer was inferior, ending a five-minute spiel with, "The fact is, ICE is trapped as a small player in the energy market. ICE has never led or innovated anything. ICE needs the CBOT to gain credibility for itself."

Next, Terry's emotions got the best of him and he launched into a dramatic rant. "ICE is trying to play up its recently discovered commitment to CBOT's storied history and heritage. Don't be fooled. It's kinda funny, how a company that shot outta nowhere a few years ago, funded by a couple of big investment banks on Wall Street, is now supposedly concerned about your history. ICE seems to be willing to say anything to convince the world that it's a better partner for CBOT, or at least to try and keep our transaction from closing." He grew louder and more agitated. "One of the other claims put out by ICE's PR machine is that Jeff Sprecher is closing on a home here in Chicago. Well, like a lot of you, I already have a home here. Not only that, I grew up here, and I've lived here my entire life. I've worked in this business for three decades. I don't believe for a minute that you can simply buy your credibility in our industry by purchasing a condo in a trendy new building. You have to earn your credibility, just as the CBOT and the CME have earned theirs and their rightful place in history."

With that, he thanked the audience and passed the microphone to Craig amidst a huge burst of applause from CBOT's members. It seemed the Merc's strategy was working, although the cheers petered out once Craig joked, "I have *two* homes in Chicago, but that's a particular problem of mine." He then tried to reassure the crowd that they didn't have to worry about the fate of CBOT members' CBOE exercise rights, which could bank them a ton of cash if CBOE went public in the future. Two months after the CME/CBOT merger was announced, the Options Exchange had filed a request with the SEC for a rule change that would vaporize the exercise rights, claiming that the formation of CME Group would mean that CBOT as an exchange— along with CBOT memberships—would technically cease to exist. CBOT had filed a brief with the SEC in February opposing CBOE's position. It was a thoroughly confusing legal battle, which is exactly why ICE had promised to retain the Chicago Board of Trade name and had structured its deal so that CBOT shareholders would own 51.5 percent of a combined ICE/CBOT exchange, thereby keeping CBOT as an entity intact.

But Craig insisted that CBOT members' exercise rights would be no safer in an ICE/CBOT combination. "They have not offered you a guarantee. They have not indicated that CBOE has consented to the form of their transaction as a way to preserve the guarantee, and like us, I'm sure you'll be waiting for that to happen for a very long time."

Those words would come back to haunt him.

At last, after 50 minutes of hearing various members of the Merc's leadership team slam ICE's offer, and after sitting through a PowerPoint presentation nearly identical to the one shown to analysts earlier in the day, CBOT members were able to ask questions. The first came from Jerry Manne, who got straight to the point. He called the Merc's original proposal "out of date," and declared that traders simply weren't going to leave money on the table. "Go back to the drawing board and come up with something more realistic, and we'll want to vote for the CME."

The room went wild. I couldn't wait to hear what the Merc team's response would be; ever since ICE came into the picture on the 15th, they had avoided any mention of raising their bid. Shockingly, they continued to dodge the elephant in the room. After thanking Jerry for his question, Terry stated matter-of-factly, "I think we have clearly demonstrated today what an inferior proposal someone else has put before you, so we agree with your comment, so thank you. Another question?"

First there was silence; then boos and intense grumbling commenced. But the members weren't going to give up. Next in line to grill the executives was Steve Fanady, who began by disclosing that he'd been a trader for half of his lifetime, and that he truly wanted to realize the dream that so many had shared for decades—the dream of the two Chicago exchanges combining to form a derivatives powerhouse. "What you've presented today are very, very compelling arguments which I have to agree with. But what they tell me is that the Board of Trade is the catalyst, it is the ingredient that lets this dream come true. . . . So as a shareholder I'm going to tell you that I will vote 'no' for this deal, and I suspect many of my fellow members and shareholders share the same sentiment and will also vote 'no.' It's not necessarily a vote for the ICE deal, but it does open the door to a reexamination of this transaction." Steve returned to his seat as another cheering session erupted.

It was Craig's turn to respond, and he joked about trying to use Terry's trick of simply saying "Thank you for your comment." I thought perhaps he had realized there was no avoiding the issue of CME's lower bid, but astonishingly, he went on to explain that their goal for the meeting was simply "to educate" the CBOT members about ICE's inferior offer. Was that going to silence the attendees? Hell no.

Next at the microphone was Harlan Krumpfes, a well-respected grain trader whose deep voice and Midwestern twang instantly commanded the room. "I'll tell ya right now, if it came to a vote, it'd be a landslide in favor of ICE, in my opinion," he warned, after faking everyone out by first praising CME's presentation for a solid few minutes. He then attempted to cut through some of the Merc's scare tactics in regard to the possible demise of the common clearing link. "Another thing that disturbs me a little . . . you talk about the capacity of the New York Board of Trade clearing operation that ICE has. Well, we have to realize there's 20 months between now and the time anything's gonna change with that clearing operation. And I don't know how long it takes to make a rocket go to Mars, but I think you can take care of that clearing operation if you're ICE in the next 20 months." He ended by assuring the Merc's executives that if they thought CBOT's traders were going to leave $1 billion on the table, "that ain't gonna happen."

After three more members made similar points, the CME team decided it was best to wrap things up. Yet instead of trying to end the meeting on a high note, Terry remained expressionless and infuriated the attendees even more with his closing comments. "I think there's been some good comments that have been made here. And I think we have clearly shown and dispelled that there's any kind of higher bid on the table for the Chicago Board of Trade than the Chicago Mercantile Exchange's. And everybody in this room—and I'll put myself in the same spot—we never bid against ourselves. We all know that. We are the highest bid today. Clearly. And we have demonstrated that. We want to thank you very much for your time and attention this afternoon." With that, he placed his hand on the laptop projecting the Merc's presentation and slammed it shut.

■ ■ ■

Three blocks away, the ICE team huddled around a speakerphone in the company's Chicago office and took in Terry's defiant statement. A beat of silence passed, and then Jeff Sprecher and his team of managers and bankers leapt out of their seats and began high-fiving each another. Jeff had correctly predicted the Merc's response; CME was not going to budge. "They aren't going to do it! They're going to try and ride it out," he marveled. ICE remained in the game.

■ ■ ■

Back at the W, CBOT members cleared out of the conference room and tables were rearranged for a CME press conference. The mood was dark. Gill was overheard saying, "It's almost like a wake, but there's no body to view."

A few hours later, the Merc's leaders emerged from their succession of meetings at the hotel. They fanned out on either side of the block as they made their way back to their offices at 20 S. Wacker. At that exact moment, the ICE team exited a nearby building where they'd been discussing the merits of their proposal with a high-profile trader.

Jeff spotted the group from CME immediately. He nudged James von Moltke and said, "Oh my god, there are the Merc guys. I'm going to the other side of the street so I don't run into them." ICE's chief strategic officer, David Goone—who'd actually been the head of product development and sales at the Merc for nine years before joining ICE— crossed the intersection with Jeff. The only CME executive Jeff had talked to since announcing ICE's bid for CBOT was Gill. They'd been on a discussion panel together at the Boca conference the afternoon of March 15, and when Jeff had approached Gill to teasingly straighten his tie, Gill flinched. "What—did you think I was going to *hit you*?" Jeff asked accusingly. The two men proceeded to trade barbs back and forth during the panel, but it was clear to Jeff that the man he once considered to be the most affable and jovial member of the Merc's management team undoubtedly "had CME running through his blood." Jeff was keen to avoid another encounter with his competition.

He didn't get his wish. After he and David made their way to the other side of the street, they were clear of Craig, Leo, and Gill, but saw that Terry was headed straight for them. The men shook their heads in jest as they approached each other. Terry looked awful, but managed to smile as he grasped Jeff's arm and wailed, "Why are you putting me through this?"

"You understand it's nothing personal," Jeff replied. He and Terry had always been on good terms, and considered themselves friends.

But once the kidding died down, the quick conversation took on a slightly more serious tone.

"Obviously I understand that," Terry acknowledged. "I'm sure this will be a very professional process—it is what it is. I look forward to working to complete this transaction, and I'm sure you do also." Terry told Jeff and David that it was good to see them, shook hands with both of them, and continued on his way. Across the street, James von Moltke was still chatting with Jack Sandner, an ex–amateur boxer and all-around likable guy, who'd served as CME's chairman for 13 years and remained on its board. The ICE team found Sandner to be incredibly gracious. As Jeff came over to him, Sandner cocked his head and commented, "You seem to walk on water these days."

All things considered, Terry and Jack had been very good-natured about the run-in. But their disheartened dispositions made it clear they were frustrated by how the CBOT member meeting had gone. Jeff, James, and David agreed that the Merc team looked "beaten up." The ICE executives, on the other hand, had just been reenergized.

March 23–26, 2007

Now that there was no doubt where their constituencies stood, the CBOT board reconvened to discuss the upcoming due diligence sessions with ICE, and all CBOT executives were ordered to clear their schedules for the subsequent two weeks. The staff at 141 W. Jackson felt the case was pretty cut and dried, and on the tenth floor I overheard countless conversations like the one between Grombacher and a data analyst. "I think as of right now, the board would vote for ICE," the economist stated confidently. "The Merc would be stupid not to raise their bid— this chance only comes once. But they're playing a game of chicken." The data analyst, like a great number of my fellow employees, felt the odds of her keeping her job were significantly better in an ICE/CBOT combination. She agreed with Grombacher's take on the Merc's stubbornness. "They're not budging on anything! I hope ICE wins."

Many on the merger team were rooting for ICE as well, even though hardly any of us owned shares of CBOT stock and therefore didn't stand to gain financially from a higher valuation of our firm.

We simply wanted our counterparts at the Merc to be put in their place. But after the excitement of ICE's unexpected proposal wore off, a new, harsher reality set in.

"If the Merc counters, or if for some reason their original deal still goes through, you know they're just going to be that much cockier, right? It might be unbearable," I worried to Janella. "And I think for a lot of people in my division, experiencing a glimmer of hope might end up being worse than if ICE had never entered the picture at all," I reasoned. Janella said someone in finance pointed out that if CME did raise its bid, it would mean that each merger team would have to scrounge for even more cost savings and synergies. "This bidding war is just going to prolong our agony," she concluded.

■ ■ ■

On March 26, ICE held an analyst call in order to respond to CME's attacks of the previous week. Jeff began by addressing Craig Donohue's claim that ICE offered a "weaker currency" to CBOT shareholders. He pointed out that in 2006, his exchange's stock was *the* best-performing stock. In any sector. Across all market caps. As in, in 2006, no public U.S. stock bested the one with the ticker symbol ICE and its 197 percent return. Next, Jeff reiterated that in regard to the CBOE exercise right issue, he was confident that since the Options Exchange was legally challenging CBOT members' entitlement to those rights— and had filed another complaint after the CME/CBOT merger was announced—that indicated the Options Exchange viewed CME Group's proposed structure as unacceptable. ICE's offer, by contrast, did not change anything about the Board of Trade's status. When an analyst probed this point again at the end of the call, Jeff phrased it another way. "We think that we can preserve the CBOT's structure as it is right now so that at a minimum, we don't make anything any worse."

Jeff saved his most expansive argument for the topic that was nearest and dearest to his heart. He viewed his exchange as a technology company first and foremost, and therefore simply could not ignore Terry's assertion that "ICE never led or innovated anything."

"We don't judge technology by how much a company can spend, or based on the head count of its IT department," he began. "It's not necessary in this day and age to spend $1 billion to develop a state-of-the-art trading platform." Then he unleashed a long list of ICE's technological accomplishments, including the fact that ICE was the only major commodities exchange in the country to offer electronic execution of both futures and over-the-counter transactions on the same screen. He also pointed out that nearly half of ICE's revenue in the fourth quarter of 2006 came from its OTC operations, whereas most exchanges—including the Merc—continued to struggle with how to break into this gigantic market.

Since, by definition, the over-the-counter market consisted of privately negotiated trades between two parties, traditional exchanges had difficulty pinpointing where they could gain a foothold. But Jeff had launched ICE in order to meet the needs of this very market, and had operated for nearly seven years with an OTC trading platform that had evolved from CPEX's technology. He'd always believed, however, that the holy grail was to find a way to clear OTC trades in addition to executing them. Ironically, it was a 1995 trip to the Chicago Board of Trade that made this lightbulb go on in his head.

When Jeff was in the midst of exploring free-market exchange options on behalf of California's government, he had headed to CBOT in order to see if there was anything he could learn that might be relevant to his cause. By this time, he'd finished his work with the Swedes at OM and had the rights to their electronic energy-trading technology. He went up to CBOT's Visitor Gallery, skimmed through a brochure, and came across a section on clearing. Jeff didn't know anything about clearing, and asked if there was someone available to explain the concepts in the brochure. John Harding, CBOT's vice president of product research and development, was called to the Gallery, and proceeded to demystify the exchange's operations for the inquisitive, tall bald man who'd showed up unannounced. Jeff then gave Harding an overview of OM's software, and told him how he was hoping to be able to apply it to the energy market. One of his remaining issues was that smaller power plants—like his own Western Power Group— would have to repeatedly post letters of credit in order to continue trading on California's proposed exchange, giving bigger utilities and energy firms an advantage. Harding replied that a clearing house would help solve that problem by figuring out an appropriate margin for each customer up front, and marking-to-market all trading positions each day.

As a result of Harding's conversation with the ambitious businessman, CBOT's executive management ended up supporting Jeff in his efforts to educate the state of California about their options. In return, Jeff shared with CBOT what he'd learned about electronic trading systems from OM, as CBOT was embarking upon its first foray into computer-based trading—an endeavor called Project A. But five years later, when Jeff was getting ready to launch ICE in 2000 and revisited his friends at CBOT to see if they wanted to partner on over-the-counter clearing, they weren't interested. Jeff sensed there was still strong opposition to electronic trading from CBOT's members, and his plan to launch an all-electronic exchange scared them.

Now, on March 26, 2007, Jeff explained to analysts how he had actually opened the door for his competitors to join him on the OTC gravy train several years prior, but they had shooed him away. He began, "When we started ICE, I visited every major derivatives exchange in North America. Yes, all the names you're thinking of. I went to visit the top management to see if we could hook ICE's OTC execution platform to their clearing houses. . . . I saw the value that a clearing house as a central counterparty with a global FCM community surrounding it could provide. That vision was not shared by any clearing house in the United States in the year 2000, as one exchange after another told me they were not interested—that this idea would not work. They said 'It's never been done,' which is something that rings familiar with the objections to our proposal that we hear today."

During the analyst call, Jeff refrained from actually naming any of the competitors he'd approached with the idea to partner on clearing. But in addition to CBOT, he'd also talked to the folks at CME and NYMEX. With NYMEX, he went so far as to offer up a stake in ICE. Gary Cohn and John Shapiro, the heads of Goldman Sachs' and Morgan Stanley's respective commodities-trading divisions, had arranged for Jeff to present his ideas to the NYMEX board. The meeting took place three days before Jeff planned to publicly announce his intention to form ICE with Goldman, Morgan Stanley, and 11 other energy and trading companies.

Jeff, Gary, and John entered NYMEX's majestic boardroom on their scheduled date and time, only to experience what Jeff deemed "the most bizarre meeting in the world." As Jeff began his presentation, NYMEX directors milled around the cavernous space, which housed a full buffet that was constantly being refreshed by an expert chef. Some men started piecing together a meal from the buffet's many options; some got in line for the roast beef carving station that was set up in the opposite corner. Undeterred by his inattentive audience, Jeff explained how his firm had developed an electronic system for trading over-the-counter commodities, and why he believed NYMEX might be interested in licensing the technology in order to launch electronic futures trading for their metals, energy, and soft commodities contracts. He also disclosed that he was interested in clearing over-the-counter trades, and thought that perhaps he could strike a deal with NYMEX to leverage its clearing house.

"I'm not looking to get into the clearing business," Jeff stated. "I'm just looking to get a clearing service going. I would be willing to route my customers' orders to your clearing house, and you could charge for it."

Richard Schaeffer, who would go on to assume the NYMEX chairmanship, but at that point was the exchange's treasurer, asked, "How much of the company are you offering?"

"I'll give you 10 percent," Jeff replied.

"Ten percent? That's an insult," Schaeffer scoffed.

Jeff was dumbfounded. "Why? I'm giving you 10 percent of my company for nothing. I'm willing to license you my platform for your use, and I'm willing to route all of my clearing to you and you can charge whatever a reasonable rate is. That seems like an unbelievable deal."

Schaeffer consulted briefly with a few other directors before responding, "The only way we'll do this deal is if you give us 51 percent."

Now it was Jeff's turn to be insulted. By that time, everyone else had set down their roast beef and all eyes were glued to the front of the room. The mood was turning hostile, quickly. So Jeff listed off the companies that would be joining him in founding ICE, and concluded, "We're going to make the announcement about the launch of our exchange in three days, so you have 72 hours to decide whether you are in or out."

The NYMEX members went nuts. They did not appreciate Jeff's blunt proposal, and the scene dissolved into chaos. Before Jeff knew what was happening, security guards had shown up and someone was shouting, "Get him out of the building!" The guards grabbed Jeff, Gary, and John, and escorted them to the street.

The three men cooled off by walking 10 minutes to Gary's office at Goldman. As they settled in to try and figure out what had just happened, word of the ICE launch leaked to Bloomberg, as did all of the other details Jeff had shared with the NYMEX team. The only thing Jeff could think was that he was glad he hadn't approached them any sooner. Despite the unplanned media preview of its launch, ICE would still go on to make its big debut three days later, as scheduled.

After Jeff received the cold shoulder from his fellow exchanges, he knew the only way to realize his OTC clearing vision was to look abroad, and that was how ICE came to purchase London's International Petroleum Exchange (IPE) in 2001. Jeff hired David Goone away from CME, and also brought aboard John Harding—whom he'd met years earlier at CBOT—to help him figure out how to get a UK-based clearing house approved to clear trades in the United States. Their plan was to connect the clearing house IPE had been using with ICE's already-existing OTC trading engine, in addition to finally getting into the exchange-traded business with IPE's flagship Brent Crude futures product (among others). Once the rest of the industry saw how successful ICE was in capturing a slice of the multihundred-trillion-dollar OTC market, other exchanges scrambled to pull together plans of their own. But by March 2007, none had come even remotely close to ICE's position. At the time of Jeff's analyst call, the Merc's OTC business accounted for less than 1 percent of its average daily trading volumes.

Jeff concluded his chat with industry analysts by musing, "As our detractors would point out, we are smaller and younger—but that makes our achievements all the more significant. We're nimble, we're able to evolve quickly, and we are busy capitalizing on opportunities that big guys miss. And there are a lot of them."

The ball was firmly back in CME's court.

Chapter 10

Suspicious Minds

March 28, 2007

Chris Malo's status update meeting with the entire business development group was a welcome break from the ICE versus CME war of words that had been playing out in the press. All of us gathered in one of the big conference rooms on the executive floor and waited for Dave, head of the ag economists, to dial in from his vacation in Puerto Vallarta. As the minutes ticked by, Bob shrugged and said, "It's early morning there . . . he's gotta be out cruising the streets looking for his daughter and her friends . . . but they're probably off filming a Snoop Dogg video." Moments later, Dave beeped in and we all shook our heads at Bob. But he was on a roll that morning. When Chris started explaining the details of a class action lawsuit an institutional investor group in Louisiana had brought against CBOT, which claimed our board wasn't giving ICE's proposal fair consideration, Bob couldn't help himself. "Hey, just because you don't have teeth doesn't mean you can't file a lawsuit!" Chris shot a look Bob's way and continued. "They brought this suit the day after ICE's announcement— we'd barely even had time to react to ICE's bid at that point."

There was more to the lawsuit than simply a contention that CBOT's board hadn't thoroughly reviewed ICE's proposal. It also asserted that the exchange's directors had not held up their fiduciary responsibilities when they accepted the Merc's offer in the first place. Though no other shareholders had gone so far as to press charges over this issue, there were certainly grumblings that CBOT's board had sorely undervalued the company. The *Financial Times* reported that in light of ICE's higher offer, some of CBOT's members viewed CME's proposal as "an embarrassment." One trader phrased it another way: "Charlie has lost his sheen."

The rest of the meeting was blissfully uneventful, but Chris, Maria, and I had a big afternoon ahead. Teams from ICE and CBOT had commenced their due diligence sessions, and the three of us had been asked to join ICE executives Chuck Vice, David Goone, and Kelly Loeffler to discuss CBOT's marketing and communications functions.

For the most part our session went smoothly and, as Maria later reported to Bernie, we found our new suitors to be sincere and engaging. However, when the three of us debriefed over lunch afterward, we agreed that although there was much that impressed us about the ICE managers we'd met and everything they'd achieved in such a short period of time, we weren't sure they fully grasped what an undertaking it would be to integrate a 159-year-old exchange and its few thousand employees.

April 11, 2007

Merger work with CME had slowed significantly since ICE's announcement. Or perhaps I should say that while our Merc counterparts were surely still running ahead with detailed planning, the CBOT team's involvement with the integration efforts had been severely cut back, not only because of the ensuing due diligence with ICE that we were all involved with, but also because the Department of Justice had started bringing people in for depositions. So when Chris Malo realized that most of his managers were in the office for once, he called us together to ensure nobody had any burning issues. Gene, head of the FIRDsters, relived his deposition for us and forewarned those who were still on the docket that the experience was "like mind chess." Chris, who'd also already faced the Feds in D.C., countered, "I'd call it something similar . . ." We all knew what he was thinking. Though the interviews sounded boring and excruciatingly long, I never heard anyone complain about the DOJ team specifically. Most seemed to agree with Gene's assessment that "the guys were just doing their jobs."

The conversation then moved to concerns about employee turnover. Steve Dickey, who headed our market data group, had lost a few key team members and was concerned because he hadn't heard anything about a raise and promotion request he'd put in for one of his remaining superstars. "We keep hearing 'run the business,' but we can't lose another person!" he argued.

Julie explained that the merger agreement with CME dictated strict "covenants" which CBOT had to remain within expense-wise, so that—if and when the deal finally closed—the Merc team wouldn't find a drastically different company than the one they thought they were buying. "We were lucky that we were able to get in your request before *everything* went on total lockdown," she explained, but Steve looked thoroughly pissed. "We can't promise that your request will be approved—or by when," she continued. "But if it is, it would be retroactive." He was still fuming.

Steve had raised an issue that was on all of our minds: There was a good chance the people we managed were starting to look elsewhere, which meant the rate of attrition was bound to start rapidly increasing. Chris segued into a discussion about the upcoming staffing process; the Merc intended to begin interviewing CBOT employees in the very near future. The head of our London office, Cathy Lyall, was dialed in on the phone and couldn't believe it. "Really?" she exclaimed. "Why would we open our people to interviews while there's this much uncertainty?"

Bob, who held Cathy in very high regard, leaned in near the speakerphone and asked worriedly, "Why, are you concerned about poaching if the deal falls through?"

"Yes," she replied. Bob put his hand to his chin and looked to be deep in thought until Cathy switched the subject and asked if she and her team in Europe could sign up for industry conferences scheduled in June.

"No," Bob declared, snapping out of his daze. He went on to explain that with so much up in the air about the merger, none of us could commit to anything past the spring months, as CBOT might be the property of either CME or ICE by that time.

One of the ag salesmen looked incredulous. "We're all just going to be sitting here with our thumbs up our butts!"

Julie had no patience for anyone who couldn't understand the situation the company was in. "Yep, that's what happens. You will either stay sitting here in the office, or your credit card will be cut off when you're overseas or at an event, because that's what they're planning to do after the deal closes." Everyone in the room—except those of us on the integration team—was downright disturbed. They couldn't imagine their lives on the road coming to a screeching halt, and truly didn't know what they would do if they were forced to be grounded for an unspecified length of time. The thought of their corporate cards being cut off was more than they could bear. Since they didn't seem to believe Julie, I confirmed that if the CME deal went through, corporate cards would be frozen, and then entirely new cards would be reissued at a later point. I refrained from adding, ". . . to those who still have jobs." Chris continued going around the table to see if anyone had other things to talk about, but the dejected looks he was met with gave him his answer.

■ ■ ■

Just when I was starting to enjoy having a chance to perform my normal job again, I received an e-mail from one of the ag salesmen—the same guy I'd seen sleeping at his desk—that made me wish I was back in a never-ending merger meeting. The e-mail was in reference to new products the ag group would be launching shortly: "e-mini" Corn, Soybeans, and Wheat. Each of these electronically traded contracts would be one-fifth the size of their original counterparts: a Corn contract represented 5,000 bushels of corn, whereas an e-mini Corn contract equaled 1,000 bushels of corn. The lower price of the e-minis allowed individual (i.e., retail) traders, and those in Asia who preferred smaller lot sizes, another way to participate in the agricultural markets. In order to appease members, however, these products would only be available for overnight trading on e-cbot so as to not provide competition for the popular agricultural e-minis that were already trading during the day on the floor. Therefore, no one had any reason to get worked up about the launch—except for me, after I saw what the salesman in question proposed for an e-mail that was scheduled to go out to tens of thousands of customers the next day. "MINI-sized, MAXI-benefits!" was his suggestion for the subject line.

I stared at the message in disbelief. This man had daughters. Did he not realize the word *maxi* usually brought to mind a feminine hygiene product? I attempted a diplomatic response.

"Something is not sitting right with me with 'Maxi-Benefits.' I would rather have it written out as 'mini-sized . . . with maximum benefits,' or something like that."

He wasn't going to make it easy for me. Within minutes he wrote back, "It was just meant to be a play on the phrase 'mini-maxi,' which is a term used in the agricultural markets. Also the mini-sized is lower case and the MAXI-BENEFITS is upper case."

I banged my head slowly against my desk and called a friend at JPMorgan. His advice was, "Why don't you ask if you can add 'With wings!' to the marketing material and see if he gets it then?"

The lone woman on the ag team took my side and replied to the e-mail chain, "I agree on the min-max concept, but perhaps not so much on the mini-maxi . . ."

It was to no avail. The pro-maxi man was not going to give up. I called Bob for help; he started choking with laughter. "Oh, Jesus. Let me handle it." I owed him one.

■ ■ ■

The already event-filled day held one last twist. After business hours, Maria's team sent a press release to the wire indicating that the CBOT member and shareholder votes on the CME/CBOT merger that had been previously scheduled for April 4 would now take place on July 9. The Merc had rescheduled their votes for the same day as well. It seemed hard to believe that everything could be resolved in less than three months.

April 12, 2007

I thought I'd get a break from talking about merger-related topics during a breakfast meeting with CBOT's advertising agency, but it was not to be. "We've been deeply entrenched for four years at CBOT. We would need advance notice if our contract wasn't going to be renewed. You guys can't just turn us off like a light switch!" cried the account rep.

"Why not?" was Chris Malo's unfazed response when I relayed the conversation to him. "That's what's happening to employees."

As it turned out, some employees feared they might be met with a far worse fate. A few hours after I'd returned from my meeting, an urgent e-mail came through from the woman who manned the tenth-floor lobby desk. She'd forwarded an alert that read, "Police are on the scene at the Chicago Board of Trade and the Chicago Mercantile Exchange after a man called in a bomb threat from a pay phone in Los Angeles. . . . The caller said there were going to be two bombs detonated at 12:20 (CDT), one at the CBOT . . . and one at the Merc." The report indicated that the anonymous caller intended the bombs to be a "message to our President."

This secretary had forwarded the news to only four people: me, Bob's assistant, the drowsy pro-maxi ag salesman, and a financial products saleswoman. The subject line of her e-mail was "How Come We Didn't Know About This?" Bob's assistant, who, like her boss, was quick on the draw with sarcastic replies, wrote back, "That's like wondering why you only sent this message to the four of us!" We weren't exactly in the know about these types of matters, but the good news was that it was after 12:20 and the building hadn't been rocked by any explosions.

Within minutes, news of the bomb threat had made its way around the tenth floor. I overheard one economist mutter, "Well, that's one way to hit our synergy numbers." Someone else shot back, "Hey, it would get them out of paying our severance packages."

At the end of the day I e-mailed Maria and asked if she had any scoop on the situation. She replied, "CBOT is committed to securing the safety of all who work in its building, but we do not comment on the specifics of our security procedures." Before I could get annoyed at her message, she called and explained that line was what she'd been repeating over and over all day to anyone who called about the bomb scare. As we were hanging up she quipped, "I'm just glad we survived one more day at work—literally."

April 13, 2007

For the first time in several weeks, Bryan Durkin asked all of the CBOT merger team leads to join him for a debriefing on our various work streams. Julie and I had a few moments to catch up as we headed to the sixth floor for the meeting. She told me she'd be spending the coming Sunday and Monday with the lawyers from Mayer Brown, preparing for her DOJ deposition on Tuesday. "It makes me nervous that they're prepping us *so* much," she worried. Fred, the cowboy-boot-wearing economist on her team, was in D.C. giving his sworn statement to the Feds at that very moment. Julie's attitude was that the long pauses Fred naturally took when he spoke would be to his advantage when the government's attorneys tried to grill him. "That's what you *need* to do. You need to collect your thoughts. Whereas my tendency is to jump in and fill the awkward silence like I'm on a bad date."

We arrived at the conference room and took our seats. Bryan wasted no time in getting down to business and began with a reminder that we must take care to keep our detailed planning documents confidential. Apparently, someone on the CME side leaked what Bryan deemed to be a "minute" decision about the trading floor to Charlie Carey. "It was the equivalent of 'Should we blow our noses with tissues or hankies?' Really small in the whole scheme of things," he stressed. "And yet I thought I was going to witness Charlie having a stroke. I thought he was going to lose it. And then I had to backpedal when he said, 'You told me nothing had been decided!'" Clearly we had no power over what our partners at the Merc were blabbing about, but I guess it made Bryan feel better to reiterate that we needed to keep our mouths shut.

Next came an update on the staffing process. Bryan indicated that the CME team had begun to take a more open-minded approach to the organizational chart. "You might be happy to hear there are some sad faces over there, because they are finally realizing what we did months ago—that this is hard. I want to look at them and say, 'NO SHIT.'"

Julie took this as an opportunity to mention that the human resources–related synergy spreadsheet the finance group had asked each team to complete was "totally screwed up" and "a waste of our time." The spreadsheet attempted to calculate savings from head-count reductions in the future organization. However, as Julie pointed out, the Merc had not only continued to hire new employees (a huge sore spot with our side, to put it lightly), but also refused to add those new employees to the baseline head-count number—which resulted in an inaccurate view of synergies.

Julie went on to say that the Merc team was getting a rude awakening with the head-count-savings projections because, "Surprise, surprise, they make more than we do over there." To date, the finance group had used an average salary figure to calculate how much money would be saved by a *reduction in force* (or RIF, the politically correct term for a mass layoff). Yet the reality was that it would be mostly CBOT staff losing their jobs. So when the actual—smaller—salary figures for CBOT employees were plugged into the formula, the resulting cost-savings number was always less than had previously been figured for each and every functional group. Our finance team lead spoke up and assured us that the Merc now realized the problem with its spreadsheet. Then he added, "They were more than fine to let *me* be the one to have to club people on the head over here, but now that they have to look deep within their own groups. . . ."

I asked if we'd be expected to wring out even higher synergy numbers, should the Merc raise their bid as a result of ICE's counterproposal.

"Yes. That's why I'm trying to turn the screws on them now, because it's only going to get worse," the finance rep answered.

"Well, this is good. We're all venting," sighed Bryan.

"I've got a better idea—do you think there's a place open right now where we can go get a drink?" Bob suggested, turning to our COO expectantly, like a puppy who was excited to go out for a walk. Alas, it was 9:30 in the morning, and no bar that we knew of was open. Otherwise I think Bryan might have actually sprung for a round.

April 16, 2007

While Julie headed to D.C. to run through questions she was likely to receive during her interview with the DOJ the following day, Fred returned from his visit to our nation's capital. I waved him over to give me the blow-by-blow of his deposition. He took a seat and said calmly,

"It wasn't bad at all. I think I bored them into submission. They are trying to rattle you." As Julie had correctly predicted, Fred wasn't one to become easily unhinged in such an intense situation. He'd found it curious that they spent a lot of time questioning him about an e-mail he'd written years ago with the subject line "Invasion of the pod people," and another—also from the distant past—that he had jokingly signed "Erwin Rommel." As in, Erwin Rommel, also known as the Desert Fox, one of Germany's most celebrated World War II military leaders. I struggled to keep a straight face as Fred wondered aloud whether the federal lawyer was trying to determine if his mention of Rommel was an attempt to draw a parallel between the general's militaristic tactics and CBOT's strategy in launching its Bund, Bobl, and Schatz (types of German debt) contract back in 2004. Either way, Fred said he answered, "Yes, counselor," but then our legal team objected because the question relied on Fred's personal opinion of Rommel. I can only imagine the conversations that took place between the DOJ attorneys as they read through all of Fred's messages for the first time. They probably had no idea what to do with him.

In addition to Fred's unflappable nature, the relative ease of his deposition might have been a result of Julie's extensive efforts to help familiarize the antitrust team with jargon and terminology that was unique to both the futures industry and our company. She'd been tirelessly assisting the DOJ for months, though her dedication came as no surprise to Fred. It was not possible for him to think more highly of her. He'd told me on several occasions that he'd "walk off a cliff for that gal. Because I know she would walk off a cliff for me." I certainly hoped the investigation wouldn't come to that.

April 18, 2007

After releasing its statement in late February that raised issues with the CME/CBOT merger, the Futures Industry Association (FIA) had not made any other comments on the ensuing bidding war for the country's oldest exchange—even after ICE shocked everyone with its 11 percent higher proposal for CBOT (announced at FIA's own conference, no less). But the lobby organization broke its silence on April 18. In response to a *Wall Street Journal* editorial that did not overtly side with either CME or ICE, but did admonish "Beltway meddlers" for worrying about the 85 percent market share a CME/CBOT combination would control in U.S.-based exchange-traded futures, FIA President John Damgard took to his laptop. His response to the *WSJ*, published as a letter to the editor and given the headline "CME/CBOT Merger Would Kill Competition," pointed out faulty arguments that the newspaper had made as it attempted to downplay concerns about what a behemoth like CME Group might mean for the industry. This did not please the executives at CME and CBOT.

"It's all-out war," Chris Malo told me that afternoon. "We just canceled a speaking engagement Bob had at an FIA event a few weeks from now. Clearly, our interests are not aligned."

Damgard's missive capped off several weeks of media speculation and industry rumors about a "New York investment bank versus Chicago exchange" conspiracy. As the FIA's membership base was responsible for about 80 percent of the business conducted across futures exchanges in the United States, and was largely made up of global brokerage firms and investment banks like UBS, Goldman Sachs, and Morgan Stanley, many started wondering if those institutions had actually orchestrated ICE's bid for CBOT. A few of those banks were, after all, the original founders of ICE, and still held small stakes in the exchange after it went public in 2005. The argument was that these firms wanted to protect their over-the-counter derivatives business from a mammoth entity like CME Group. So if CME upped its offer for CBOT, the banks might extend credit to ICE in order to keep the bidding war going. Even if the Merc still triumphed, it would have paid billions more than originally planned—and ICE's stock price would have risen in the meantime—so supporting ICE was a no-lose bet for Wall Street.

Chris wondered aloud whether Goldman Sachs in particular might also be partially responsible for the ongoing DOJ investigation into the CME/CBOT merger, because "Goldman underwrote ICE's IPO and is one of its shareholders, and Hank Paulson, who used to run Goldman, is now the head of the U.S. Treasury." This was by no means the first conspiracy theory involving the firm sometimes referred to as

"Government Sachs," however; its ex-executives had been taking high-profile positions in Washington D.C. since World War II.

The *Chicago Tribune* had added fuel to the fire the previous week with an article that began, "Some of New York's biggest investment banks would like to make sure top-ranked Chicago becomes the Second City when it comes to exchange-traded derivatives." They quoted University of Maryland law professor and former CFTC director Michael Greenberger as saying, "This is hand-to-hand combat, Chicago versus New York. It's a massive power play by New York and global banks against the Chicago futures infrastructure." Russell Wasendorf Sr., founder of *SFO* (Stocks, Futures and Options) magazine, and chairman and CEO of PFGBEST, one of the largest futures brokerage firms in the country, agreed. He believed the Wall Street firms—which made up the majority of the FIA's board—were afraid CME Group might serve to challenge their lobbying power. "There is not a single member of FIA's board that gives a fetid dingo kidney whether my firm exists or not. The organization has its roots in New York, where it was founded in 1955, and it has always given short shrift to Chicago, the home of the U.S. futures industry," he wrote in a biting editorial.

One person who chose not to believe the conspiracy rumors was past CBOT board member Chris Hehmeyer. "The New York banks—oftentimes people think they're much more of a monolith than they really are. They're very competitive with each other. So for them to get together and be that organized? I guess it's *possible*. But it's still to me more like these rumors are a result of the Merc trying to keep their bid low: '*Aaaahhh, it's the New York banks!*'"

Another guy pouring doubt on the Big Apple conspiracy was John Lothian, who used his newsletter as an opportunity to try and talk sense into those troubled by the rumors. He'd already raised the same point I'd been puzzling over: If the investment banks were so desperate to protect their over-the-counter revenues, why would they want to support ICE, the only major exchange in the country that had actually made significant headway into the OTC market?

Lothian did his best to bring people back to reality: "Be afraid; be very, very afraid!! *Or*, you can be a Chicagoan who is very confident about the value of the city, its people and exchanges, no matter who owns them. . . . Chicago is a great city and a great place to live and be a trader. It is a magnet for traders from all over the world, just as it has always been, and will continue to be."

He grew so agitated by gossip about an East Coast versus Midwest plot that he eventually wrote a two-page-long commentary on the issue. "For all the baloney in yesterday's *Tribune* fear-mongering scare-story about the intentions of the big bad New York bankers, local Chicago reporters and their stories have completely ignored what I believe to be the much greater threat to Chicago's futures markets: innovation and competition loss." He went on to compare how the Merc and CBOT had both recently launched real estate contracts, and had taken drastically different approaches in doing so. He argued that if the exchanges had been combined, only one of those ideas would have seen the light of day. "The city of Chicago loses, not wins. Do you want one lottery ticket or two in the big drawing?" Lothian opposed the end of the intense rivalry between CBOT and CME—and the creativity in contracts it often spurred—and believed this situation was what the New York firms wanted to avoid, too. "What the bankers fear is the concentration of existing futures products on a single exchange and the pricing power that would give that entity." Banc of America Securities analyst Chris Allen sided with Lothian. In his view, for the Wall Streeters, "it wasn't about the over-the-counter business; they hate monopolies, as anyone would."

I never heard the Merc's executive team address the "loss of innovation" argument, but they did have a response for those worried about CME Group's potential pricing power. As Craig had discussed with me during my meeting with him in December, each contract at both CBOT and CME—as well as most other exchanges—was already essentially a monopoly, because of federal regulations preventing futures from being bought on one exchange and sold on another. The exchange that was the quickest to build liquidity in a contract usually became the sole controller of that market because traders wanted to do business where open interest was high. That's just the way it was in the futures industry, and a CME/CBOT merger wasn't going to change that situation at all. In addition, Craig reminded the media that it was not in his company's best interests to raise prices, because his customers would trade more frequently if fees were low. Exchanges benefited from higher volumes more than they did higher fees. He also claimed that about $62.5 million in cost savings would be passed on to the Merc's customers every year once it had consolidated with CBOT.

And so the pro-CME and pro-ICE arguments wore on, with factions on each side standing their ground. Soon it became easier to ignore the unbroken stream of articles about what might happen next. Except for when I checked in with my Merc partner, Chris Mead, and he said things like, "Hey, so in our build-out plans for the CME Group web site, we need to make sure the IT guys are keeping things very flexible, because let's face it, there's gonna be another merger. In fact, there's gonna be another merger in six months." I had no idea what he was talking about, but figured his buddy leading CME's merger efforts probably shared information he shouldn't have.

April 19 to May 3, 2007

Despite ICE's still-much-higher bid hanging over CBOT and CME like a threatening thunderstorm, the Merc moved full steam ahead with its staffing plans. Janella in human resources sent an e-mail to all senior managers informing us that we would be invited to interview at some point between April 23 and May 4. I found the last sentence of her message hilarious, though I'm sure it wasn't intended to be: "Even if you do not think that you are interested in a position at CME Group, we encourage you to engage in these interviews and to keep an open mind."

On my way into the office the next day I stopped by Julie's desk to see how her deposition had gone. She said she'd kept her answers so incredibly short that during the lunch break our lawyers told her, "You know, you could say a *little* more." But she never changed her tactics. "I just wasn't going to put myself through that." All in all, however, she was just pleased to have the experience behind her and hoped she wouldn't be called back.

I brought her up to speed on the latest gossip making its way around our floor, and then told her how Chris Mead had hinted about another looming merger. "Do you think he could be right?" I asked. She got a look on her face like she was trying to remember something.

After a moment, she said she vaguely recalled the same head project manager I'd been thinking of—Chris's friend—making a similar comment. "I think he might've mentioned 'another deal on the table.' I can only imagine that it would be with one of the Asian exchanges—Tokyo Grain, maybe?"

Chris and his friend were off by a few months with the timing, and Julie was dead wrong about the target, but there was in fact a second exchange already in the Merc's crosshairs. At that point, however, Julie and I had bigger things to worry about—like the fate of *our* company . . .

■ ■ ■

Near the end of April, Chris Malo gathered all of the merger team members he could find on the tenth floor, waited until we had settled into a conference room, and announced, "ICE has stated that they have completed their due diligence."

Though I hadn't talked a lot with my fellow CBOT managers about the details of their due diligence sessions with the team from Atlanta, I was surprised by how earnestly most people had cooperated with the requests for documents, information, and meetings over the past few weeks. This surprised me because even though the rank and file at CBOT still were hoping for ICE to emerge victorious, I noticed that those in more senior positions had slowly shuffled back toward the CME camp. It probably came down to greater familiarity with the Merc team, its clearing platform, and its culture—even though everyone continued to despise the haughty attitude that pervaded 20 S. Wacker. Simply put, CME was the devil they knew, and ICE was the devil they didn't know.

"Well, we gave them everything," Bob said. "AND we gave it to 'em in braille!"

"Ah, shut up, you fargin' ICEHOLE!" Tom Hammond yelled, which served to unleash a volley of other *Johnny Dangerously* quotes. Needless to say, from that point on the term "icehole" was used much more frequently around the office.

Once Chris had the room under control again, the conversation turned to the current state of affairs at CBOT. Chris indicated that we needed to start making a Plan B in case the CME deal was not voted through in July. Although we were still "running the business" as directed back in October, the fact was that several employees had quit, the IT team had held off on technology upgrades, and no one in business development had been allowed to make travel plans to visit customers or attend industry events past June. Further, trading volumes for both CBOT and CME showed signs of an April slowdown. The Merc's shares slipped 3 percent when analysts predicted CME could experience its "first year-on-year decline since November 2003."

"People might think the bubble is bursting on growth. CME really can't afford to lose this deal," Chris opined. Bob was convinced that the New York Stock Exchange, now technically NYSE Euronext, was going to put in a bid for us as well. "I'd be shocked if they didn't," he declared. Those watching the situation from the outside also felt a third player might emerge, especially now that the merger votes had been pushed back to July 9. "We believe an elongated timeline increases the likelihood of another rival bidder," wrote Credit Suisse analyst Howard Chen to investors. His peer Edward Ditmire at Fox-Pitt, Kelton had an even stronger opinion: "It seems completely unreasonable that the big exchanges in this world, knowing that CBOT is officially in play, would not be evaluating whether or not that would be a good fit."

While everyone on the merger team shuddered at the thought of having to go through another round of due diligence with an as-yet-unknown suitor, there was a group of people who couldn't be happier about the situation: CBOT members. A good chunk of them were looking to completely cash out after the exchange finally settled on a merger partner. Until that point, their stock holdings just kept climbing higher. As Bryan Hynes, an associate CBOT member, told *Dow Jones Newswires*, "It's always great to be the guy at the bar with a bunch of girls who want to go home with you."

Chapter 11

Land of Confusion

May 10, 2007

The lull in merger work—and all other kinds of work—wore on. And the gap between the CME and ICE bids grew ever wider. What had been a $1 billion difference between proposals in mid-March was now a $2.2 billion gulf. ICE's stock continued to hold steady—or at points, rise—while the Merc's kept falling. "There's a hometown discount, but not this kind of a discount," CBOT member Lee Stern pronounced. Yet there were still no signs that the CME team intended to increase their offer.

Near the end of the day, out of the corner of my eye I saw Bob charge down the rows of cubicles behind the kitchen, pausing at each person's workstation a moment before moving on. Eventually he made it over to me.

"You okay?" he asked.

"Uh, yeah—what's going on?" I replied, wondering if maybe there'd been another bomb threat—or if the mouse a saleswoman had sworn she'd seen a week earlier was wreaking havoc again.

"Some guy got beaten up pretty badly in the elevator. We think there was a fight between a couple of the traders from the firm across the hall. I'm making sure everybody knows that we're gonna keep the front lobby door locked the rest of the evening." Just as he ran off to continue spreading the news, Maria called to check in on me. "I heard about the fight," she said.

"What the hell? Does this kind of thing go down all the time?" I asked.

"It's been known to happen," she laughed.

An hour later, if it weren't for a concert I was rushing to get to, I probably would've been reluctant to venture out to the scene of the crime at the elevator bank. Thankfully, I left the building without incident. As I waited at the LaSalle and Jackson Street bus stop, I e-mailed Anita—Maria's counterpart at CME, and the accountable executive for our merger team. CBOT employee interviews had finally commenced with the Merc's hiring managers, and mine was scheduled with Anita for the following morning. I wanted to confirm we were still on. She wrote back soon after and said she'd see me in her office at 10 A.M.

May 11, 2007

Very early on May 11, I checked my BlackBerry while on the way home from my concert. Anita's assistant had e-mailed me at six minutes past midnight, apologizing because we would have to reschedule my interview. I immediately knew another surprise was around the corner—there was no way an assistant would be working at such an hour otherwise.

My hunch proved correct. Right before 8 A.M., Bernie sent a message to all exchange employees, informing us that CME had upped its bid and that CBOT's board had recommitted to the Merc's merger proposal. Two months after it began its courtship, ICE had been officially snubbed.

Curiously, the Merc's new offer still valued CBOT lower than both ICE and the market did. As part of its sweetened bid, CME had raised its CME-CBOT share exchange ratio from .3006 to .35, in addition to announcing a $3.5 billion, $560 per share CME stock buyback plan that would commence at the close of the merger for those interested in participating. (CME's stock had been trading near $530 the week the revised proposal was announced.) The Merc's press release stated that the buyback would be financed through the exchange's available cash balances, in addition to a $2.5 billion commitment from Lehman Brothers. Buybacks like this usually came into play when an acquiring firm wanted to win over shareholders of its target firm, while rewarding its own investors at the same time. When this tender offer was factored in, CBOT's owners would be getting about $196 per share for signing their exchange over to the Merc. ICE's offer valued CBOT at $198 per share, while the market was trading CBOT at over $200 per share.

CBOT's constituents were not pleased. "What they've done is readjust their original under-the-market offer to another under-the-market offer," blasted Burt Stone, a full CBOT member. Burt's fellow member Leonard Goldstein put it another way: "They are really not acting as if they want to buy us. I'm a trader, they are a trader, and if I'm in the pit bidding $194 and the guy next to me is bidding $185, there is no way he is ever going to get the trade. It's that simple." Another member, Carl Zapffe, was downright angry at the exchanges' management teams: "These guys are wedded at the hip, and they don't realize that they can recommend a bad deal until they are blue in the face and it won't swing one single vote. As for me, this new .35 merger ratio is a joke and I am insulted."

After all of his talk back in March about the Merc having the superior proposal and refusing to bid against itself, how did Chairman Terry Duffy explain his firm's increased offer? His adjusted stance was that over the course of detailed planning, it became clear that combining CME and CBOT would save more money and generate more revenue than previously anticipated, so the Merc changed its proposal accordingly. He also couldn't help but add that ICE's bid was still based on an "extremely overinflated" share price.

Steve Fanady, one of the CBOT members who criticized the Merc deal during the Q&A session held in March, was livid. The buyback offer in particular had him seeing red. "This is amateur night at the Chicago Mercantile Exchange. This is not how you conduct a merger and acquisition," he fumed. "You pay for the premium for all the synergies you say you're going to get. What they're proposing to do is to use smoke and mirrors to get a value that the market has already given me. That's called fuzzy math, and I'm not voting for it."

There did exist shareholders, however, who were happy with the Merc's revised bid. Burt Gutterman, a CBOT member since 1971, had actually been content with the original deal because he felt CME's trading and clearing platforms were far superior to ICE's. His take on the Merc's tender offer was, "ICE doesn't have the wherewithal to borrow and provide that kind of liquidity for members who choose to leave."

John Lothian couldn't resist putting in his two cents, of course, and banged out a commentary dedicated solely to the Merc's new bid. After reiterating that he owned stock in neither CBOT nor CME, and pointing out that at the end of April, Eurex had announced it would be paying a 48 percent premium to purchase the International Securities Exchange (ISE), he observed:

> It seems the CME thinks they only need to improve on their previous bid, while I would expect shareholders would think any bidder should improve on the current [market] price. . . . The CME is right, they have offered a powerful, value-laden deal for the CBOT moving forward. The problem, I believe, is that moving forward many CBOT shareholder/members are going to be more worried about retirement, golf balls and grandkids than whether any deal is accretive to future earnings. . . . The CME is and has been a great stock to hold, but a lot of CBOT members are looking to make a trade, not an investment, when they sell the exchange.

His points were valid. But they may have been overshadowed by his more controversial comments that took dead aim at Bernie and Charlie.

> The problem for CBOT shareholders wanting to wait out a higher bid for the CBOT is that time is running out. With no disrespect intended to the current CEO of the CBOT, it appears to me that CBOT Chairman Charlie Carey has become the de facto CEO of the CBOT. The current CEO does not survive the CME merger, other than in an advisory role for a limited time, and has 20 million reasons to go along with what Chairman Carey and his board of directors want to do. And clearly, Charlie Carey wants the CME deal where he will be the Vice Chairman of the combined company's board of directors. Would CBOT members hire Charlie Carey to be CEO, or

would any $10 billion company, for that matter? But given the current realities, I believe that is the situation for the CBOT.

It would be a gross understatement to say that Lothian's diatribe did not go over well on the sixth floor of 141 W. Jackson; the "20 million reasons" line was the last straw for Bernie. In his mind, the May 11 commentary capped off nearly two years of "Lothian getting himself into topics he shouldn't be in." It was hard to believe that CBOT's CEO used to be a strong supporter of the *John Lothian Newsletter*. He'd helped to expand its distribution shortly after its summer 2000 launch by forwarding it to all of his contacts at Cargill. He even came up with its tagline: "Irreverent, but never irrelevant." What's more, there was once a time when Lothian referred to himself as "a big Bernie fan, and a CBOT fan." What, then, had led to the dysfunctional relationship between the writer and the exchange?

■ ■ ■

John Lothian—the middle son of a wholesale electrical supply sales-man and a high school teacher—was raised in the upscale suburb of Glenview, Illinois, about 20 miles north of Chicago. When he was 17 and on break from school at his family's summer home in Williams Bay, Wisconsin, John applied for a job working for a soybean trader who lived in the area. He'd drive the trader into the city, run various errands for him during the day, and read as much as he could about the markets whenever he had a few spare moments. By the time John went off to college at Purdue University, he knew what he wanted to study: finance and journalism. After graduating in 1983 with degrees in both, he landed a job as a reporter for Commodity News Services, which later morphed into Knight Ridder Financial News. But his career as a journalist was cut short a year later during the farm crisis of 1984, when the U.S. agriculture industry severely contracted—and the media companies covering the space went right along with it.

Over the next 13 years, John gained experience in the brokerage side of the futures business, and also tried his hand at trading. But it was a visit to his alma mater for a football game that had the biggest impact on the rest of his career. He saw how Purdue's new dorm rooms had built-in Internet connections for each student. "They are going to come and steal our jobs! I need to get in front of this," he thought. From that point on, his growing interest in technology led his associates to use him as a guinea pig for anything related to conducting business through a computer. In 1997, he was asked to oversee the creation of the electronic trading division at Price Futures Group, a brokerage firm headquartered within the Chicago Board of Trade building.

Around that time, John began to explore financial message boards and web logs, as well as investigate viral marketing tactics. He realized that starting an e-mail-based newsletter would be a thrifty way to not only network within the industry, but also spread the word about Price Futures Group's services. By the summer of 2000, the *John Lothian Newsletter* was born—he branded it with his name so that its recipients wouldn't think it was spam, and included links to all of the day's top industry-related stories. Every once in a while, he would write short commentaries on any happenings or events that were of particular importance.

Over the next few years, John's musings built him a reputation as a derivatives industry commentator, and he began to be invited to speak at industry events—including FIA Boca and the exclusive Swiss Futures and Options Association's annual conference in Bürgenstock, Switzerland. On December 26, 2002, the *Wall Street Journal* published a profile on the six-foot-seven broker/blogger, after sitting on the finished piece for about five weeks. John liked to quip, "It only took the slowest news day of the year and the birth of Christ for me to get in the *Wall Street Journal*." The article served to promote John's newsletter to employees of the securities industry, and its circulation skyrocketed.

All this time, John had a largely cordial relationship with both CME and CBOT. Of course, whenever he'd write something positive about CBOT, CME's management would think he was in their rival's pocket, and vice versa. In 2004, however, things gradually started to change. John had been a big supporter of CME bringing in Jim McNulty to help lead its demutualization and IPO. It just so happened that John knew McNulty from their younger days, as McNulty had a connection to the soybean trader John had worked for in Wisconsin. When Leo mounted his boardroom coup that pushed McNulty out of the company, John began to question CME's board, its new management team, and their intentions.

Things were still friendly between the newsletter-creator and CBOT, though. The same year McNulty left CME, CBOT was taking on NYMEX with its controversial, electronically traded metals contracts—a move John applauded. In October 2004, Bernie enthusiastically introduced John as the keynote speaker at a metals seminar jointly hosted by their two companies.

A year later, the relationship started to head south. John took exception to the dismissal of CBOT board member Carol Burke, who got into a tussle with Charlie over the hiring of his cousin as the exchange's outside legal counsel. John also had harsh words for how CBOT's leadership handled—and limited—employee participation in the firm's upcoming IPO. He pounded out several scathing commentaries with titles such as, "The CBOT Needs a New Chairman," "The Cost of the CBOT's Political Culture," and "The CBOT Is For Sale." He knew his relationship with the exchange would never be the same afterward, but felt it was his responsibility to his readers to explain why CBOT's actions gave him pause. Now he believed the CME/CBOT merger threatened the competitive spirit of his industry, and he was not going to stay quiet about it.

■ ■ ■

After giving everyone the morning to digest the terms of the Merc's new bid—and the fact that our company had finally said, "Thanks, but no thanks" to ICE—Chris Malo held an impromptu meeting in Bob's office with the business development managers. My boss's take was that we were "in the sixth inning—this thing is still very fluid, and anything could happen." He also mentioned that two publications had run stories the day prior about our board's latest—and supposedly secret—meeting to review both deals, citing "a CBOT director" as their source. Rick McCombs, an attorney at Mayer Brown who represented us in the DOJ proceedings, had apparently gone berserk about the leak and Chris had overheard him screaming, "We're going to find that fucker, and he is going to jail!" Bob, who had also witnessed Rick's rants firsthand, nodded and confirmed solemnly, "Every other word is fuck."

The group then started deliberating the various what-if scenarios based on the stock prices of the three exchanges. "Since both CME and ICE are offering all-stock transactions, the market sped up this whole process. CME had to do something—as its share price kept falling, the gap kept widening," Chris summarized.

Chuck Farra, our Asian markets specialist, asked what we were going to be able to do for staff if the merger vote had to be bumped back again. Chris gave a vague response. "Retention was discussed at the board meeting. They realize the stress this is putting on employees, especially if it goes past July. Their decision will be communicated."

Next, Chris shared that the scope of the DOJ investigation had continued to narrow, and that consequently the CBOT and CME management teams were even more confident than they were before that the merger would not be challenged. The DOJ would release its final judgment in advance of the July 9 shareholder and member meetings.

Most of the business development managers were still convinced that the New York Stock Exchange would come in at the eleventh hour. Chris tried to quell that speculation by explaining how our bankers had run an extensive analysis to determine what other exchanges could afford to buy us, considering our current stock price. Because of this analysis, CBOT's directors would be able to quickly assess any deal that might materialize from another company. "We know that putting in bids past specific levels would become dilutive to certain would-be purchasers—it would make their own stock prices go down." However, he didn't come right out and deny that NYSE was no longer in the realm of possibility, and closed the meeting down by saying there was always a chance a player they hadn't considered in their analysis could come out of nowhere.

May 15, 2007

A lot of people I'd come to enjoy working with chose to leave CBOT during the time that had elapsed since the original merger announcement. But it was Franco Campione's departure that hit me—and many others—the hardest. Franco was an energetic young guy who'd been at CBOT for nine years and had played a large role in building CBOT.com. The Merc team adored him, which was why it was somewhat of a shocker that he'd turned in his resignation and was heading to Spectrum, a hedge fund administration firm headed by none other than Carol Burke, the ex-CBOT board member whose ousting John Lothian had railed against at the end of 2005. While I shuddered at the thought of having to endure a web site integration meeting at CME without Franco to keep me sane, I was happy for him. But to CBOT's executives, Franco's news was a tough blow. Bryan Durkin was especially frustrated—our COO now had even more reason to be concerned about CBOT's technology team. They'd lost 80 people since October, and other companies in the industry were heavily recruiting the highly skilled staff that remained. "It's only going to get worse," Franco warned.

As Franco was one of the people at the exchange whom everyone loved—and whom no one thought would ever willingly leave—20 minutes after the IT whiz told the human resources group about his impending departure, Chris Malo marched into my office, clearly disturbed. "Why would someone go through this for seven months only to quit when there's just sixty days left?"

"Who's saying there's only sixty days left?" I asked, and was met with the infamous stone face. "Because I'll tell you what, Chris, on this floor, no one thinks this thing is ending any time soon."

He shook his head. "I just don't get it."

"I don't think you're looking at it from Franco's point of view," I challenged. "He's got a newborn and a young son, and there's absolutely no certainty about when this thing's going to close. So I think it makes perfect sense for him to leave if he has a good offer in hand. But now what *we* have to worry about is the fact that everyone else around here thought Franco was one of the few shoo-ins for a job at CME Group. When word gets out that he—of all people—is choosing to leave rather than stick around and see what happens, anybody who wasn't already sending out resumes is probably going to start."

Chris kept shaking his head. He responded to my final point by sharing that the management team was considering notifying employees about a "kicker" they'd receive—some type of extra bonus—if the merger proceedings dragged out past the end of July.

"WHAT? Why would you want to tell anyone that now?" I almost shouted.

"Well, so that people know it's coming," Chris replied, not understanding my reaction.

"Yeah . . . unless the deal still closes in July—or better yet, on July 31—and then everyone's going to be bitter about the extra money they could've had. I definitely would not communicate that information until you are absolutely *certain* that people *will* get the kicker."

"Ugh, you're thinking just like our members," he scolded.

We went back to talking about why Chris truly believed that everything would be settled within the next 60 days. The CBOT and CME leadership teams were banking on the Department of Justice giving the merger the all-clear, and felt that CME's stock would get a boost once that happened. In fact, they thought the stock would get such a bump that the $560 buyback plan might become moot, because shares could be trading higher than that at the close of the deal. As far as the July 9 meetings were concerned, Chris indicated that everyone was confident the Class A shareholders would vote the merger through. The CBOT executives figured the Class A constituency would only be concerned about whether the CME/CBOT union looked to be strong from a long-term investment perspective. However, a majority of both Class A and B shareholders needed to select "For" on their ballots, and it was the Class B shareholders—most of whom were individual members who'd spent decades on the trading floor—that Chris and others felt might cause problems. "A lot of them don't care about the overall viability of the combination; they just want the highest price so they can retire. This is their last trade."

Second Half of May 2007

One of the lighter moments the CBOT team enjoyed during the course of the CME/ICE bidding war was the arrival of "the interns." I would not have known that they'd begun their rotation through our group if it hadn't been for Bob. He came over to my desk and ordered me to call Julie and ask for her take on the interns. He stood and watched as I picked up the phone. Julie answered on the first ring, and I looked up at Bob as he smiled and waited for my reaction to whatever Julie was going to say.

"You tell Bob that I am *not* going to prejudice your opinion before you've even met them!" she replied and hung up. I relayed her statement to him. He pursed his lips at his foiled plan. "Okay, I won't tell you anything either," he said. "Except this—they're majoring in communications, but they're minoring in finance, 'so, like, we get numbers,'" he mimicked in a high-pitched voice.

A day or so later, I finally met the two young and quite attractive women who would go on to spend a number of weeks helping out with small research projects on our floor. After I'd seen them, I sent an e-mail to both Julie and Bob that simply read, "Oh sweet lord baby jesus." To say the girls were inappropriately dressed for the workplace would not be an exaggeration. They had teased hair and wore very short shorts and heavy makeup. I considered it a real possibility that I might get a tan simply by standing near them. They were bubbly and giggly, and their presence surely provided a welcome distraction for more than a few of the men on the premises. However, after some of us overheard the interns refer to a powerful board member more than once, we quickly figured out that they were either related or otherwise connected to this director, which made everyone a bit uneasy. As a co-worker put it, "Now we have to be careful not to say anything like, 'Fuck grains!' or 'Can't we just make the floor go away?'"

■ ■ ■

For two weeks following the release of CME's revised bid and CBOT's subsequent recommitment to the CME/CBOT merger, the only statement from ICE indicated that the firm was "evaluating its options." While Jeff Sprecher's team regrouped and planned their next move, an executive at another exchange unwittingly did them a huge favor. Nelson Chai, the CFO of NYSE Euronext, told industry analysts he believed ICE had effectively put itself "in play" by making a bid for CBOT. On top of that statement, he did not rule out the possibility that the Big Board might be one of the firms considering a purchase of the Atlanta exchange.

Chai's comments sent ICE's shares soaring. The Merc team watched the stock ticker in horror; their rival's offer for CBOT grew to be $1.6 billion higher than their own—again. What's more, word broke that ICE had entered into an agreement with Innisfree M&A, a premier proxy solicitation firm. That meant they intended to reach out to CBOT shareholders directly in an attempt to corral "Against" votes before the CME/CBOT July 9 deadline. It wasn't necessarily a hostile move, but it served to freak everyone out all the same. And as if that weren't enough, the day after the ICE/Innisfree news hit, the Atlanta exchange announced a May 31 meeting with CBOT shareholders. "We are extremely pleased to be hosting this event in response to the overwhelming number of requests we have received from CBOT members for a face-to-face meeting," Jeff stated in a press release.

While the ICE leadership team had been engaging in individual discussions with CBOT shareholders for the previous two months, it was believed that Jeff had refrained from meeting with CBOT members as a group because the exchange's board had asked him not to. But at this point, all bets were off. John Lothian, for one, had been eagerly awaiting an ICE/CBOT member meeting, and was glad CBOT's board wasn't standing in Jeff's way any longer. "For an exchange that has championed transparency, integrity and fairness of its markets, it is about time those values were applied to the ICE's interest in acquiring it as well," he sniped in his newsletter.

■ ■ ■

Two days before Jeff's big meeting, details from a CME/CBOT joint proxy emerged. The proxy had been filed with regulators and laid out the formal terms of the merger. It was intended to give investors all the information they'd need about the deal, its potential risks, and—of course—exactly how and when they could begin voting in advance of July 9. The media jumped all over a few key points in the document, such as the $288 million breakup fee that CBOT would be required to pay "if the merger is not consummated." Another revelation the press had a field day with was that CBOT had purportedly asked ICE several different times to enhance the "financial and legal" terms of its proposal. The main sticking points were that CBOT's board wanted Charlie Carey to remain chairman of an ICE/CBOT amalgamation, and they also wanted the authority to appoint the majority of the combined exchange's 16 directors. Further, they wanted an even higher valuation from ICE in order to assuage their concerns over the upstart's ability to handle CBOT's transaction and clearing volumes. ICE had refused these requests.

The revelations of the past several days made our weekly merger communications conference call especially intense. Anita kicked things off by asking Maria how worried the CBOT team was about the possibility of the Class B shareholders putting the kibosh on the whole deal. "We're worried," Maria responded gravely. Anita wondered aloud if perhaps CBOT members who were supportive of the merger might not proactively contact reporters and share their take on the situation. Those speaking out against the merger had a tendency to be much more prominent in news articles; the pro-CME faction needed better representation.

Then the conversation turned toward trying to guess what ICE might do next. "We don't want to act like it's a hostile takeover until it *is*," cautioned Maria. A woman on Anita's team said that ICE would have to file with the SEC if it intended to make any such move. Maria replied, "The counsel we've gotten is that if they do file, CBOT will have to be very tight-lipped, and CME would have to drive any subsequent messaging." Regarding the upcoming meeting with CBOT's members, Maria relayed that our PR firm felt Jeff Sprecher would concentrate on encouraging "Against" votes for CME, rather than continue to plug his own offer. "Well, it just all depends on what the New York banks are telling him to do, now doesn't it?" shot back a member of the Merc's team.

The call ended with Anita reminding everyone she'd see us at the highly anticipated detailed planning review scheduled for the next day. The review served as the official end of the second phase of integration planning, and each team would be presenting its plans to executives from both exchanges. Then we'd be in the home stretch of finalizing preparations for the July 9 meetings, and—assuming the merger was voted through—getting everything in order for the official debut of CME Group.

At the end of that same day, May 29, a number of CBOT managers jumped into a conference room to discuss what might happen during ICE's meeting with CBOT members on the 31st. We shared what we'd each heard about the meetings CBOT's executives had been conducting with firms and individuals who held the biggest blocks of A and B shares, or were otherwise particularly influential. Stockholders were still having a tough time with the billion-dollar-plus difference between the offers. Maria captured the overall sentiment best: "The issue is that the facts are moving away from us. The facts are simply not in our favor."

"But there's a $1.8 billion savings loss if the common clearing link goes away, and an outright cost, *and* a loss of functionality if we went with ICE," Gene Mueller, head of the FIRDsters, argued.

"Yeah, I can't believe any firm would forego its fiduciary responsibility and leave that $1.8 billion on the table—they'd be worried about getting sued," Bob agreed. Maria relayed that the CME team's latest plan was to shoot a video to mail to shareholders that would point out "the fallacies in ICE's proposal" and reiterate the strengths of their own offer. Bob threw his hands up in anger. "*A VIDEO?* How does that help with the impression that they're cold and arrogant? There's something to be said for face-to-face meetings!"

Long after the sun had set, we continued to debate how everything might play out. But none of the scenarios we'd envisioned for the immediate future came to pass. To our credit, no one else had predicted ICE's next move, either.

Chapter 12

Fight for Your Right

May 30, 2007

At 7:01 A.M., an e-mail from CBOT's head project manager signaled another imminent twist in the CME/ICE bidding war. The detailed planning review—the important milestone we'd been working toward for over four months—had been canceled. No reason was given. But as I scrolled through my other messages, I figured it out pretty quickly. "ICE and CBOE Enter Exclusive Agreement Regarding CBOE Exercise Rights as Part of ICE's Proposed Merger with CBOT," declared an ICE press release.

The week after FIA Boca, Jeff Sprecher had arranged a meeting in Chicago with CBOE's CEO, Bill Brodsky, just as he said he would. Jeff was confident that Bill would engage with an independent party like ICE if presented with a logical solution to the exercise rights conundrum. Jeff understood that the exercise right privilege (ERP) issue represented a major cause for concern among full CBOT members, since they conceivably had much to gain if they could resolve the quandary to their satisfaction, and subsequently clear the way for CBOE to go public. He felt the Merc's proposal had completely failed to take the issue into consideration; CME had pledged $15 million to continue the court battle against the Options Exchange, but that was it. One of the ideas Jeff had proposed to the Morgan Stanley executive team early on was that he would try to strike a deal with CBOE to put a specific value on the exercise rights, and then offer a payout to those who held them. But the key was to ensure the Merc couldn't turn around and promise the same thing after ICE made its announcement. So for the 10 and a half weeks following Jeff and Bill's quick conversation at the Boca Raton Resort, ICE and CBOE had been negotiating the terms of an exclusive arrangement.

They ended up agreeing that each full member of CBOT who held a CBOE exercise right would receive $500,000, and ICE and CBOE would split the financing—only if ICE and CBOT were to merge, of course. There were various ways an ERP holder could receive his payout: cash, future ICE/CBOT stock (up to $250,000), or CBOE debentures (up to a face value of $250,000) that would be converted into CBOE stock, should the Options Exchange ever go public. If CBOT's ERP holders agreed to give up their exercise rights in return for the payment Jeff and Bill had outlined, the likelihood of the class action lawsuit dissolving and CBOE finally being able to proceed with an IPO would substantially improve. In the meantime, no one was getting any money for his exercise right until CBOE went public, and CBOE wasn't going to go public until this issue was resolved.

"Unlike the acquisition of CBOT proposed by CME Holdings, which provides no value for the exercise right eligibility of CBOT members, and no certain resolution to this critical issue, the ICE-CBOE proposal would provide CBOT Full Members with immediate value for their exercise rights and the ability to hold equity in CBOE following its planned demutualization," Jeff said in the release. "This exclusive agreement with CBOE affirms ICE's consistently stated intention to provide a constructive resolution to this long-running dispute. We are eliminating a costly and potentially open-ended distraction that would otherwise persist following a completed merger between ICE and CBOT. We believe this agreement enhances our already superior proposal to merge with CBOT and underscores ICE's innovation and leadership."

Reactions flowed quickly. "This puts IntercontinentalExchange in the catbird seat. It's a huge achievement," remarked Larry Tabb, founder and CEO of Tabb Group, a financial markets research and advisory firm. CBOT member Jerome Israelov, who stood to gain from the deal, was a little more blunt. "It's disconcerting to me that Joe Blow comes out of the woodwork and settles a dispute which we have been fighting for 35 years. It certainly gives Mr. Sprecher a leg up." And of course there was no way John Lothian could refrain from adding an incendiary note about ICE's latest curveball at the start of his newsletter. "If the CBOT is going to change course from the one plotted by Charlie Carey and his board, Sprecher's display of leadership and vision might just be the thing to attract CBOT members to follow him. On the other hand, the CME squandered their opportunity to demonstrate their listening and leadership skills when they met with the CBOT members at the W Hotel in Chicago. . . . Serious questions were raised in my mind about the CME leaders' ability to deal with the often contentious CBOT membership."

■ ■ ■

After everyone had absorbed ICE's news, Chris Malo called me to check in.

"So what do you think? Will it be enough to sway the members?" I asked.

"For some of them, nothing will ever be enough," he figured. "But for others, this is their last chance to make a lot of money—to keep themselves from flippin' burgers to pay the bills during retirement." He reasoned they might be happy with getting an extra half-million in cash now, instead of waiting possibly years longer for a final judgment in the lawsuit.

Later that day, I stopped by Julie's office to get her thoughts on the situation.

"Just like Boca, this was a brilliant move. Everything ICE has done has been so well timed and calculated," she conceded. "It was smart of them to go after the Class B shareholders, because they'll be the most disruptive." We then pondered whether the ICE/CBOE deal might be enough to push back the July 9 votes scheduled at both CME and CBOT. Julie said the CME/CBOT proxy statement that had recently been filed was about 300 pages long, and if CME didn't change its offer, the document would be mailed as-is to shareholders very shortly. She thought the Merc's proposal had to be absolutely finalized a certain number of days before the vote, but wasn't positive. "Maria would know for sure," she said.

Unfortunately, I wasn't going to be able to talk to Maria any time soon. She and her team continued to be ridiculously swamped; they had spent the day crafting a letter to CBOT members in an attempt to head off hysteria about the ICE/CBOE deal, and reiterate—again— the strengths of CME's offer, particularly for the B-share contingent. I imagined they were already bracing themselves for the type of messaging they'd have to pull together after Jeff Sprecher held his meeting with CBOT members the following afternoon.

May 31, 2007

It was a very unproductive day at 141 W. Jackson. Outside it was rainy and dreary, and inside everyone was on pins and needles, waiting for the clock to hit 3:30 P.M. That was when ICE's meeting with CBOT members would commence at the Westin River North—and also when the rest of us planned to dial the published teleconference number in order to listen in.

When the designated time arrived, Jeff Sprecher, his management team, and several of his board members were met with a standing-room-only crowd of more than 400 people in one of the Westin's conference rooms. Countless others were watching via webcast or had joined over the phone.

After the ICE team introduced themselves, Jeff began his address by telling the story of how he visited CBOT in the mid-1990s, and how the exchange helped him get his start in the industry. "Now I'll fast-forward ten years. Today the Board of Trade is being prepared to be gutted by its crosstown rival, and I believe you have a superior alternative."

Oh yeah, this was going to be a good meeting. I could feel everyone around me on the tenth floor bristle with anticipation. Jeff then launched into the background of ICE, reviewed its accomplishments, laid out what he felt made his firm's proposal better than the Merc's, and addressed the concerns he'd heard about ICE's ability to scale its trading and clearing platforms. He ended his prepared remarks by urging people to contact ICE directly with their questions in the future, and "not rely on people with conflicted agendas."

Next came the part we'd all been waiting for: the Q&A session. ICE representatives with microphones moved across the room to try and reach those who were itching to speak. Before things got going, Jeff gave a droll shout-out to his competitors at CME by reminding attendees to speak clearly, because "there's a whole bunch of ears pressed to the speakerphones over on Wacker Drive—so we want to make sure that everybody can hear all of the questions."

Harlan Krumpfes, who'd been one of the lucky six to confront the Merc's management team in March, was first to the microphone. He began by thanking ICE for "bringing this thing to life." He then dared to challenge the reign of Ceres, the Roman goddess who watched over the financial district from her perch above our building, when he said to Jeff, "I told somebody the other day, I said, maybe we ought to take that statue on top of the Board of Trade down, I'm serious, and put your statue up there, because you're the new God."

"I'll tell you what, I'd be very happy if you'd just let me have an office in there and help you run your business," Jeff replied.

But that was the last of the wild compliments ICE's CEO would receive. Like he'd done at the Merc meeting, Krumpfes started out with pleasantries, but soon turned critical and proceeded to slam the ICE/CBOE exercise right valuation. "Do you think $500,000 is a fair value for a $2.5 million membership?" he asked. CBOE seats were indeed trading at that record-high amount after the ICE/CBOE deal had been announced.

Jeff launched into a detailed explanation of how he came to agree to the $500,000 number. He went through his calculations, which showed that if CBOE members suddenly had a change of heart and decided to recognize all of CBOT's ERP holders as full members of their exchange—and then subsequently split the equity of their company equally among all of the resulting 2,000-plus members—CBOE seats would each be worth about $1 million, instead of the $2.5 million they were presently going for. However, the reality was that unless a court of law instructed them otherwise, the CBOE members were never going to agree that CBOT was entitled to a stake in their exchange. Therefore, since it was impossible to predict how—or, more importantly, when—the ongoing CBOT/CBOE lawsuit would end, Jeff thought that splitting the $1 million figure down the middle and rewarding CBOT members a near-term payment was extremely fair. "I think it's a winner, relative to the amount of time that it's going to take to try to unlock that extra $500,000 of value," Jeff told his audience.

Krumpfes continued to question the mathematics, and at one point blasted, "I think that's a bad trade. I think that's a horseshit trade, okay?"

"I appreciate you not holding back, by the way," Jeff cut in, which served to lighten the mood for a few moments.

It was hard not to feel sorry for the ICE team as over the course of four hours, more than 25 members—some with four or five questions each—took turns condemning various aspects of the Atlanta exchange's proposal, with particular emphasis on the exercise-right deal. "Obviously, partly why I'm here is I want to hear your feedback on constructing the deal, because I'm just trying to be an honest broker on a thirty-five-year problem that I didn't create. I create other problems, but not that one," Jeff assured his audience.

Each time a Class B shareholder asked a particularly tough question, the conference room in which CBOT's executive management team was listening to the call erupted in cheers. "Now *that's* Chicago!" Bernie would exclaim. Members demanded more CBOT representation on an ICE/CBOT board, feared what would become of the trading floor and their fee discounts, second-guessed Jeff's promise to keep the firm headquartered in the Windy City, and—unsurprisingly— brought up the New York bank conspiracy. Well into the meeting, an elderly member approached the microphone and summed up the feelings of his brethren quite pointedly. "I'm rather old," he began.

"I'm aging up here," Jeff shot back, amid much laughter.

"But I'm seventy-eight. And I've been a member of this exchange for over fifty-five years. So I've seen a lot of things come and go and go down. For us older fellows, we would like to see more cash."

"All right, thank you, sir," Jeff replied.

As the afternoon turned into early evening and the hits kept coming, the Morgan Stanley bankers—who were either physically witnessing the scene or listening over the phone—eventually began to take the spirited reactions from CBOT members as a good sign. "At first the response was a little bit of, 'What right do you have to negotiate a settlement on our behalf?' but I do believe the members respected Jeff for getting up on stage and taking the heat. That helped him," James von Moltke observed. "The CBOE agreement was a creative solution to a problem that had been around for decades, but it was novel and hard to understand. We put something superior on the table, but because it was there, the members could shoot at it. If you've got nothing, there's nothing to shoot at."

Von Moltke's fellow banker Chris Lown couldn't get over how everyone in the room seemed to know each other, which certainly wasn't the case in a typical shareholder meeting. "The CBOT owner-ship is so concentrated in one city; their kids grew up together, they all live by each other," he marveled. "There is a kind of familiarity you wouldn't have in other deals. The situation is just so rich with conflict, emotion, and history—far beyond any other public company."

After the Q&A session wound down, those who still wanted to talk broke into small, informal groups and mingled with the ICE exec-utives and board members. When it was all said and done, the bankers felt the meeting went significantly better than the Merc's had two and a half months prior, and Jeff found it "invigorating to be up there." He knew some of the men were attempting to get a rise out of him with their questions, but overall he interpreted the mood of his audi-ence to be one of "interest."

The truth was, it was difficult for anyone to know what was really going through the members' minds. At both the Merc meeting and the ICE meeting, they were doing what they did best: trading. No one was surprised they were trying to squeeze every penny they could out of both suitors. Until members were able to start voting on the CME/CBOT deal, it would be impossible to accurately gauge which side they were on.

Early June 2007

As expected, Charlie and Bernie sent another letter to CBOT mem-bers the week after ICE's presentation. It was much more strongly worded than the others had been, and spoke of the dire consequences of a merger with Jeff Sprecher's seven-year-old exchange. "Our entire franchise would be at risk," they warned. For his part, Craig Donohue discredited the ICE/CBOE exercise right deal every chance he could get. "It's a clearly inadequate solution," he stated. "It's a poor structure. I think it hurts CBOT members rather than helps them . . . [they are] far better off hanging in there with the litigation and getting the upside."

The CME team remained confident in their offer, and together with CBOT on June 8, they mailed their joint proxy statement to shareholders. There was only one more month to go before the big vote. While the thick prospectuses were making their way across the country, word began circulating that ICE and CBOE were resuming discussions in order to incorporate CBOT members' feedback from the May 31 meeting into their exercise right agreement. "What we are trying to do is negotiate something that is fair to all," Bill Brodsky stated during an industry conference in New York. "I am not going to say that anything is going on, but I wouldn't rule anything out either."

Elsewhere in Manhattan, New York Stock Exchange executives were kicking up dust once again. At a presentation to Wall Street analysts, CEO John Thain hinted that the Big Board's April acquisition of Euronext, the second-largest derivatives exchange in Europe, wasn't the end of his firm's expansion into the futures markets. However, he didn't foresee organic growth. "For us to get a big position in the U.S., we have to acquire something," he stated.

NYSE CFO Nelson Chai also continued to stir the pot. "We can take a swing," he said, when asked if his team was ready to make another acquisition even though they were still in the midst of integrating with Euronext. "We can walk and chew gum." Analysts focused in on four possible takeover targets: NYMEX, CME, CBOT, and ICE. Shares of all exchanges, except NYMEX, rose—and ICE led the gains.

■ ■ ■

CME and CBOT executives were busy meeting with shareholders and members in major cities around the globe and attempting to make a case for their merger, so I wasn't expecting to see much of my boss for a while. But one day he had a break, was in Chicago, and called me to the executive floor so that he could give me an update. He reported that they'd been hearing mixed comments regarding both the ICE and CME offers. The CBOE exercise right issue was the Class B shareholders' biggest concern. ICE's persistently rising stock price, which served to continue widening the gap between the two proposals, was also one of the most frequent topics of conversation. However, members seemed uneasy about how ICE might diminish their fee discounts in the future. Chris said that in every meeting, he reminded whomever he was talking to of the reasons they'd want to stick with CME: strategic fit, higher synergies, better operational efficiencies for member firms, and the threat of ICE not being able to execute everything it had promised in the time frame it had laid out. He felt that all in all, the meetings were going very well.

The CME and CBOT leaders were not even attempting to sit down with the most vocal dissenters. "You can't convince them of anything, and you can't have a rational conversation with them," Chris explained. However, that didn't mean the naysayers weren't eager to meet. Once word got out that the powers that be at the two Chicago exchanges were making the rounds, Chris started fielding calls left and right. He said that angry members would dial the general Office of the President line, and when Chris would answer, the conversation would go something like this:

Member (agitated): WHO IS THIS?

Chris: This is the Office of the President.

Member: Who are YOU?

Chris: I'm Chris Malo, executive vice president of business development and marketing.

Member: Well, why haven't I been told about these meetings that are going on?

Chris: They are invitation-only. Let me take your information and someone will get back to you.

His eyes flashed as he concluded that the dissenters were starting to feel like they were the ones left out of something—that they were no longer the ones in the know. And it was bugging the hell out of them.

"You're not worried about the A shares, then?" I asked.

"No, we know who holds those and have figured out that we should be fine there," he replied. Before I went back to my desk, he told me he was pretty sure the CME and CBOT votes would still take place on July 9, and that the merger would pass. "But I remember when you interviewed, I told you I never thought CME and CBOT would come together in the first place—so I guess I could be wrong again!" he added with a laugh, accompanied by a "Who knows?" gesture.

Mid-June 2007

At 5:24 P.M. on June 11, Bernie sent an e-mail to all CBOT employees, proclaiming that the DOJ had closed its investigation of the CME/CBOT merger. There had been rumors that the staff overseeing the case did in fact want to block the Chicago union, but had been overruled by their superiors. All we knew for sure was that the antitrust division had stepped aside, and its official statement said, ". . . the evidence does not indicate that either the transaction or the clearing agreement is likely to reduce competition substantially." The following afternoon, the senior project manager at CME sent the entire merger team a message explaining that we could now move "more aggressively" to "accelerate integration."

That same day, however, ICE submitted an enhanced proposal to CBOT's board. The revised offer addressed many of the concerns raised at ICE's March 31 meeting with CBOT members. If shareholders didn't want to receive ICE/CBOT stock after the merger, ICE now offered to pay cash instead—up to $2.5 billion. In addition, the updated document outlined member fee guarantees for the next seven years. It also allowed for the CBOE exercise right settlement to be more than $500,000 per person if there were fewer ERP holders than originally anticipated. Further, as long as the agreed-upon total percentage of CBOE equity was not exceeded, the full value of the ERP settlement for any given member could be paid entirely in pre-IPO CBOE shares, cash, or ICE/ CBOT shares (instead of the previously stated $250,000 limits for either of the stock components). Finally, ICE had reserved 5 of 12 board seats for CBOT designees through the year 2014. When asked by a reporter if the enhanced bid represented his company's final stance, Jeff Sprecher avoided answering directly, and instead replied, "This is a dynamic situation. Our offer, in our minds, has always been superior."

■ ■ ■

Two days after ICE turned in its updated proposal, CME followed suit with a revised bid of its own. The first major amendment was that CBOT's Class A stockholders would receive a special dividend of $9.14 per share at some point after a successful CME/CBOT merger vote, but before the legal close of the deal. Full members would each gross at least a quarter of a million dollars from the dividend alone—only if they voted the deal through, of course. CME's sweetened offer also contained points pertaining to the CBOE exercise right issue. ERP holders had a choice: They could take a $250,000 cash payout in return for selling their exercise right to CME within 45 days of the close of the merger, or continue as a member of the lawsuit in the hopes of getting a higher settlement—with a guarantee that CME would pay them $250,000 if the court battle was ultimately unsuccessful. The Merc also eliminated the $15 million cap on legal fees connected to the case. Finally, they offered representation on the CME Group board in the form of a five-person committee who would have veto power over rule changes—like member fees—until 2012.

Bernie sent an e-mail to CBOT staff that went over the highlights of the Merc's new offer. He also mentioned that our board had carefully reviewed both of the revised proposals it received, and concluded that CME's was still the better bet for our company. Craig Donohue's interpretation was a bit more pointed when he spoke to journalists about the latest developments: "ICE has been rejected not once, but twice." An analyst at CIBC World Markets, Niamh Alexander, summed up what the rest of us were thinking: "The deal will be won now on intangibles not easily quantified. It's not a simple question of economics in this member-influenced shareholder vote, rather a 'hearts and minds' campaign from here."

The afternoon CME made its enhanced deal public, Chris Malo gathered the managers of his division together to go over the flurry of new information we'd received that week. "I'd say we're now in the bottom of the ninth," he told the group. Ted Doukas followed up with the obvious question: "But what if the game goes extra innings?"

The only seriously disconcerting update that came out of the meeting was that Chris had learned shareholders must proactively vote "For" the merger, or else their ballot would be counted as an "Against" vote. Meaning, if someone didn't vote at all—under the assumption that uncast votes would go with the board's recommendation—their vote would be added to the "Against" tally. Maria knew her team was going to have to get in front of this potentially huge debacle and start communicating the consequences of a "no vote" as soon as possible.

■ ■ ■

The following week, the ICE team demonstrated they were not going to sit idle while CBOT shareholders tried to make up their minds. On June 18, the Atlanta exchange announced an exclusive licensing agreement with Russell Investment Group, which granted ICE sole rights to futures based on the widely followed Russell equity indexes. The kicker was that CME was presently processing about 218,000 Russell contract trades per day, which represented nearly 10 percent of its average daily volume in the stock index futures category. Russell Investment Group had never signed an exclusivity contract before doing so with ICE, so now CME would be forced to de-list its Russell products in 2008. Sandler O'Neill analyst Richard Repetto estimated this move would cost CME about 3 percent of its earnings.

The day after ICE's announcement, CME fired back with a press release touting the expansion of its current relationship with Standard & Poor's, which would bring an electronically traded mini-version of its S&P Small Cap Stock Index futures contract to the exchange. Further, the Merc planned to offer incentives that would encourage market participants to transfer their open interest in Russell 2000 stock index futures contracts to the new S&P product. The team at 20 S. Wacker was finally prepared to respond to any surprise ICE threw their way.

Some members of that team also seemed to have been a bit humbled by everything that had transpired since mid-March. On our merger communications call, Maria said she thought the July 9 vote was going to happen. Anita, however, was more cautious. "Well, I know July 9 will come and go—but just what is going to happen on that day, I'm not sure!" she replied with a nervous laugh. Next, we reviewed ads that were placed in the *Chicago Tribune* to encourage shareholders to begin voting. Anita had not been informed of the "no vote" glitch, where uncast ballots would be counted as "Against" votes. "Why is it like that? Who is responsible for that decision?" she raged. We had no answer for her—it was a mystery as to why the rules had been structured in such a bizarre way. Further, everyone conceded that despite our best efforts to plead with shareholders to do otherwise, most people were probably not going to vote until the deadline. "I don't think we'll know the results until *late* on the ninth," Maria guessed.

"Yeah, they're traders, they're gonna wait 'til the last minute," Anita agreed.

Late June 2007

It hardly seemed the ICE versus CME drama could escalate any further, but it did. On June 21, Jeff Sprecher upped the ante with a no-holds-barred letter to CBOT stockholders and members. Its first line read, "Your Board of Directors has agreed to a bargain basement sale of your company to the Chicago Mercantile Exchange in a transaction that would leave over $1.3 billion of your money on the table." That was just a warm-up. Jeff accused the Merc executives of "misleading scare tactics," and of improving their offer—which they had previously sworn to never do— only because ICE had forced their hand with its "innovative value enhancements." He reiterated why ICE's stock was the stronger currency, why its CBOE ERP solution was better, and why his team would be able to finish scaling their trading and clearing platforms to accommodate CBOT's business six months before the common clearing link agreement expired in 2009. The letter ended, "DON'T SELL CBOT SHORT! VOTE AGAINST THE CME SALE!"

Later that day—thanks to ever-fluctuating share prices—ICE's offer for CBOT passed the $12 billion mark.

∎ ∎ ∎

The ICE team remained busy. On June 22, they announced an agreement to acquire the Winnipeg Commodity Exchange (WCE)—Canada's only commodity futures exchange, and home to the world's leading Canola contract. Winnipeg's products had been hosted on CBOT's electronic trading platform, but would be moving to ICE's system by the end of the year. Overall, WCE's business was immaterial to CBOT's revenues, but from the ICE team's perspective, the acquisition would give their exchange an opportunity to develop energy markets in Canada. "By God, that summer home in Saskatchewan is looking better and better!" Bob cried as a bunch of us settled in to his office to trade thoughts on the day's news. We had been expecting Terry Duffy and Craig Donohue to send CBOT shareholders a letter that morning, and they did. In it, they stated that the vote on July 9 would be "the most important vote in the CBOT's 159-year history." The letter reviewed all of the ways in which a CME/CBOT pairing was preferable to a merger with ICE, and emphasized the fact that together, the two Chicago institutions would form the world's largest and most valuable exchange, with the most diversified revenue streams. They concluded, "As members and shareholders of CBOT Holdings you are sophisticated market participants. You understand risk. The choice is clear: vote "YES" [to] the CBOT/CME combination."

ICE had also anticipated CME's letter, which was why they hired a slew of people to stand outside every entrance to 141 W. Jackson and hand out flyers which screamed "Don't Be Sold Short" in large, bold font. The flyers contended that in order to justify the decision to move forward with a lower offer, CBOT's board was attempting to "disparage ICE and instill fear so you will accept CME's inferior bid." At the bottom of the one-pager, shareholders were encouraged to vote against the CME/CBOT deal, and reminded that they could continue to change their vote up until July 9, as only their most recent entry would count.

Nobody knew how to read the situation anymore. "If they delay the July 9 meetings, how far will they push them out?" I asked Chris. He scanned all of the long faces in Bob's office before answering.

"If it's still just CME and ICE vying for us, probably just a few weeks. If another party comes in, probably longer."

■ ■ ■

Citing an SEC rule, the media reported that June 25—10 business days before the July 9 meetings—was the last day the Merc could change its bid without having to postpone the merger vote. However, it didn't appear CME would be making any final moves. The morning of the 25th, Craig and Terry sent another letter to CBOT shareholders entitled, "Setting the record straight on the CME/CBOT merger: know the risks of dealing with ICE." They wrote that they wanted to make sure everyone voting on the merger had "the facts they need to see through the ICE propaganda." Then they outlined several points in ICE's offer that they considered extremely perilous, and included quotes from a wide range of financial analysts, reporters, consulting firms, and CBOT members to back up their statements. It was a wise strategy that relied on objective, third-party sources to legitimize the Merc's assertions.

I was reading through the letter when Tom Hammond popped his head around the corner. As always, his face was pink and shiny, and he was smiling.

"Did you see the goodbye message from the interns?" he snickered. I had indeed. The girls had sent a one-sentence e-mail with the subject line "THANK YOU" to the entire company. "Now that they're gone, I can tell you what I did. I told the interns we were all worried about Bob because he was getting older and seemed to be forgetting things all the time and couldn't hear very well anymore. I said to them, 'If you're ever walking with Bob, you need to keep reminding him where he's going because he'll get halfway there and not know where he is.' They looked at me all wide-eyed and nodded their heads that they'd do it. Isn't that great?"

"You are *so bad!*" I exclaimed in mock disgust.

"I also told them that he could only hear out of his right ear so they always needed to be sure that they were on that side of him and to shout really loud. It was classic."

Before he left, he said he thought things were going to start getting wild, despite the fact that it seemed like CME was not going to up its bid any further. "Trust me, people have been running around like crazy today already—we just lost a huge block of votes." I could only assume he had inside information about one of the scheduled client or investor meetings that hadn't gone well. As he stepped away, his jolly face turned unusually serious. "I don't think I can stay here if this thing doesn't go through," he said softly, more to himself than to me. With that, Tom and his blond tuft of hair disappeared down the hall.

The Merc did not make any other changes to its proposal that day. We were finally in the home stretch, hurtling toward the July 9 vote.

Chapter 13

Down Under

June 27, 2007

Chris decided to hold the weekly business development meeting in Bob's office, as several people had already congregated there to share the latest gossip. ICE's proxy solicitation firm had begun contacting CBOT shareholders in the hopes of garnering votes against the CME/CBOT merger; Julie had received a call from them, as had others. "They even called my mother!" Chuck Farra, our soft-spoken Asian markets specialist, piped in. "She got all confused and shouted, 'We didn't order any ice!' and hung up on them." Everyone doubled over as Chuck looked down at the floor shyly and smiled to himself. I asked whether or not the vote might be so close that a recount would be necessary. Bob's eyes lit up and he immediately blurted, "Yeah, are there going to be hanging chads with this thing? We better check and see if Al Gore's a shareholder—if he's involved in any way whatsoever, we're screwed."

The next topic of discussion was a meeting CME had scheduled with our members for the following afternoon. The sentiment was that Craig needed to be "a backup dancer" during that discussion, as he often rubbed traders the wrong way. "He's too corporate for those guys. He doesn't speak their language. It's being held in the soybean pit, for chrissakes—he just needs to let Terry do the talking," Bob opined. However, it was Terry's "we don't bid against ourselves" comment that had pissed everyone off the last time. If tomorrow's meeting ended as abruptly as the March meeting had, the consequences could be disastrous for the Merc.

Chris moved on to a bit of good news for his merger-weary team. Institutional Shareholder Services (better known as ISS), an independent U.S. proxy advisory firm, had finally weighed in with a recommendation that CBOT shareholders vote "For" the merger. ISS's take on the deal had been of great concern to both CME and CBOT's management, because up until recently, they sensed the group was not going to lend its support. Bernie had spent a lot of time making presentations to ISS and answering their questions over the past two weeks, and his efforts had paid off. "So that was a big relief," Chris explained. "Many institutional holders of our stock literally *must* vote the way ISS recommends, or risk being sued by their own shareholders. So this was a huge win for us and will carry a lot of weight."

"Wait a second," I interjected. "I know they're a private company and everything, but didn't Caledonia just come out against the merger?"

My question was met with dead silence. Everyone stared at me, lost for words.

"*What?*" Bob eventually uttered.

"Right before I came to this meeting I saw that in a headline, I swear!" I insisted. This set the room abuzz as Bob cranked around in his chair to search for the news on the Web. He found it, and summarized part of an article that confirmed what I'd said. Caledonia Investments Pty Limited, a privately held Australian investment firm—and CBOT's largest stockholder with about 7 percent of the Class A shares—had indeed cast its 3.5 million votes against the merger. Bob knew just how to sum up the situation: "Shit. This changes everything."

"The Caledonia guys" held significant influence over the members, and were therefore treated like rock stars by CBOT's board and staff every time they touched down in the States. The firm's joint chief investment officer, Will Vicars, served as the exchange's main point of contact. I'd never met Will, but was aware that the assistants on the executive floor always looked forward to visits from the tall, handsome Australian. As my boss had explained when he first clued me in to Caledonia's importance, between the investor's youthful appearance, charming personality, and killer accent, "You could say that the ladies around here love him."

Upon hearing that Will had chosen not only to cast Caledonia's votes against the merger, but also to communicate his decision to a select few members of the press, Chris cut our group meeting short and ran back to the executive floor. He looked panicked.

■ ■ ■

Will Vicars' shrewd move was 41 years in the making. Born and raised very comfortably in an eastern suburb of Sydney, Australia, he'd been fascinated by financial markets ever since he was a young boy. His family saw how curious he was about investing, and subsequently sought out people and activities that could help him learn more; his grandmother even asked an accountant to run play-money trading simulations with him. By the time he was 11, however, Will had grown bored of imaginary scenarios. He wanted to invest real funds. So he saved up $100 and put it into shares of a mining company. Throughout his school years, he continued buying shares of different firms, and also enjoyed tracking "penny dreadfuls"—extremely cheap and volatile stocks that had a lot of upside potential. At the University of Sydney, he sought out books on the art and psychology of investing, such as Benjamin Graham's *The Intelligent Investor*, while earning his BA in economics. He graduated in 1986, and then spent the next 11 years working in the fixed-income and equity markets before he and his wife decided to take a yearlong sabbatical with their two young children. By that point, Will was a portfolio manager at Bankers Trust—though it wasn't until after he'd turned in his resignation that he realized his six-week-old daughter would not be able to travel abroad, as she had yet to receive the proper immunizations.

The Vicars clan was subsequently grounded for the time being, but fortunately Will's friends Ian Darling and Mark Nelson were nice enough to provide him with an office at their company, Caledonia, so that he could continue to keep an eye on the markets, as well as work with them on a few investments. Will had gotten to know Ian and Mark over the course of his career—they ran in the same social circles, and hit it off because of their shared admiration of American businessman extraordinaire, Warren Buffett. Ian and Mark had become Buffett disciples in the early 1980s, and in 1995 made the first of many long treks from Australia to the Berkshire Hathaway annual shareholder meeting in Omaha, Nebraska. Warren Buffett and Berkshire Hathaway memorabilia decorated their offices back in Sydney—they collected everything from books to baseball caps to bobbleheads. The two men proved to be such huge fans that they earned their own chapter in Andrew Kilpatrick's 2,000-page tome, *Of Permanent Value*, otherwise known as "the Buffett Bible." Ian would eventually go on to direct a documentary about the Berkshire Hathaway annual meeting, entitled *Woodstock for Capitalists*.

Will Vicars was also a big believer in Buffett's investment philosophies, and through his interactions with Ian and Mark over the first half of his yearlong leave—when he'd stop by their offices between trips across the Australian states of Victoria and Queensland—it became clear that he fit in well at Caledonia. In the summer of 1998, after Will and his brood returned from six months in Provence, France, and Umbria, Italy, it seemed only natural for him to accept a partner position at the small, close-knit firm.

At the time Will Vicars joined Caledonia, the company was just starting to extend its investment management services to high-net-worth individuals outside of its owners' families. When the firm had been founded six years earlier, its main purpose was to manage the equity portfolio interests of the Darling family—the descendents of John Darling, a successful South Australian wheat exporter in the late 1800s, otherwise known as "the Grain King of Australia." In the early 1900s, Darling's son, John Darling Jr., had continued to grow the wheat empire, but had also expanded into silver and lead mining, as well as steel production. A significant percentage of the family's inheritance could be traced back to Darling Jr.'s part-ownership in the Broken Hill Proprietary Company (BHP), where he'd been a director for over 20 years. Today, BHP (renamed BHP Billiton after a 2001 merger) is the world's biggest mining company, as well as Australia's largest business.

Will's inaugural year with Caledonia was the same year the Australian Stock Exchange became the first stock exchange to demutualize and go public, and the Caledonia team made a fortune on its IPO. Within 24 months, they'd repeated their success when both the Sydney Futures Exchange and Germany's Deutsche Börse went public. The Aussie investors figured out that the majority of exchanges around the world would eventually demutualize, so they began to buy memberships in as many of them as they could.

Late in the summer of 2003, John Murray, a stockbroker at Bell Potter Securities—one of Australia's leading investment advisory firms—organized a multicountry trip to several exchanges in order to see where they each were in the process of not only demutualizing, but also converting from open outcry to electronic trading. He invited Will to come along. During the trip, in every city across every nation he visited, Will heard one statement over and over again: "The Chicago Board of Trade is done." CBOT and the Deutsche Börse–owned Eurex had recently (and bitterly) ended their trading-platform agreement, and everyone in the futures industry believed that as soon as Eurex launched its retaliatory attack and went head-to-head with CBOT's U.S. Treasury contracts, CBOT would be decimated. The members of the world's oldest exchange were simply too set in their ways, too slow to react to the threat of competition, and too afraid of electronic trading to be able to withstand a blow from the aggressive Europeans.

Once the investment group reached Chicago, they had lunch with John "the bloody giant" Lothian on a Friday afternoon, and asked for his take on the situation. The industry commentator echoed the grim predictions of others. "CBOT's broke, it's gone, it's over. The Germans are going to kill it—it's got months, if not weeks, to live."

John Murray, Will, and a small number of other foreign investors were scheduled to go to CBOT and talk with Bernie Dan later that same day; it was the last stop on their long, globe-spanning journey. Will was extremely jet-lagged, and—after everything he'd heard about CBOT's dire prospects—felt the meeting would be relatively pointless. His preference was to try and jump on an earlier flight back to Australia. But John Murray had known Bernie since the mid-1990s when Bernie was heading the CIS Singapore operation, and had faith in his old friend. "Look, you gotta meet him and hear what's going on," John pleaded to Will. "It'll only take an hour and then we'll get out of there," he promised.

The men reluctantly headed to 141 W. Jackson after they agreed that canceling on Bernie just didn't seem right. Once at CBOT, they found its CEO more than ready to review all of the strategic initiatives his company had under way. Will's observation was that Bernie was "as relaxed and confident as anyone—almost like the Cheshire Cat, sitting there inside this big building with no one in the outside world having the foggiest idea how well it was doing and how it was turning around . . . Everyone had said, 'CBOT's gone.' But when you met Bernie, you realized very quickly that it wasn't."

Back in Australia, the Caledonia team ran a series of financial projections after Will had returned with a favorable impression of CBOT. As they were investors rather than futures industry insiders, they didn't pay much attention to all of the warnings they'd heard about the Eurex threat. As Will put it, "We didn't get caught up in the noise—we just looked at the raw numbers." The Australians determined that buying seats at CBOT was a no-brainer, but knew there was an obstacle they'd have to overcome first; the exchange's rules were set up in such a way that any seat holder had to declare a "reason for membership." Acceptable reasons were limited to trading-related activities: An individual or corporation needed to hedge their cash market positions, a firm intended to set up a brokerage operation in the pits, an individual desired to speculate in the financial markets, and so on. The rules didn't allow for seats to be purchased simply as an investment in the exchange—that had never been done before. The point of buying a membership was almost exclusively tied to the ability to enjoy heavily discounted trading fees.

Bernie, however, appreciated what Caledonia wanted to do, and proceeded to convince Charlie and the rest of the board to change the membership rules. Will could guess what was going through the CBOT CEO's mind. "Bernie smartly looked at us and thought, 'Geez, here are some Martians from another bloody place that see value where nobody else does—I'm going to use them to aid my cause to get this machine moving and bring it into the twentieth century.'" Within two months of Will's first meeting with Bernie, CBOT had adjusted its membership criteria, and Caledonia purchased its first of several seats that it would accumulate over the next two years.

Shortly after Caledonia became a member firm, it started making a 20 percent return on its investment by leasing out its seats. Doing so enabled Will to qualify for a spot on the Lessor Committee, chaired by distinguished CBOT member C.C. Odom II. A larger-than-life Texas character, C.C. bought his full membership for a mere $46,000 in 1973, and had been deeply involved in the exchange's operations ever since, energetically chairing 25 of the more than 45 committees on which he'd served over the decades. C.C. and Will struck up a friendship, and Will began to learn how critical it was that CBOT continue to expand its electronic trading operations and move toward demutualization. The Texan, the Australian, and Bernie—the Irish kid from the west side of Chicago—slowly but surely began to plant seeds within the membership base about what changes needed to be made in order for CBOT to not just survive, but prosper. Since Caledonia had believed in the company at a time when the rest of the industry had already written its death notice, members were keen to listen to whatever Will had to say. Even the most risk-averse members had to think twice when Will proposed an idea they would have otherwise resisted—a fact that was not lost on Bernie.

Eventually, Bernie arranged for the Caledonia team to address CBOT's board of directors about particularly sticky issues; Will would sit at the head of "a table eighty feet long with a microphone at one end, like the United Nations," and speak his mind. By that time, he was fully aware that he held an enormous amount of political power at the exchange. So when the board was renegotiating Bernie's employment agreement—at the same time the company was preparing to go public—Will threatened to vote against the demutualization unless the CEO's contract was finalized quickly. As a result, the directors had to call an emergency weekend meeting to hash everything out. Will thought it was "stupid and naïve" of them to even think about organizing a road show for investors without certainty of management, and believed that Bernie had proven to be much more than a turnaround agent: He'd put a structure in place for the future of the exchange, and had assembled a team that was moving the company in the right direction—a direction that was guaranteed to make everyone a lot of money.

■ ■ ■

When the CME/CBOT merger agreement became public the morning of October 17, 2006, Will was sound asleep on the other side of the world. Once the news reached him, his reaction was, "This is fantastic." Four months later, Bernie encouraged Charlie, Terry, and Craig to fly to Australia and get to know CBOT's largest shareholder—and so they did. It was a prescient idea, because mere weeks after their visit, ICE announced its counteroffer. At first, Will was skeptical about the Atlanta exchange's intentions; Caledonia had actually invested in ICE shortly after its 2005 IPO, but when Jeff Sprecher made his surprise move at FIA Boca, Will's initial judgment was that the whole thing seemed like a scripted publicity stunt. As time went on, though, his attitude changed. "The more you scratched with Sprecher, the more you found out how enthusiastic and real and smart he was . . . Sprecher was an anteater; he was always turning over logs and finding things that CME had to address." As a result of Jeff's impressive strategizing during the bidding war, the Caledonia team decided to increase their holdings in ICE.

In the months that had passed since CME and CBOT's October announcement, Caledonia's clients and business associates were confused as to why the firm hadn't made any statements about the pending merger, especially in light of CME's escalating bidding war with ICE. But the investment team's silence had been intentional. The Australians were watching the situation unfold from afar, and waiting for the perfect moment to strike. In their minds, it was pointless to come down on one side or the other before the DOJ divulged the results of its investigation. However, once the antitrust issue was out of the way—and CME showed no signs of intending to increase its offer any further—Will Vicars proceeded to turn the deal on its head by directing his broker to cast Caledonia's 3.5 million votes against the merger. He had not spent three and a half years assisting CBOT's management team in building the exchange into a valuable company just to turn around and sell it for $1 billion less than he believed—and the market had proven—it was worth.

Meanwhile, at 20 S. Wacker, CME's management had been so focused on outmaneuvering ICE that they were absolutely thrown by this threat from within. Throughout the bidding war, Terry and Craig had held their cards close to their chests and displayed nothing but confidence to the outside world. But they had met their match in Will Vicars. The battle for CBOT was now a high-stakes poker game between skilled players who were all exceptionally clever—and equally determined to win.

■ ■ ■

A few hours after Chris Malo had excused himself from our group meeting and hoofed it to Bernie's office to find out what was going on with Caledonia, he called to let me know that he was going to be in New York the rest of the week for more client and member discussions. He relayed that so far, only 2 of the 100 firms they'd been talking to were voting against the merger—but those discussions had taken place before Caledonia went public with its decision. He also said that word was spreading among the members that they would have to pay capital gains tax on the $9.14 per share dividend if the merger went through, which upset them. Had CME chosen to up the stock-for-stock exchange ratio from its present .35 level instead, members would've been able to control the timing of their tax hits by simply not selling shares until they wanted or needed to. Therefore, the consensus about the conditional dividend seemed to be, "Those motherfuckers are trying to bribe us!"

The reason Chris and other CBOT executives were aware of these reactions in the first place was because they had access to the "Trade-talk" message board. Before CBOT went public, it had hosted an online listserv that members could access in order to get news or share thoughts on industry issues. But once the exchange began the demutualization process, the board was advised against continuing to sponsor the listserv. So in February 2005, multiple seat owner Steve Fanady told Charlie that he'd be more than willing to take on the responsibility of hosting and monitoring Trade-talk going forward. He then transformed the listserv into a more robust, invite-only online community. As the CME versus ICE battle intensified, Steve saw participation on the board increase significantly, and would post detailed financial analyses of the two offers in order to help his fellow traders separate fact from rumor. CBOT's leadership team viewed Trade-talk as an essential tool to help them keep in touch with "the heartbeat of the jungle." And on

June 27, they knew the jungle's inhabitants were experiencing serious palpitations.

Before Chris hung up, I wished him luck with his next round of shareholder and member meetings. It sounded like he was going to need it.

■ ■ ■

As other CBOT and CME officials jetted around the country or hustled through boardrooms across Chicago in a last-ditch effort to sell the merger to their constituents, Bernie frantically tried to reach Will Vicars. Regrettably for CBOT's CEO, the day before Caledonia's broker submitted the firm's devastating "Against" vote, Will had boarded *In the Mood*, his 68-foot Oyster yacht, and set sail on a 10-day excursion.

The first time Bernie called his largest shareholder in an attempt to make sense of the move, Will was watching the sun rise over the calm waters outside of Queensland's Hervey Bay—a resting and calving area for humpback whales before they migrated north. With his wife, 12- and 9-year-old daughters, and 6-year-old son in tow, he intended to cruise to Lady Musgrave Island, near the southern tip of the Great Barrier Reef. Needless to say, cell phone reception wasn't exactly stellar at the far ends of the earth. But Bernie was persistent in his attempts to get through to the game-changing Australian.

"Will, can you hear me?" Bernie said anxiously when the call finally connected. Will ran to the back deck of his boat and held his phone tightly to his ear. He could barely make out a word of what Bernie was saying.

"Yeah, I'm here," he replied.

Bernie knew he probably didn't have much time before they were cut off. "Look, there have been a lot of changes to CME's proposal, and I want to ensure you understand the different components of what they're off—"

"What?" Will yelled.

"I said I want to make sure you understand what the Merc's offering!" Bernie shouted above the static. "And I'm also wondering why you went public with your vote."

"You know that CME can pay more," Will replied loudly, while checking the reception bars on his phone. He glanced toward the bow of his yacht, where his young son stood catching little rim fish and giggling with Hoggy, a local who'd come on board to give the family fishing lessons.

"Yeah, we all know they can pay more—it's been written in the press a thousand times," Bernie said, his voice starting to break up over the spotty connection. "But the reality is that we're right at the tipping point. This deal could completely fall apart, and that would be disastrous for the Board of Trade."

Will shrugged his shoulders—he had nothing more to say. He wasn't going to budge. Bernie hung up, frustrated, and Will happily returned to Hoggy's lesson. His family had anchored overnight off the coast of Fraser Island, and on their side of the world, the day was just beginning. Yet in spite of the early hour, before his call with Bernie, Will had already spoken to journalists from *Crain's Chicago Business* and *Bloomberg* who were eager to quote his reasons for dismissing CME's proposal. He didn't mind that work was cutting into his vacation, though; the calls signaled that his master plan was progressing. And he had no problem with letting the executives in Chicago sweat it out for a little bit longer.

June 28, 2007

The chatter around the break room Thursday morning indicated that the battle for our company had reached a fever pitch. Both ICE and CME had taken out full-page ads in the Business section of the *Chicago Tribune*, hoping to grab the attention of shareholders and sway their votes. CME's spot, entitled "Consensus Builds," showcased 10 somber quotes from influential people in favor of the merger—from Chicago's Mayor Daley and Illinois Senator Dick Durbin to prominent traders and analysts.

ICE's ad, by contrast, blared, "Attention CBOT Holdings Stockholders: THE PRICE IS WRONG. Don't be fooled by CME's supposedly enhanced offer. . . . It's a sweet deal for the slow-growing CME—but a bad deal for you. . . . ICE has consistently offered more value for CBOT—and CME has repeatedly lowballed you. Don't let your Board sell you out and undervalue your Company by millions of dollars. CME has resorted to scare tactics and low-road rhetoric to sell you on their inferior deal. But the simple fact remains: CME Undervalues CBOT and Your Board Has Failed You. DON'T LET CME STEAL YOUR COMPANY! . . . Vote NO on July 9!"

Slightly different approaches.

July 2, 2007

We had finally reached the last full week before the merger vote, and the situation had officially turned into a circus. ICE pulled out all the stops and hired people to stand outside the CBOT building and give away flyers and T-shirts (!) supporting its cause. The most creative thing that came out of the Merc, however, was an ad with the head-line, "Don't Put Your Future on ICE"—a play on words that had been exhausted months earlier. CME kept running staid ads that were laden with charts, graphs, and third-party quotes—one was simply a full page of signatures from CBOT members who supported the merger. ICE proceeded to rely on shocking statements and ads that hit mem-bers where it hurt them most. My personal favorite featured a huge mountain of cash. Above it read: "How many reasons do you need to vote NO?" Under the pile of bills followed: "How about more than a billion?"

No one could deny that the ad made a valid point—the value of ICE's offer stood at $11.7 billion, while CME's still lagged at $10.6 billion. However, a closer look at the copy disclosed that ICE wasn't actually attempting to call out the differential between the two bids. Rather, it was trying to inform readers that the Merc could still afford to pay over $1 billion more for CBOT than it was currently offering. The spot also featured four analysts' quotes that backed up this asser-tion. Now that the July 9 vote was a mere week away, ICE's message had switched from "Here's why you should want to merge with us," to "Here's why you need to vote against them."

That afternoon it was time for another merger communications team conference call. Maria began, "I wanted to let everyone know that our PR firm is drafting a press release for us in the event that the merger doesn't pass, because, let's face it, both companies are going to have to have a plan for what we're each going to do if that happens." I could almost feel a little gust of wind as Maria's statement knocked the CME team speechless across town. They had been refusing to even mention the word "ICE," much less consider the possibility of not winning the vote. No one said anything. After dropping that bombshell, Maria had to jump off the call. Members of the media and shareholders with questions about voting procedures had been contacting the exchange every few minutes, and her team needed to get out yet another letter clarifying everything.

As expected, the latest letter to members was released before the end of the day. "We are writing to encourage you to VOTE NOW for the upcoming July 9, 2007, special meetings of CBOT Holdings stockholders and CBOT members. Every vote is important. . . . The failure to vote is the same as a vote AGAINST the merger." The document went on to describe in excruciating detail exactly how to complete a vote online, over the phone, or via mail. It also gave answers to frequently asked questions, such as, what is the deadline to vote online? Do I have to vote both my A shares and my B shares or will one vote cover everything? Who do I call if I have other questions?

By all accounts, it was a mess. So many letters and e-mails had gone out, so many presentations had been given, so many meetings had been held, so many articles had been written, and so many rumors had run wild—on top of the fact that both ICE and CBOT had mailed similar-looking proxy voting materials to CBOT shareholders—that no one knew which way was up. As Ginger Szala, group publisher and senior editor of *Futures* magazine pointed out, "entire forests were sacrificed in this battle of releases."

While CBOT's management team was doing everything it could to encourage early voting (so that they could start forecasting the end results), they were aware that any given vote could be changed multiple times up until the cut-off point. So despite their best efforts to analyze the submissions that had already come through, no one truly believed that the final outcome would be known until after the in-person shareholder and member meetings on July 9.

July 5, 2007

Maria and I saw each other briefly during the Thursday morning elevator ride up to our respective floors. She grumbled that she hadn't slept very well because she was so stressed. After she had stepped out and faded from view down the hallway, another person in the elevator told me the newest rumor was that Maria and the executive team had been working over the Fourth of July on something that ended up getting canned. Had the CME team been scrambling to make last-minute adjustments to their offer . . . but then scrapped the effort?

At my desk, I read the latest *Crain's Chicago Business* article, which contained quotes from Caledonia's Will Vicars. "If they stay with the current bid, I think they will lose it. . . . The membership should say no to the current terms and stay resolute." He went on to declare that if CME's executives did not decide to raise their bid to ensure they win the vote, that move "would be extraordinarily foolhardy." Caledonia had obviously not changed its "Against" position from the week prior.

I moved on to an article from *Reuters*. In it, Kevin Ward, a CBOT member, shareholder, and floor trader for 25 years, stated, "There's a large group of individual traders, like myself, who view Caledonia as our spokesman. A bunch of people are going to do what Vicars does." The piece also noted how Jeff Sprecher was viewed as a "dynamo," who—no matter what ended up happening—would be considered the one responsible for driving more money into CBOT members' pockets. Another floor trader summed up the sentiments of many members: "There's quite a few of us that like the horse and the jockey—the horse being the CME and the jockey being Sprecher. That creates a lot of confusion."

I stopped by Julie's office to see if she had caught wind of any scoop. She said that a few people at the Merc had shared with her that Craig was "running around, all upset" over at 20 S. Wacker. She shook her head in disbelief and continued, "Bob and I were just talking about this. We don't understand why the CME guys are so surprised. They had the chance to seal this deal months ago by raising their bid then and getting this thing over with earlier, but now it has dragged on for months. They just kept the window open for more things to go wrong." Yet despite the precarious situation CME faced, she didn't think they were going to change their offer at this late date. After all, there was only one business day left before July 9.

What neither Julie nor I were aware of, however, was that the CBOT and CME executives had been analyzing a critical mass of early vote submissions, and their projections had removed all doubt that the merger truly was in jeopardy. Chris Malo, still on the road meeting with customers but privy to the voting results that had come through so far, e-mailed Bernie: "It is not mathematically possible for us to win at this point."

Bernie's response?

"I know."

Chapter 14

Take the Money and Run

July 6, 2007

Throughout Will Vicars' week-and-a-half-long vacation, several people connected to the CME/CBOT merger had begged him to reconsider Caledonia's "Against" vote. Bernie had called a few more times after their stilted June 27 conversation, and CBOT board director C.C. Odom II had been in touch daily. "Are you really serious about this?" C.C. asked in an e-mail. "Yes, I'm serious. I will bloody block this thing," Will replied.

Caledonia's savvy investors knew something about power plays. In fact, just seven months earlier during the merger of the Australian Stock Exchange and the Sydney Futures Exchange, they had championed a shareholder protest that landed their preferred candidate the title of CEO in the combined firm. Their successful moneymaking strategies had even caught the attention of one of the world's richest men— billionaire Ken Griffin (the same Ken Griffin who was featured in CME's fall 2006 advertising campaign). The Citadel hedge fund CEO had requested a meeting with Will and his Caledonia partner Mark Nelson after learning about their phenomenally lucrative multiyear streak of investing in exchanges. Ken seemed perplexed as to how his own firm had missed out on such an opportunity. The three businessmen talked for about 15 minutes during one of the Australians' trips to Chicago, before the CME/CBOT merger had been announced. Will's interpretation of their conversation was that Ken "couldn't understand how people from God knows where could just come along, steal all of these memberships, and then go back to Sydney and sit there and wait."

Though Will had modestly told Ken that he attributed his firm's prosperity to "being in the right place at the right time—and having a little luck," the fact was that when the CME/CBOT merger was announced, the Caledonia team had already been pouring money into exchange memberships for over a decade. They had anticipated that the Australian Stock Exchange's high-flying IPO would be reproduced by other exchanges across the globe, and had felt particularly confident about CBOT's future prospects. For that reason, they proceeded to accumulate a 7 percent stake in the exchange.

Now they were certain that a significant percentage of the CBOT membership base would mimic whatever they did. So they saw no reason to roll over and accept the Merc's present offer when they believed the company could, and should, pay more. But that didn't stop C.C. Odom from continuing to hound his Aussie friend.

Will understood that several people at the exchange were probably starting to worry that he was completely irrational—giving them such an impression had always been a part of his strategy. However, when Bernie called him from Chicago in the very early morning hours of July 6, the pure panic in the CEO's voice made Will pause. Will had just returned from his sailing voyage, and now stood with a phone to his ear, taking in a panoramic view of Sydney Harbour from his twenty-first-floor office in Circular Quay. It was another glorious, sunny day in Oz. His eyes drifted from the Opera House to the Harbour Bridge while Bernie listed out one grisly prediction after another about CBOT's fate, should the vote fail to pass.

"Look, it's going to be catastrophic for the Board of Trade if this deal doesn't get done!" Bernie finally concluded. He sounded genuinely afraid.

"I want to talk to Terry and Craig," Will replied.

Bernie hung up, and then immediately dialed his counterparts at the Merc. The clock read 2 A.M., and Terry and Craig were suffering through the fourth hour of an emergency board meeting they'd called in order to debate what, if anything, they should do about the rapidly deteriorating situation. It was one of the rare times that all 20 of the Merc's directors found a way to make themselves available at a moment's notice—with some even dialing in from India and Germany. As soon as Bernie's message came through, however, CME's chairman and CEO excused themselves from the discussion, scurried down the hall to find another conference room, and called Will Vicars.

He answered right away. "The price is wrong," Will stated bluntly. But since Terry and Craig had strict limitations on how they were legally allowed to respond to such remarks, they mostly remained quiet and listened to Will's demands for several minutes. After ending the conversation, they returned to their board meeting and decided that the time had arrived to summon their secret weapon: Phupinder Gill. Gill wasn't on CME's board, and could consequently speak with the Caledonia liaison more freely than his fellow executives had been able to. Further, he was indisputably more personable, and everybody knew it.

Indeed, Will was a big fan of the Merc's boisterous and shoot-from-the-hip president, and was happy to chat with him. But he wasn't ready to lift his irrational act just yet. His firm had the right to change its vote up until the cut-off—which was still three days away—whereas he assumed the CME team was now quite desperate to turn the tide in their favor as quickly as possible. Therefore, the Australian proceeded to give Gill both barrels about how much more he thought CME should pay. He wanted the Merc to raise its proposed stock-for-stock exchange ratio from .35 to .40.

"No, no . . . we really cannot move that much more," Gill protested, his voice dripping with distress. Will figured he was bluffing. So he suggested that Terry and Craig continue to push back on the company's directors, and told Gill to call again when there was something new to report.

Unbeknownst to Will, the CME team really was prepared to walk. "Anyone who wants to play a game of chicken at this hour is truly on his own—we are done," Terry had stated before sending Gill off to make the fateful call. When the Merc's president returned with bad news, Terry took a deep breath and then went back into the conference room to address his board. He explained that Gill would soon be calling the Caledonia director one final time, and therefore the

Merc's leadership needed be on the same page about what Gill could agree to. "I need an answer now. I am not waiting any longer. So you have all of five minutes to make a decision," he snapped.

■ ■ ■

Before long, Will's phone rang once more.

"Here's where we are: we are not going to get to .4," Gill explained in a hushed tone. "The vote is on the edge—this thing is going to fall over." He sounded like he was at wit's end, and went on to use every emotive and plea known to mankind in order to get the powerful shareholder to respond.

But Will didn't respond. It was as if—instead of being 9,000 miles apart—the two men were nose-to-nose, staring each other down. The tension crackled through the phone line. Eventually, Gill broke the silence.

"Perhaps we can move a touch," he sighed. "Where will you deal?"

Will took a moment to gather his thoughts. He knew the game had been played out, and that the logical thing to do would be to make a decision right then and there. He still believed the Merc could afford the .4 exchange ratio, but recalled Bernie's anguished warnings of what might happen if Caledonia continued to fight for a higher payout and the merger vote didn't pass as a result. The truth was, Will really did want the deal to close, and thought anyone who didn't see the synergies between the two Chicago exchanges must be "absolutely barking mad." So he finally relented and said, "We can meet in the middle."

"Done," Gill replied, without hesitation. He then asked Will if he would make a statement indicating his full support of the merger, write a message on Trade-talk to confirm that he approved of the deal's new terms, and—of course—actually change Caledonia's block of votes to "For." Will said he would do so straightaway. The call ended, and on opposite sides of the globe, both men exhaled with relief. It was over.

Or so they thought.

■ ■ ■

CME's board meeting adjourned in the wee hours of July 6, and then CBOT's directors assembled at dawn in order to officially approve the updated deal. Those of us uninvolved with the early-morning negotiations learned about CME's final move—and Caledonia's subsequent change of heart—from an urgent message waiting at the top of our e-mail inboxes.

"CME and CBOT Agree to Increase Merger Offer," trumpeted the joint press release, which included high-spirited quotes from Bernie, Charlie, Terry, and Craig. Will Vicars sent out his promised statement on behalf of Caledonia, as well:

> We have always supported this merger from a strategic rationale and long-term growth perspective. We continue to believe this combination makes massive sense for the industry, for the shareholders of both companies and customers. Now, with CME's latest enhancement, we fully endorse this merger and will vote in favor of this transaction.

With the exception of the stock-swap ratio changing from .35 to .375, everything else about the Merc's proposal remained the same. The merger votes were still on for July 9; it turned out that the SEC's supposed "no changes to the deal within 10 business days of the vote" rule that had been referenced by every major industry publication two weeks prior was not actually a rule, but a recommendation. The Merc team knew this, and had purposely waited until the bitter end to raise their offer in order to make it difficult for ICE—or another player—to retaliate before the shareholder and member meetings.

While the value of the ICE and CME proposals fluctuated throughout the day, the .375 ratio served to increase the Merc's deal approximately 7 percent. Now it was very close to—sometimes slightly higher than, sometimes just a tad lower than—ICE's $11.7 billion bid. Would it be enough for the members?

"This is our best and final offer, and we will not change it," Craig announced in a conference call to analysts. "We don't like to lose," he continued, moving on to highlight the support of the eminent Australian investors. "We believe there's a significant number of other CBOT shareholders who regard Caledonia and their view as important."

He was correct.

"I've got to go back and change my vote," stated Ray Cahnman, a renowned trader and the chairman of TransMarket Group LLC, a firm that controlled several voting memberships. "The fact that they got Caledonia changes the whole ball game . . . [they] are very shrewd and very experienced."

■ ■ ■

When I arrived at the office, Chuck Farra passed by me on the way to get his morning coffee fix. We both paused outside of the break room. "So, do you think it's finally over?" I asked. "Oh, yeah, definitely," he replied, nodding assuredly. "I was in the elevator a few minutes ago with Jay Homan, and he told me he was going to vote the same way Caledonia did, so he was on his way down to the pits to make sure everyone else switched over their votes, too. They do whatever he says." I knew Jay was a prominent oat trader who had become somewhat of an institution at the exchange over the past 30 years, so I was not surprised to hear he held that kind of sway. "But I thought all those floor guys swore they wouldn't budge unless the Merc bumped the ratio to .4?" I countered. Chuck shrugged and replied, "I think at this point they all just want this thing over with. They know it's as good as it's gonna get. This way, everyone saved face because the ratio was a compromise."

"Let's just hope nothing else happens," I laughed nervously.

The mood on the tenth floor was mixed. Some of my co-workers had really wanted ICE to win, and therefore they prayed that Jeff Sprecher would up the ante once again by Monday. So far, however, there'd been no response from the ICE team after the Merc's latest move became public. Other CBOT employees were annoyed that CME's board waited until the absolute last minute to show their hand. And there remained a few people who held out hope that the New York Stock Exchange would swoop in out of nowhere with a bid of its own—like a knight in shining armor—and derail everything.

■ ■ ■

The rest of July 6 passed without incident. A reporter managed to reach Will Vicars while he was enjoying a glass of wine after a late dinner at Buon Ricordo, one of Sydney's premier Italian restaurants. "I think this is an extraordinary opportunity unparalleled in the industry, for all constituents: customers, shareholders, and users of the products," he raved, when asked to confirm that he was now fully behind the CME/CBOT deal. Meanwhile, increasingly confident statements were coming out of the Merc, including one from Terry in which he boasted that CME Group "will be a force to be reckoned with."

Before we left the office that day, I assured David and Keith that I would call them over the weekend when I received word that the vote had passed. My co-workers and I believed Will and Terry's comments were signs that the majority of Class A and B "Against" votes must have been switched, and that there was no longer any doubt that the merger would be overwhelmingly approved.

We were mistaken.

July 9, 2007

Merger team members from both CME and CBOT had been expecting a triumphant e-mail from our executives late on Sunday evening, but no such message ever came through. Surely our two boards had been tracking votes incessantly all weekend, and the cut-off for online and over-the-phone submissions had been midnight on the eighth, so why hadn't we heard anything? "Do you know what's going on?" I e-mailed Janella during my El ride into the Loop on Monday morning. It was shaping up to be a hot, muggy day in the city.

Janella replied that she was also in the dark, and then forwarded a news blurb stating that "unidentified people" connected to ICE had indicated that the Atlanta-based exchange would not be continuing its fight for the Chicago Board of Trade. Indeed, Jeff Sprecher had decided at the outset of his campaign that if the Merc ever raised its offer within throwing distance of ICE's, it would be "pencils down" for his team. They all knew that if they pushed things any further, it might result in a hit to their share price, which had increased by 20 percent since the start of the bidding war. However, it was not as though CME's rivals were depressed about calling it quits. As the *Wall Street Journal* pointed out, ". . . the Atlanta upstart exchange has raised its profile by an amount that few PR and ad budgets could afford." Now the leaders of ICE—and their Morgan Stanley advisers—waited anxiously along with the rest of the financial services industry to see whether CME and CBOT were finally going to seal their deal.

■ ■ ■

Once I'd reached 141 W. Jackson, after an hour of waiting on the edge of my seat for even the smallest hint of news, I couldn't take it anymore. I jogged down the hall to see if Julie was at her desk. She was, but had her back to the open door of her office as she scrolled through e-mails. I cleared my throat, and she turned around with a knowing "I bet I can guess why you're here!" smile on her face.

"I'm sorry to bother you, but I can't stand this. It's too quiet around here—it's eerie. Have you heard anything at all?" I asked.

In a low voice she replied, "So the B shares passed—but now everyone's worried about the A shares."

"*What?*" I hissed.

"All I know is that the latest data was showing that the A-share vote would not pass—and not because people voted no, but because some people didn't vote at all." I smacked my hand against my forehead as she added, "There's basically a telethon under way right now on the executive floor in order to get people's votes in. I think they've been at it all weekend."

"But I thought the cut-off was last night?"

She shook her head quickly to correct me. "That was only for the online and phoned-in entries. Technically someone can still vote— or change his vote—up until the shareholder meeting at 3:00, so our guys have been making calls to encourage people to either fax their proxies in, or show up at the meeting and physically cast their votes in person."

"Good God, this is exactly the opposite of what everybody was worried about! What a total nightmare," I whispered, still stunned.

"I know. Can you believe it?" she said, and shook her head once again.

■ ■ ■

Three more excruciating hours passed before an e-mail came through from Bernie shortly before noon. It was an invitation for all department heads and officers of the exchange to join him at the W Hotel the following morning to discuss "the outcome of this afternoon's vote." *Hmm.*

About 15 minutes later, Chris Malo appeared in front of my desk with a huge smile on his face. It was the first time I'd seen him in a while. He still had a healthy tan, but looked like he could use a good night's sleep.

"So . . . ?" I leaned back defensively in my chair, bracing for his response.

"We got the votes," he replied cheerfully. His voice was crackling and hoarse, but his grin signaled that the final outcome of his weeks spent in back-to-back calls and meetings more than justified a scratchy throat.

"What happened? I was talking to Julie earlier and she told me about how the A shares were a concern," I said.

"Yeah, they were, and we were making calls, but now we've tipped the scale," he answered.

"So there's *no doubt*—it's a done deal?" I asked. I couldn't wrap my head around the fact that nine months of turmoil had finally—and instantly—come to an end.

"It's a done deal!" he reiterated. "We had a goal, and we just threw everything at it these past few days. Now all that's left is the pomp and circumstance of the meetings," he gushed. "Hey, I gotta run, but I'll see you in a couple of hours." With that, my boss flashed yet another big smile and took off.

I wanted to interpret his confidence as a sure sign that the bidding war was truly over—that my co-workers and I were about to get some closure at long last. But considering everything that had transpired since October, I couldn't.

At 2 P.M. I met some of Maria's staff a few blocks east on Jackson Street, in the lobby of the Union League Club of Chicago. The opulent, exclusive club—home to one of the nation's largest privately held art collections—seemed like an appropriate venue for history in the making. The member and shareholder meetings were going to take

place in the chandelier-laden second-floor conference room at 2:30 and 3:00 P.M., respectively, and Maria was already upstairs helping to ensure everything was running smoothly. CME would commence its vote at 3:00 in the UBS Tower across town, and after all of the meetings had concluded, the executives from both sides would sit down together for a press conference.

The communications team and I were supposed to help check people in, so we climbed the wide spiral staircase up to the first landing, where the atmosphere was nothing short of electric—and the temperature was soaring. In fact, July 9 would go down in the record books as Chicago's hottest day in 2007, with a high of 94 degrees. The air-conditioning simply couldn't keep up with the hundreds of men milling about the floor, waiting for the festivities to begin. They slapped each other on the back, shouted greetings, shook hands, and dabbed their foreheads with handkerchiefs. When I asked for identification in order to complete the check-in process, most seemed surprised—as if I should have known who they were. But on the whole, the members were exceedingly friendly, and I found myself cracking up more than once at the cheesy lines they'd throw out, such as, "Some say today's a day that could melt ICE!"

Their giddiness was understandable. After all, nearly everyone I checked in held at least one CBOT membership seat that was now worth around $7 million. They'd earned the right to bask in their victory however they saw fit.

Amidst the chaos, I spotted Bryan Durkin standing stiffly off to the side with his back to the wall. Just a few days before the meeting, he'd undergone an urgent, seven-hour-long surgery in an attempt to head off some disintegration in his spine that could have left him a paraplegic. There was no way he was supposed to be out and about. I rushed over to him.

"*What are you doing here?*" I scolded. "You should be recovering and resting!"

He grinned, nodded at the bustling activity surrounding us and said, "Well . . . there's kind of a few things going on . . ."

That was dedication. But I was seriously afraid one of the members would attempt to give him a bear hug and break him in two. He insisted that he felt fine and that his operation had gone well. I vowed to keep an eye on him, and returned to my post. Within moments, he began slowly and carefully shuffling across the room to chat with a shareholder who'd beckoned.

■ ■ ■

Eventually, the meetings commenced. They lasted less than 10 minutes each, and not one member or shareholder asked a question when given the opportunity to do so. But really, what was left to say? Everyone just wanted to hurry up and make the deal official. And finally— shortly after 3:00 P.M. on July 9, 2007—it was.

■ ■ ■

By 3:45 P.M., a press release had hit the wire, introducing CME Group as "the world's largest and most diverse exchange," and celebrating the fact that the Windy City would continue its reign as "the center for risk management worldwide." Terry and Craig joined Charlie and Bernie to address reporters in a small conference room away from the hoopla on the second floor. Maria, her team members, and I stood several feet behind the rows of seated journalists and listened in.

"Some of you are traders—why was this a good trade for Chicago?" asked one reporter.

"This is the *greatest* trade in the history of Chicago, and I think it's one of the few trades where both sides are big winners," Charlie began.

"This is the best deal in the history of the derivatives space!" Terry elaborated. The two friends went on to reminisce about their initial merger discussion during their December 2005 lunch at Gene & Georgetti, with Terry concluding, "Sometimes that feels just like yesterday, and sometimes that feels like a really, *really* long time ago."

Eventually, one member of the press candidly inquired, "While there weren't any questions at either CBOT meeting, at the CME meeting, someone asked why you upped the bid at the last minute. Did you not think you were going to win otherwise? Craig, you listed four reasons for doing that, but you never mentioned the ICE deal, which I find unbelievable. Are you meaning to imply that ICE had *nothing* to do with you raising your bid?"

Craig smiled a thin smile. "Well, there was only time to list four reasons," he replied wryly. "No, why we reevaluated our offer was because, one, CBOT's stock has been performing strongly; two, we had raised the amount of synergies we identified through the merger planning process; three, the long-term growth of the combined firm was compelling; four, there had been movement in the marketplace; and . . . you know, five would be ICE," he admitted, as the four executives looked at each other and laughed.

Soon, however, CME's leaders would let down their guard and reveal just how miserable ICE's interloping bid had made their lives. "This has been a very anxiety-ridden process we've been going through," Craig explained. "It has taken its toll on a lot of us." He divulged that as the vote neared, he was literally jumping every time his cell phone rang—dreading what surprise twist might be next. Terry described the 117 days that had transpired since ICE's FIA Boca announcement a bit more colorfully: "It was us getting our teeth kicked in."

As the media representatives chuckled at Craig and Terry's confessions, I heard a low gasp from one of the women standing next to me. "What's the matter?" I whispered. "An e-mail just came through from Jeff Sprecher—to all CBOT members and shareholders," she whispered back. Everyone within earshot whipped out his or her BlackBerry and began reading the message. In a freakishly timed move, just as the CME and CBOT executives began to discuss the bidding war with ICE, Jeff had fired off a one-page letter to the traders and investors he'd gotten to know since March 15, thanking them for their "willingness to engage in a dialogue over the past several months." He also gently reminded them that "ICE's involvement has created nearly $3 billion in additional value through our willingness to recognize the true worth of your company." Someone behind me said softly, "Or in other words, 'Because of us, you each have—at minimum—a few extra million in your bank account. You're welcome.'"

While many people described the CEO's letter as "classy," there was no doubt that its final paragraph served up a thinly veiled challenge:

The future winners in our industry may not be the biggest or oldest players. Success will be determined by the ability to adapt quickly to changing markets and innovate responsively in creating new products and serving customers around the globe. ICE will remain focused in these areas, and we look forward to the opportunity to work with you in the future.

■ ■ ■

The remainder of the week would disappear into what seemed like a never-ending series of goodbyes. On Wednesday, Chris Malo held the final business development meeting. Julie explained to our division that we still had another month to wait before staffing decisions were finalized. "I've worked here my entire career, so I understand the mixed emotions that everyone has about this situation. But we have to ask you to sit tight a little while longer." After suggesting what we should attempt to focus on in the meantime, Chris began to wrap things up by gently revealing that on Friday, he, Bernie, William Farrow, and our CFO Glen Johnson would be leaving the firm. This news came as a huge shock to many of the employees who'd been at the company for decades; only two days had passed since the vote, yet significant change was already under way.

To try and soften the blow, Chris then shared some moving words about his experience at CBOT, and ended by saying, "It has been a tremendous honor and privilege to work with all of you. I have learned so much from my time here, and from each of you, and I want to sincerely thank you for that." He turned to Bob, who'd been staring at the table and twiddling his fingers nervously as the conversation wound down. "Bob, do you have anything else to add?"

Our head of sales paused, and then glared at Chris and complained, "Jesus, you're like the priest at my mother's funeral—you already said everything *I* wanted to say!"

The mock fight broke the mounting sadness in the room, but not for long. After the laughter had subsided, Bob grew unusually serious, and briefly made eye contact with each of us before clearing his throat. "I want to thank all of you, too, for your patience over the past year.

This is probably the last time we'll all be together, so I want you to know that leading this team has been the highlight of my career." One by one, the faces around the table dropped, and I watched as quite a few of my co-workers frantically tried to blink back tears. Suddenly, the situation had become very, very real.

The next evening, emotions would continue to run high during the send-off party that Bob and Bryan Durkin hosted for Bernie, Chris, William, and Glen at the Metropolitan Club on the sixty-sixth floor of the Sears Tower. With a breathtaking view of the city as their back-drop, the departing executives each made a short, heartfelt speech, and then Bob raised his glass to toast Bernie. Next came a video Maria's team had pulled together that covered our CEO's six years at the exchange. As it played, the love and admiration for the man who'd brought the company back from the brink of failure was palpable— though Bernie seemed a bit embarrassed by all of the attention. For the most part, he had managed to stay out of the spotlight, even amidst the flurry of news coverage following the successful merger vote. The peo-ple gathered in his honor that night, however, knew without a doubt that the Chicago Board of Trade would never have been at the center of a multibillion-dollar bidding war had Bernie Dan not dedicated his every waking moment since July 2001 to the company's spectacular turnaround.

■ ■ ■

Ironically—or perhaps poetically—CME Group's first day of busi-ness fell on Friday the 13th. Those who entered our headquarters' dramatic, three-story marble lobby that morning were greeted with flowing banners that read, "Two Legacies, One Future." John Lothian couldn't resist one last dig after he saw the gigantic signs. With a tongue-in-cheek nod to the Merc's famed Pork Belly contracts and CBOT's long-standing Soybean futures, he wrote: "The runner-up motto was: 'CME Group: The Pork and Beans Exchange.'" (To his credit, Lothian's quip came at the end of a congratulatory note to both the CME and CBOT teams for getting their momentous deal done.)

By the end of the day, each merged division had gathered for a wel-come meeting at the W Hotel. As I headed inside for the marketing meet-and-greet, Fred and the other economists were leaving the building. They looked happy. "I think this is gonna be good," Fred remarked, grinning from ear to ear. Later, one of the salespeople reported that Bob had been "swarmed like a movie star" upon stepping foot in the hip hotel—apparently he'd already built up something of a fan base for himself over at the Merc.

To be sure, by the end of the week that had kicked off with the extraordinary merger vote, everyone was starting to get excited about what lay ahead for the $30 billion behemoth that was CME Group. But back in the waning daylight hours of July 9—before traders, members, and employees had come to accept that the Chicago Board of Trade as they knew it was gone—a bit of remorse quite naturally set in shortly after the shareholder meetings. "What isn't showing in the balance sheets or the proxy statements is what the Board of Trade means to a lot of us. It's really a bittersweet situation," said James Cashman, a CBOT director and 30-year member who hailed from a long line of legendary grain traders. "It's a special relationship that's hard to explain."

Another wheat trader, Jerome Israelov, echoed Cashman's sentiments: "I don't think it's quite sunk in yet that it's essentially the end of an institution that's been here for a century and a half."

However, the realization that the Chicago Board of Trade's 159 years of independence were over—and that it was now the property of a rival it had spent 109 of those years quarreling with—had in fact begun to sink in to some of us already. An hour after the press conference concluded, the merger team leads were invited to a celebratory happy hour at the Merc's private club. Yet almost no one I was close to from CBOT planned to attend; they all cited various pressing issues that were waiting for them back at the office. I suspected the real reason they weren't up for free drinks was that nine months of nonstop stress had finally taken its toll on each of them, and the last thing they wanted to do was be around anyone who was reveling in the end of the company they'd poured their hearts and souls into for the majority of their careers.

So I decided to call it a day, and walked alone from the Union League Club to the Jackson and LaSalle Street bus stop. When I was a block away from my destination, the scorching heat finally broke amidst a flash of lightning and a loud roll of thunder. Within seconds, the sky opened up and began pummeling pedestrians with a furious rain. Moments later, large pools of water had formed wherever the sidewalk was uneven, and hopelessly drenched people ran desperately for shelter. The downpour was so intense that I had to take my chances when crossing the intersection in front of the Board of Trade—it was hard to see more than two feet ahead.

The storm raged on, but since I was already soaked, I stepped aside to let others huddle under the tiny bus stop shelter. My thoughts drifted back to the merger vote that had brought a beloved institution's remarkable story to a close, and I gazed sadly at the gorgeous Art Deco building that had served as my second home for the past year. Even in such miserable weather, 141 W. Jackson was nothing short of stunning. My eyes traveled to the ever-present goddess at its peak. As the rain poured down upon the Chicago Board of Trade, it almost looked as though Ceres was crying.

Epilogue

Mid-August 2007 to Mid-June 2010

The event everyone had been dreading—the reduction in force, or RIF—was carried out one month after CME Group commenced operations. I talked with Bob shortly before our division's D-Day; he was visibly distraught over having to break the bad news to a significant percentage of his staff. "Waiting for this RIF to hit has just been brutal. Bryan's a wreck, and Julie had to get a night guard because she's grinding her teeth!" he wailed after sharing that he hadn't been sleeping well, either. "But at least the severance package is good, and anyone who's been here for a while will have a lot of time to look," he figured.

August 16, 2007, did end up being an utterly awful day that came and went in a blur of tears, angry protests, and sad good-byes. But thankfully, nearly everyone I knew who was let go has since landed on his or her feet, with the majority of ex-CBOT employees finding other positions in the futures industry. Several of my old co-workers were even recruited back to CME Group over the course of the past three years.

About two months after the deal closed, Will Vicars and Mark Nelson of Caledonia traveled to Chicago and went out for a celebratory dinner with Craig, Gill, Terry, Charlie, and Bryan at—where else?—Gene & Georgetti. During that same trip the investors met Leo Melamed for the first time. The notorious ex-chairman introduced himself by remarking, "You've probably read a lot about me—there have been books and interviews and a lot of speculation about what I've done." He then flung his arms open dramatically and concluded, "But none of it really encapsulates *all* that I have done."

It was also on this visit that Will learned about the CBOT and CME executives' intense three-day scramble for votes after Caledonia threw its support behind the deal. His take was that "logistically, it sounded like a nightmare." When asked if he was intentionally trying to be evil by holding out for so long, he laughed. "No . . . no! We didn't want to create enemies—we always intended to be long-term shareholders of the exchange. I didn't realize all of that was going on." After a short pause he added, "But I did find it a bit comical afterwards, though."

■ ■ ■

All of CBOT's electronic business—an average of 3.7 million trades per day—successfully transitioned from e-cbot to CME's Globex platform as planned in early 2008. The consolidation of the CBOT and CME trading floors at 141 W. Jackson also went off without a hitch four months later.

By that point, CME Group had its next deal well under way. In March 2008 it signed an $8.3 billion merger agreement with NYMEX. Eager to avoid another Caledonia-type situation, CME Group's management formally secured the blessing of NYMEX's largest shareholder, private equity firm General Atlantic LLC, via an official "voting and support agreement" before moving forward with the deal. However, finalizing the acquisition was not without drama. One NYMEX member waged a high-profile lawsuit against NYMEX, its directors, and CME Group, claiming that the New York exchange was being grossly undervalued. Another band of vocal members threatened to vote down the deal if certain concessions weren't made. The leader of the dissidents, Bobby Sahn, had always been critical of NYMEX's board of directors, and once told the *New York Post* that they "should be given a cigarette, taken outside and shot" for approving what he considered to be unjustified bonuses for the exchange's chairman and vice chairman. Craig Donohue knew Bobby was influential, so he took a helicopter from Manhattan to Long Island in order to meet with him and ensure that his group would not derail the mid-August vote. Whatever Craig said, it worked, because the acquisition closed on August 22, 2008. With the addition of NYMEX's metals, energy, and soft commodity contracts, CME Group now controls 98 percent of the exchange-traded futures market in the United States.

■ ■ ■

Though many assumed Jeff Sprecher was in ICE's Atlanta headquarters when he sent out his congratulatory letter to all CBOT members and shareholders after the CME/CBOT merger vote passed on July 9, 2007, he and NYMEX CEO James Newsome were actually in Washington D.C., testifying before the Senate Permanent Subcommittee on Investigations. In the fall of 2006, the hedge fund Amaranth Advisors had collapsed after losing $6 billion through speculative futures trades. Near the end of 2005, Amaranth had begun repeatedly exceeding accountability limits for its natural gas positions held at NYMEX, which had long dominated the market for energy futures. Yet the hedge fund was allowed to continue trading on the New York exchange for over seven months in 2006 amidst several warnings and a CFTC investigation. Eventually NYMEX turned up the disciplinary heat, which prompted Amaranth to transfer the bulk of its trades to ICE, whose natural gas swaps were not subject to position limits because the Commodity Futures Modernization Act of 2000 (CFMA) exempted these products—among other electronic energy derivatives—from CFTC regulation.

This controversial exemption was inserted into the CFMA at the last minute by Texas Senator Phil Gramm, who received $100,000 in campaign funds from Enron, and whose wife Wendy used to chair the CFTC and then served as a director at the now-defunct energy giant. The provision became known as "the Enron loophole," because it allowed EnronOnline—which took one side of every trade on its system—to manipulate the energy market. ICE, however, did not engage in any trading on its own system, agreed with the Senate Subcommittee that the Enron loophole should be closed, and also agreed to position limits for its energy products that were comparable in size and volume to NYMEX's. "We don't believe we've been successful because there's been some sort of regulatory arbitrage between us and the incumbent. Over time, we've taken that argument off the table," Jeff stated. "We have been successful by being faster and more creative, exploiting technology, and trying to have better relationships with our customers."

Alas, the Amaranth debacle was not the end of government hearings for those in the derivatives industry. In 2008, as oil prices skyrocketed to $147 per barrel, Bear Stearns and Lehman Brothers crumbled, and *bailout* became a household term, Jeff Sprecher, Craig Donohue, Terry Duffy, and several other financial services executives testified in front of the Senate and House of Representatives a number of times. Since CME Group's NYMEX-branded West Texas Intermediate and ICE's Brent Crude contracts are world benchmarks for the price of oil, the two exchanges found themselves in the spotlight when politicians blamed speculators for increased prices at the pump. The media then followed suit, furthering the false notion that futures trading affects the underlying physical supply of oil, and that an increased number of speculators in the market is enough to drive up prices—even though derivatives contracts cannot exist in the first place without two parties agreeing on the future price of the underlying commodity in question. The issue even became a point of debate during the 2008 U.S. presidential election (Senator John McCain's senior economic advisor was none other than Phil Gramm). Several reports ended up concluding that a supply-and-demand imbalance, geopolitical issues, and a falling U.S. dollar were behind the severe gas price trend. As a past NYMEX annual report put it, "We don't make the prices. We make the prices known." Data also proved that the same index and hedge funds that were vilified for their speculative positions were actually exiting the market when oil prices were rising.

Nevertheless, efforts to increase regulation and oversight of exchanges, as well as to limit speculation, continue to rage on.

The biggest reason for the government's rekindled interest in futures markets, however, is that much of the country's lingering financial crisis has been blamed on the widespread use of over-the-counter (OTC) derivatives such as credit default swaps (CDSs). In the fall of 2008, ailing insurance company American International Group (AIG) revealed that it had entered into multihundred-million-dollar—and in some cases multibillion-dollar—CDS transactions with nearly every major Wall Street investment bank, so the U.S. government invested $182.5 billion in the firm in the hope of heading off a domino-like collapse of institutions deemed "too big to fail."

Now the U.S. government and the financial services industry are grappling with how to untangle the intricate web of OTC derivatives transactions—which Warren Buffett famously termed "financial weapons of mass destruction" in his 2002 Berkshire Hathaway shareholder letter—and prevent another meltdown. The prevailing solution, embedded in the July 2010 Dodd-Frank financial reform legislation, calls for banks and securities firms to move their largest and most standardized over-the-counter contracts onto exchanges or through clearing houses.

Jeff Sprecher anticipated the need for a more transparent credit derivatives market months before AIG's problems were made public, and began moving ICE aggressively into the CDS space in mid-2008. He worked with his Morgan Stanley banking team once again to complete ICE's $625 million purchase of Creditex, a technology firm that had successfully launched electronic trading for credit default swaps four years earlier.

Creditex focuses almost exclusively on CDS trade execution, so in order to also bring clearing services to the credit derivatives market, in October 2008 ICE announced its intention to acquire The Clearing Corporation, the 83-year-old clearing house that began its life as the Board of Trade Clearing Corporation (BOTCC). The Clearing Corporation's infrastructure was leveraged to form ICE Trust, which today operates as a subsidiary of ICE and a member of the Federal Reserve. So far it's winning the battle for the CDS clearing market.

By the end of April 2010, the ICE subsidiary had processed $5 trillion in underlying transaction value, while the CME Group's CDS clearing solution—launched a few days before ICE's in December 2009—had processed $190 million. A small number of other exchanges, including NYSE Euronext and Eurex, also plan to compete in the CDS clearing space, but had not made significant headway as of September 2010. Goldman Sachs, however, announced the launch of its own derivatives clearing unit in July 2010. In addition to pursuing over-the-counter clearing for credit default swaps, many exchanges are also currently salivating over the gigantic OTC market for interest rate swaps ($349 trillion in notional value versus $32.6 trillion for credit derivatives at the end of 2009).

Governments around the world—and the economically battered general public—are looking to companies like ICE and CME Group to provide more stability to the OTC market through their clearing services, but this solution does not completely guarantee avoidance of another crisis in the future. "Clearing houses aren't infallible, and no one should assume that they're infallible and will solve all problems," Jeff cautioned. "But they will improve the situation."

■ ■ ■

Since July 2007, in addition to integrating CBOT and NYMEX, forming partnerships with several other exchanges around the globe, breaking into the CDS OTC space, launching hundreds of non-CDS OTC contracts through its ClearPort clearing service, and taking a 90 percent ownership interest in Dow Jones Indexes, CME Group also ended the three-year legal battle over CBOT members' CBOE exercise right privileges. At the end of July 2009, the Delaware Court approved a settlement valued at roughly $1 billion, granting each ERP holder who met specific conditions 18,774 pre-IPO shares in the Options Exchange, a $1.25 dividend on each of those shares, and a one-time cash payment of $235,000. With the lawsuit out of the way, CBOE finally demutualized and went public on June 15, 2010. It was the last major exchange in the United States to do so.

Already there is talk that CME Group and ICE will be battling it out once again, this time for CBOE. The more interesting rumor, however, is that—faced with potential revenue losses stemming from mandates in the Dodd-Frank Act—Wall Street investment banks will soon be looking to buy their way into the futures industry.

■ ■ ■

IntercontinentalExchange, now 10 years old, continues to shake things up. In its relatively short existence, it went from only providing electronic trading services to the energy market, to operating three regulated exchanges, two OTC markets, and five clearing houses, with products across five asset classes. Its latest triumph was the $600 million purchase of the London-based Climate Exchange, the European Union's leading emissions, or cap-and-trade, market. The first quarter of 2010 was ICE's strongest to date, and, as of mid-August 2010, its ICE Trust division has cleared $11.2 trillion in notional value of OTC credit default swaps across the United States and European Union.

■ ■ ■

Looking back, Bernie Dan views his six years at the Chicago Board of Trade as the highlight of his career. "It was an exhilarating time," he said somewhat wistfully, recalling how he was "tested early on in the politics of working in a member organization," and then proceeded to lead the exchange through its demutualization and IPO, and eventually the merger. "I had to constantly be on guard and up-to-date, totally aware, energetic, and positive amidst all this uncertainty. Given my personality, it was a great time for me." What brought him the most satisfaction, however, was watching CBOT's employees rise to challenge after challenge. "We developed a lot of people—we gave them a chance and gave them a ton of responsibility, and they responded. It was kind of bittersweet when it was all over."

When Jeff Sprecher reminisces about his bid for the Chicago Board of Trade and considers the position CBOT shareholders would've been in today had they owned 51 percent of an ICE/CBOT combination, he can't help but wonder if any of them regret voting the CME deal through. "I fundamentally believed at the time, and still believe today, that it was the wrong deal for the market. I really believe that CME, which is this unbelievably great company with 100 years of history, and CBOT, which was an unbelievably great company with 150 years of history, by putting themselves together have limited what can happen to them in the next 150 years. My motivation in 2007 was that I thought others might see that. . . . I thought the market would've wanted an Avis and a Hertz." Still, regarding his counterparts at CME Group, he has nothing but positive things to say. "I get along with all of those guys," he insists. "I would have a drink with any one of them."

The feeling seems mutual. "To this day, I have a good relationship with Jeff," Terry Duffy shared. But, like Jeff, he remains convinced that his own deal was the right one for CBOT. "If we didn't create the efficiencies with CME and CBOT, I shudder to think where these exchanges would be," he asserted, and went on to credit his pal Charlie Carey with realizing—at the end of 2005—that the globalization of the industry was accelerating the need for the Chicago exchanges to band together. "The hardest thing to do when you're a 150-year-old institution is say, 'We're going to go merge with someone else.' What he did was very difficult." Terry is also particularly proud of the deal because it showed that mixing business and friendship can be successful. "Charlie and I proved that."

As for Charlie, when asked whether he would do anything differently if he had the chance to relive the merger battle all over again, his answer came quickly and confidently:

"No."

Where Are They Now?

Everyone at both CME and ICE who appeared in this book was still in their respective positions at either firm as of September 2010. What follows are updates from my ex-co-workers at CBOT, as well as four others who were crucial to the story.

Ex-CBOT Employees

Bernie Dan consulted to CME Group for a year following the merger, and near the end of that period became involved with MF Global, the world's largest exchange-traded derivatives broker. The brokerage had already begun to struggle in February 2008 after a rogue trader made an unauthorized transaction and lost the firm $141.5 million, but things turned really ugly when Bear Stearns' collapse precipitated a liquidity crisis across the financial services industry the following month. Bernie was subsequently brought on board as MF Global's North American chief operating officer in June 2008, promoted to global COO and president three months later, and then one month after that replaced the departing CEO. The firm's share price had dropped a whopping 90 percent over the course of 2008, so Bernie found himself back in turnaround mode. He spent the majority of the next year and a half traveling the world, restoring MF Global's credibility among regulators, shareholders, customers, and employees. The company's stock increased 125 percent during that time. Near the end of March 2010, Jon Corzine—former chairman of Goldman Sachs and ex–New Jersey governor and senator—took the reins when Bernie announced that he was resigning in order to spend more time with his family. Though he still remains active in the futures industry through his involvement with various committees and boards, by and large—for the first time since he was nine years old—Bernie is attempting to take it easy.

Bob Ray is the managing director of international products and services at CME Group, and relocated to London in early 2009. While he's very busy overseeing the exchange's business and sales strategies across Europe, Asia, the Middle East, Africa, and Latin America, he still gets a bit fired up when reminiscing about CBOT's metals complex, which was sold to NYSE Euronext (its first foray into the U.S. futures market) in March 2008. At least it didn't go to the Germans.

Bryan Durkin is the chief operating officer and managing director of products and services at CME Group. After the close of the merger, he ensured that the rest of the CME/CBOT integration efforts went smoothly, and then turned his attention toward the firm's consolidation of NYMEX's operations in 2008. Today he is responsible for leading the company's technology and enterprise computing, enterprise solutions, products and services, and global operations divisions.

C.C. Odom II was elected to CME Group's board at the close of the merger, and continues to play an influential role at the combined exchange. In addition to his board responsibilities, he runs Odom Investments and Argent Venture Capital, trades Gold and Silver futures online, and can be found in the midst of the chaos on the floor whenever he's visiting Chicago from his home state of Texas.

Charles "Chuck" Farra is the director of international products and services at CME Group. He's responsible for developing client relationships across several countries, with a particular focus on emerging markets in Latin America.

Charlie Carey has served as CME Group's vice chairman since the close of the merger. In light of CBOT's previous foray into Brazil (the exchange had launched a South American soybean contract in 2005), Charlie was deeply involved in the formation of CME Group's electronic-trading and product-distribution partnership with BM&F Bovespa, the leading exchange in Latin America. He is also a partner at the clearing firm Henning and Carey, and remains active in the markets by trading grains, Treasuries, and foreign exchange futures on a daily basis.

Chris Malo took a year off after the close of the deal in order to pursue personal interests and spend time with his family. In June 2008 he rejoined corporate America as chief financial officer and partner at Sun Trading LLC, a Chicago-based proprietary trading firm. There, he oversees financial and administrative functions for the company, as well as several business development initiatives.

Daniel Grombacher was promoted to director of financial research and product development at CME Group, where he continues to work as a senior research economist specializing in interest rate and credit markets. He spearheaded the development and subsequent January 2010 launch of the Long-Term "Ultra" Treasury Bond contract, which ranks as the most successful U.S. interest rate futures debut in exchange history.

Dave Lehman was promoted to managing director of commodity research and product development at CME Group. He's responsible for maintaining the viability of current agricultural and commodity contracts, and developing new opportunities in both the exchange-traded and OTC markets.

David Mitchell (a.k.a. "Rod Stewart") left the financial services industry shortly after the close of the merger, and decided to pursue his passion for fashion. He currently works in New York City for Ralph Lauren's RRL brand, and his goal is to one day design a men's clothing line for a business of his own.

Franco Campione rejoined his old CBOT co-workers at CME Group in May 2009. As the manager of Internet solutions, he drives the information technology strategy behind, and oversees all project development for, CMEGroup.com.

Fred Sturm was promoted to director of financial research and product development at CME Group, and has played a role in several new interest rate product launches, including the mightily successful Ultra T-Bond futures contract. What gives him the greatest pride, however, is the fact that he's "still on active duty with Julie Winkler's crew. There's no better place."

Gene Mueller left CME Group in mid-2009, and in the fall of that same year founded Omega Financial Training Ltd. Omega offers educational seminars and consulting services that focus on technical analysis as well as agricultural and fixed-income futures trading strategies.

Janella Kaczanko left CME Group in June 2008, and today is the vice president of human resources at MF Global. She is responsible for recruiting, employee relations, training, and development at the firm's 900-person Chicago office.

Julie Winkler is now the managing director of research and product development at CME Group, and is responsible for the creation and growth of all commodity, interest rate, currency, energy, metals, and equity index products. She also manages research initiatives, works actively on expanding the firm's strategic partnerships internationally, and sits on the board of the Green Exchange Venture, which provides trading and clearing of emissions allowances and credits.

Keith Rice is currently the manager of online marketing at CME Group. He played a major role in the integration of both CBOT.com and NYMEX.com into the CME Group web site, and now helps facilitate and launch online initiatives for several product groups across the exchange.

Maria Gemskie remained at CME Group until April 2008, and today is the vice president of corporate communications at MF Global. Her primary responsibility is to manage the visibility and brand reputation of the firm, in addition to overseeing its public relations strategy and internal communications.

Ted Doukas joined ICE in early 2008 and is a director in the business development division of ICE Futures U.S. He is responsible for managing the growth of the Russell Index futures and options complex.

Tom Hammond joined ICE, and took over as president and chief operating officer of ICE Clear U.S. (the exchange's domestic futures clearing division), two months after the CME/CBOT deal closed. It is rumored that he can still be found at CBOT's "satellite office" on a regular basis.

Tom McCabe was vice president of operations and quality assurance at CME Group until January 2008, and then joined OneChicago as its chief operating officer. OneChicago is an exchange that offers single-stock and exchange-traded fund (ETF) futures, and is jointly owned by CME Group, CBOE, and Interactive Brokers.

William M. Farrow III was recruited by ex-CBOT CEO David Vitale, with whom he also worked at First Chicago, to join the executive team at Urban Partnership Bank. William serves as president and chief operating officer at the mission-based financial institution, which focuses on community development lending in low- and moderate-income neighborhoods.

As for Those Outside of CME, ICE, and CBOT

Chris Lown remains at Morgan Stanley, and is now co-head of the global financial technology practice in the firm's financial institutions group. He continues to be active in the exchange sector, most recently advising ICE in its $600 million purchase of the Climate Exchange.

James von Moltke left Morgan Stanley in June 2009 and joined Citigroup as the head of corporate mergers and acquisitions. He is responsible for all of Citi's internal transactions, most notably the sale of several Citi Holdings businesses, such as CitiFinancial and Primerica, which was successfully spun off from the firm through an initial public offering on April 1, 2010.

John Lothian remains a broker at Price Futures Group, and continues to help the derivatives world expand its social media and networking tools. He founded MarketsWiki.com, which went live at the beginning of 2008, and has also launched blogs and newsletters dedicated to options, metals, interest rates, and environmental trading, among other niche areas. Rest assured that he has been upholding his reputation as "the conscience of the industry," and still provides his special brand of commentary in the *John Lothian Newsletter*.

Will Vicars continues to circle the globe for Caledonia, which remains invested in CME Group, as well as several other exchanges. In fact, with 33 memberships to its name, Caledonia was the third-largest seat holder at the Chicago Board Options Exchange—on top of owning 103 exercise rights. Between the 80,000 pre-IPO shares that each of its seats translated into, and the mix of cash and stock Caledonia received as part of the ERP settlement, the Australian investors enjoyed a spectacular and well-deserved $159 million windfall when CBOE finally went public in June 2010.

Notes

Chapter 1   Welcome to the Jungle

page 11   *Not only did their seats translate*   Ann Saphir, "Little Discontent Over Deal at CBOT Meeting," *Crain's Chicago Business*, May 1, 2007.

page 12   *The Chicago Mercantile Exchange*   Galen Burghardt, "Off the Charts: Futures Volume Soars to Record Highs,"   Global Futures and Options Volume chart, *Futures Industry Magazine*, January/February 2002.

page 12   *The fact was that electronic trading*   CBOT 2005 Annual Report, 7.

Chapter 2   Into the Groove

page 20   *So even though CBOT*   CBOT 2006 Annual Report, 27.

page 27   *Bernie was asked to serve*   "CBOT Announces Appointment of David Vitale as President and Chief Executive Officer," *Korn/Ferry International Press Release*, February 22, 2001.

Chapter 3   This Is How We Do It

page 31   *Unlike stocks, which can be*   Larry Harris, "Breaking the Futures Monopoly," *Forbes.com*, November 6, 2006, www.forbes.com/2006/11/03/options-monopoly- cboe-cme-oped-cx_lh_1106options.html.

page 31   *CBOT's metals contracts were scandalous*   Gail Osten, "Grabbing the Golden Mouse by the Tail: Precious Metals Jump onto the Screen in Chicago," *SFO Magazine*, October 2004.

page 31   *Indeed, when asked about CBOT's apparent*   Daniel P. Collins, "Is NYMEX Game for a Fight?" *Futures Magazine*, November 2004.

page 32   *Within 14 months, however*   CBOT 2005 Annual Report, 9.

page 32   *By the time I arrived at the exchange*   CBOT 2006 Annual Report, 6.

page 32 *When CBOT launched its competing contracts* "Second City Targets Big Apple," *Futures Magazine*, September 2004.

page 33 *In other words, the open interest level* Keystone Marketing Services, "Understanding Volume and Open Interest in Commodity Futures," http://tfc-charts .w2d.com/learning/volume_open_interest.html.

page 36 *Limits for Corn futures* Fred Seamon, "Speculative Position Limits and Hedge Exemptions," CME Group Research and Product Development White Paper.

page 36 *Six hundred contracts represented* "Major Crops Grown in the United States," U.S. Environmental Protection Agency web site, www.epa.gov/ oecaagct/ag101/cropmajor.html.

page 42 *To satisfy the stream of curious tourists* David Roeder, "A Far Cry from the Pits," *Chicago Sun-Times*, February 1, 2007.

page 43 *Margin amounts varied by the risk* *The Chicago Board of Trade Handbook of Futures and Options* (New York: McGraw-Hill, 2006), 19; Todd Lofton, *Getting Started in Futures*, 5th ed. (Hoboken, NJ: John Wiley & Sons, 2005), 32.

Chapter 4 Don't Speak

page 51 *Leo was infamous for having* Emily Lambert, "Up from the Pits," *Forbes*, January 28, 2008.

page 51 *After the CME/CBOT merger* Aaron Lucchetti and Susan Carey, "Two Men—Soft-Spoken CEO and an Exchange Veteran—Savor Chicago Merc's Triumph," *Wall Street Journal*, October 19, 2006.

page 52 *By 2006, the system had been upgraded* 2006 Globex statistics provided by CME Group, May 7, 2010.

page 53 *A photo of a two-by-four* Leo Melamed with Bob Tamarkin, *Escape to the Futures* (New York: John Wiley & Sons, 1996), 154.

page 53 *More recently, rumor had it* Jeremy Grant and Doug Cameron, "Pugilists from the Pits," *Financial Times*, October 20, 2006.

page 54 *Its trading volumes, led by* Galen Burghardt, "Off the Charts: Futures Volume Soars to Record Highs," Global Futures and Options Volume chart, *Futures Industry Magazine*, January/February 2002.

page 55 *Later we would learn that* David Roeder, "Where the Wooing Went Down," *Chicago Sun-Times*, November 2, 2006.

page 55 *Good evening, gentlemen.* Ibid.

page 56 *CME's board meeting was planned* "Donohue, Dan See Opportunity in CME-CBOT Pact," *Bloomberg News* (transcript), October 17, 2006.

Chapter 5 Wanna Be Startin' Somethin'

page 60 *There were also stories* Julie Johnsson, "Board of Trade CEO Stands to Collect Millions in Merger," *Chicago Tribune*, October 18, 2006.

page 60 *. . . to how cafes near the CME* Susan Chandler, "Eateries Fear Flight of the 'Yellow Jackets,'" *Chicago Tribune*, October 18, 2006.

page 61 *That's where he met Terry Duffy* Emily Lambert, "Up from the Pits," *Forbes*, January 28, 2008.

page 62 *Case in point: Chicago Mayor* Jeremy Grant and Doug Cameron, "Pugilists from the Pits," *Financial Times*, October 20, 2006.

page 67 *What's more, the small, Atlanta-based* Steven Smith, "ICE vs. NYMEX Battle Heats Up," RealMoney from TheStreet.com, February 6, 2006.

page 67 *The one we saw the most was* Doug Cameron and Kevin Morrison, "CME Grapples with Possible Metals Conflict," *Financial Times*, October 18, 2006.

page 72 *Although CME Group would control* "Making the Future—Financial Exchanges," Economist.com, May 25, 2007.

page 72 *He thanked the lawyer* Interview with Jeff Sprecher, March 22, 2010.

Chapter 6 Dirty Laundry

page 74 *Born in Malaysia and a citizen* David Roeder, "How Will These Guys Fit the Merc Here?" *Chicago Sun-Times*, October 25, 2006.

page 75 *In fact, even Leo thought of Gill* Leo Melamed, *For Crying Out Loud: From Open Outcry to the Electronic Screen* (Hoboken, NJ: John Wiley & Sons, 2009), 68.

page 75 *Within a year, he'd left CBOE* Ibid.

page 75 *In 2006, CME's clearing house* Clearing homepage on CMEGroup.com, http://www.cmegroup.com/clearing/index.html (accessed July 6, 2010).

page 75 *. . . settled 2.1 billion transactions* CME 2006 Annual Report, 18.

page 75 *The agreement made CME Clearing* CBOT Chairman's Letter to Members, January 16, 2004.

page 75 *Further, if customers' positions* Bryan Durkin and Edward Gogol, "The CBOT-CME Common Clearing Link," *Futures Industry Magazine*, May/June 2003.

page 75 *The CCL deal and others like it* CME 2006 Annual Report, 8.

page 77 *What makes the OTC market attractive* "Over the Counter, Out of Sight," *Economist*, November 12, 2009.

page 78 *At the closing bell* Derived from information in *The Chicago Board of Trade Handbook of Futures and Options* (New York: McGraw-Hill, 2006), 145.

page 78   *The lack of price transparency*   Bank for International Settlements, "OTC Derivatives Market Activity in the Second Half of 2006," May 2007, 7.

page 78   *—which might not be so worrisome*   Central Intelligence Agency, *The World Factbook 2006*, "Economy" section, www.cia.gov/ library/publications/ the-world-factbook/.

page 79   *Under the Bush administration*   Matthew Leising, "U.S. May Reject Chicago Merger, Former Official Says," *Bloomberg News*, March 22, 2007.

page 79   *When the ex-chairman caught wind*   Melamed, *For Crying Out Loud*, "Cabal" chapter.

page 79   *The story told to the media*   Aaron Lucchetti and Susan Carey, "Two Men—Soft-Spoken CEO and an Exchange Veteran—Savor Chicago Merc's Triumph," *Wall Street Journal*, October 19, 2006.

page 79   *The story told to the media*   Ann Saphir, "Ex-CEO Is Back to Haunt CME," *Crain's Chicago Business*, June 29, 2009.

page 80   *But since CME's stock fell nearly*   Meredith Derby, "Chicago Merc Shares Drop on CEO News," TheStreet.com, August 19, 2003.

page 80   *He had planned to become*   Ann Saphir, "Merc's Power Couple Faces Stress Test," *Crain's Chicago Business*, October 23, 2006; Emily Lambert, "Up from the Pits," *Forbes*, January 28, 2008.

page 80   *He went on to earn not one*   Melamed, *For Crying Out Loud*, 96.

page 80   *After a short stint at the law*   CME Group Management Bios, CMEGroup .com, http://investor.cmegroup.com/investor-relations/management.cfm? bioID= 7652 (accessed July 6, 2010).

page 80   *Craig's background didn't exactly make*   Emily Lambert, "Up from the Pits," *Forbes*, January 28, 2008.

page 80   *He was also a complete workaholic*   Abbie Hansen, "Playing Center Court," *Drake Blue*, the magazine of Drake University, Spring 2008.

page 80   *I'd never seen his Bentley convertible*   Ann Saphir, "Crunch Time at CME," *Crain's Chicago Business*, November 1, 2008.

page 82   *Operations Sourmash and Hedgeclipper*   Bob Tamarkin, *The Merc: The Emergence of a Global Financial Powerhouse* (New York: Harper Business, 1993), 355.

page 82   *Forty-six indictments*   Federal Bureau of Investigation, Chicago Division web site, http://chicago.fbi.gov/history.htm (accessed July 6, 2010).

page 83   *Three out of twelve*   Arlene Michlin Bronstein, *My Word Is My Bond: Voices from Inside the Chicago Board of Trade* (Hoboken, NJ: John Wiley & Sons, 2008), 10.

page 86   *The situation had turned so hostile*   Aaron Lucchetti, "CBOE Finds Knock on IPO Door," *Wall Street Journal*, January 17, 2007.

page 87 *The personnel moves underscore the fact* Ann Saphir, "Merc–CBOT Lay Out Post-Merger Exec Team," *Crain's Chicago Business*, January 24, 2007.

Chapter 7 Under Pressure

page 92 *CBOT fined its traders as well* Ann Saphir, "What Rules Will Rule?" *Crain's Chicago Business*, November 13 2006.

page 95 *Craig Donohue had continued to make* Jesse Thomas, "NYMEX CEO Sees Solid CME Deal on Energy, Metals Listings," *Dow Jones Newswires*, February 6, 2007.

page 95 *Then there was the matter* Ann Saphir, "Little Future in Gold," *Crain's Chicago Business*, February 5, 2007.

page 97 *FIA acknowledges that the merger* "FIA Statement on the Proposed CME–CBOT merger," FIA web site, February 16, 2007, www.futuresindustry .org/press-center.asp?i=1146 (accessed July 6, 2010).

page 97 *Craig Donohue retorted that the FIA* David Roeder, "Making the Case for Merger," *Chicago Sun-Times*, March 7, 2007.

page 97 *We have a lot of support from . . .* Doug Cameron, "CME Accuses Banks of Inflated Profits," *Financial Times*, March 14, 2007.

page 97 *We understand where opponents . . .* Ibid.

page 97 *Quotes such as "Acquirers tend to favor . . .* Joann S. Lublin, "Do You Cut and Run or Stay in Your Job After an Acquisition?" *Wall Street Journal*, March 6, 2007.

page 99 *Its trading volumes were a fraction* Aaron Lucchetti, "Newcomer ICE, Chicago Merc Try to Sell Rival Bids to CBOT," *Wall Street Journal*, March 21, 2007.

Chapter 8 ICE ICE Baby

page 102 *CME leaders planned to host* Ann Saphir, "CME Trying to Build Support for CBOT Acquisition," *Crain's Chicago Business*, March 14, 2007.

page 103 *Our valued customers, who will also* "CME and CBOT Announce New Timelines for Electronic and Floor Trading Migrations Post Merger Close," CBOT and CME joint press release, March 14, 2007.

page 105 *You gotta do what you gotta do,* Aaron Lucchetti and Bernard Wysocki Jr., "Futures Fight: Upstart Makes a Play for the CBOT," *Wall Street Journal*, March 16, 2007.

page 108 *It's a very bold move.* Nandini Sukumar and Elizabeth Stanton, Matthew Leising, Edgar Ortega, and Dan Lonkevich, "IntercontinentalExchange Bids $9.9 Billion for CBOT," *Bloomberg News*, March 15, 2007.

page 110 *The go-go 1980s were in full swing* Danielle L. Scott, "Leveraging Opportunities in the Current Economic Climate: Audio Interview with Jeff Sprecher, ICE Chairman and Founder," *Graziadio Business Report* 12, no. 2 (2009).

page 115 *Or will you work with my colleagues* "ICE – IntercontinentalExchange Proposes to Merge with Chicago Board of Trade," Thomson StreetEvents transcript of the March 15, 2007 call, filed with the SEC by ICE, Commission File No. 001-32650.

page 116 *Since John Thain, CEO of the* "For Thain, Much Left to Do," *Bloomberg News*, March 9, 2007.

page 116 *It's clear the Board of Trade . . .* Ann Saphir, "'You've Got a Bidding War Now' for CBOT," *Crain's Chicago Business*, March 15, 2007.

Chapter 9   War

page 117 *But since analysts, reporters, and the* Darrell Hassler and Bruce Blythe, "Traders Put Cash Over Chicago Loyalty with New Bid for Exchange," Bloomberg.com, March 19, 2007.

page 118 *CBOT's volumes, which were cleared* James P. Miller and *Bloomberg News*, "Merc Calls ICE Bid 'Inferior,'" *Chicago Tribune*, March 21, 2007.

page 118 *. . . For people to raise issues as if . . .* Daniel P. Collins, "ICE Proposal Moves Forward—an Interview with Jeff Sprecher," *Futures Magazine*, March 20, 2007.

page 118 *. . . While it is easy to throw out . . .* Ibid.

page 118 *. . . Both would have the ability . . .* Jim Kharouf, "Users Weigh Best Deal for CBOT," *FOWeek*, March 26, 2007.

page 119 *CBOT's board had asked Jeff* Ann Saphir, "ICE's Sprecher Outlines Plans," *Crain's Chicago Business*, March 21, 2007.

page 119 *But that sit-down had yet* "CBOT Holdings' Board of Directors Authorizes Discussions with IntercontinentalExchange, Inc.," CBOT press release, March 19, 2007.

page 119 *Considering ICE's significantly higher* Susan Diesenhouse, "ICE Head Wondering: Where's Red Carpet?" *Chicago Tribune*, March 22, 2007.

page 119 *The media picked up on a note* Ann Saphir, "CME Can Afford to Outbid ICE by Big Margin: Analyst," *Crain's Chicago Business*, March 20, 2007.

page 119 *Next, CBOT sent another press release* "Chicago Board of Trade Postpones Special Meeting for CME Merger," CBOT press release, March 20, 2007.

page 119 *Craig Donohue told reporters* Dave Carpenter, "Merc Fires Back at 'Significantly Weaker' Offer for CBOT," *Chicago Sun-Times*, March 21, 2007.

page 119   *The CME rhetoric will not fool . . .*   Anuj Gangahar and Doug Cameron, "CBOT's Market Value Soars as Suitors Trade Blows," *Financial Times*, March 21, 2007.

page 119   *This war of words between their suitors*   Ibid.

page 119   *. . . and ICE's offer stood to put*   Ann Saphir, "CBOT Torn over Rival Offers," *Crain's Chicago Business*, March 26, 2007.

page 120   *Beginning in late April, traders could*   Ann Saphir, "Who Will Get CBOT? Exchange to Offer Contracts to Bet," *Crain's Chicago Business*, March 22, 2007; Howard Packowitz, "New Exchange to List Futures on CBOT Merger Battle," *Dow Jones Newswires*, March 23, 2007.

page 121   *We have a 109-year history . . .*   Peter Robison and Otis Bilodeau, "Refco, Name Tarnished, Has 'Several Days' to Fight for Survival," *Bloomberg News*, October 14, 2005.

page 121   *Two hundred fifty members gathered*   Ann Saphir, "CBOT Torn over Rival Offers," *Crain's Chicago Business*, March 26, 2007.

page 122   *CBOT had filed a brief*   Jim Kharouf, "CBOT Fires Latest Rounds in Exercise Rights Battle," *FOWeek*, March 9, 2007.

page 124   *He ended by assuring the Merc's executives*   Ann Saphir, "CBOT Members Call on CME to Raise Bid," *Crain's Chicago Business*, March 22, 2007; Susan Diesenhouse, "CBOT Icy Toward Merc Bid," *Chicago Tribune*, March 23, 2007; David Roeder, "Show 'em," *Chicago Sun-Times*, March 23, 2007.

page 124   *With that, he placed his hand*   Interview with Steve Fanady, April 20, 2010.

page 125   *Gill was overheard saying*   Doug Cameron, "Plenty of Life Left in Exchanges Battle," *Financial Times*, March 29, 2007.

page 126   *Across the street, James von Moltke was*   Emily Lambert, "Up from the Pits," *Forbes*, January 28, 2008.

page 127   *As in, in 2006, no public U.S. stock*   Aaron Lucchetti, "Shareholder Scorecard—A Closer Look: Inside the Leaders and Laggards," *Wall Street Journal*, February 26, 2007.

page 131   *At the time of Jeff's analyst call*   CME 2006 Annual Report, 28.

Chapter 10   Suspicious Minds

page 133   *One trader phrased it another way*   Doug Cameron, "Plenty of Life Left in Exchanges Battle," *Financial Times*, March 29, 2007.

page 135   *The lower price of the e-minis*   Jim Kharouf, "CBOT Mini Ags to Go Electronic," *FOWeek*, April 9, 2007.

page 135   *In order to appease members*   "CBOT Announces May 14 e-cbot Launch Date for Mini-Sized Ag Contracts," CBOT press release, April 12, 2007.

page 136   *After business hours, Maria's team*   "Chicago Board of Trade Reschedules Special Meetings; Board of Directors' Review of ICE Proposal Continues," CBOT press release, April 11, 2007.

page 137   *The report indicated that the anonymous*   STNG Wire Reports, "L.A. Bomb Threat Sends Police to CBOT, Merc," *Chicago Sun-Times*, April 12, 2007.

page 141   *In response to a* Wall Street Journal   "The Future of Futures," *Wall Street Journal*, April 11, 2007.

page 141   *His response to the* WSJ   John Damgard, "CME/CBOT Merger Would Kill Competition," *The Wall Street Journal*, April 18, 2007.

page 141   *As the FIA's membership base*   FIA web site, www.futuresindustry.org /about-fia-.asp (accessed July 7, 2010).

page 142   *This was by no means the first*   Marcus Baram, "Government Sachs: Goldman's Close Ties to Washington Arouse Envy, Raise Questions," *Huffington Post*, June 2, 2009, www.huffingtonpost.com/2009/06/02/government-sachs-goldmans_n_210561.html.

page 142   *They quoted University of Maryland*   Susan Diesenhouse, "N.Y. Banks Back ICE in Futures Power Play," *Chicago Tribune*, April 10, 2007.

page 142   *He believed the Wall Street*   FIA web site, www.futuresindustry.org /board-members.asp (accessed July 7, 2010).

page 142   . . . *The organization has its roots* . . .   Russell Wasendorf Sr. and Jim Kharouf and SFO editorial staff, "Kings in the Corners," *SFO Magazine*, April 2007.

page 142   *But it's still to me more like*   Interview with Chris Hehmeyer, March 26, 2010.

page 143   . . . *It is a magnet for traders* . . .   John Lothian, *John Lothian Newsletter*, April 10, 2007.

page 143   *What the bankers fear* . . .   John Lothian, "Lead Commentary: Innovation and Competition Story Lost amid Chicago-NY Struggle for Supremacy Hooey," *John Lothian Newsletter*, April 11, 2007.

page 143   *In his view, for the Wall Streeters*   Interview with Chris Allen, Ticonderoga Securities, March 26, 2010.

page 144   *He also claimed that about*   Loren Fox, "Today Chicago, Tomorrow . . . " *Institutional Investor*, March 2007.

page 146   *The Merc's shares slipped 3 percent*   Ros Krasny, "CME Q1 Profit Up, Shares Slip on Early Q2 Trends," *Reuters*, April 25, 2007.

page 146   *His peer Edward Ditmire*   Jesse Thomas, "Longer CME/CBOT Timeline Could Open Door to New Bidders," *Dow Jones Newswires*, April 16, 2007.

page 146   *As Bryan Hynes, an associate CBOT member, told*   Ibid.

Chapter 11   Land of Confusion

page 147   *What had been a $1 billion*   Aaron Lucchetti, Edward Taylor, and Alistair MacDonald, "CBOT Weighs Options," *Wall Street Journal*, May 11, 2007.

page 147   *There's a hometown discount . . .*   Ann Saphir, "ICE's CBOT Bid Now $2 Bil. More Than Merc's," *Crain's Chicago Business*, May 8, 2007.

page 148   *As part of its sweetened bid*   "CME and CBOT Revise Terms of Merger Agreement," CME and CBOT joint press release, May 11, 2007.

page 148   *CME's stock had been trading*   Matthew Leising and Edgar Ortega, "Chicago Merc Agrees to Pay More for Board of Trade," *Bloomberg News*, May 11, 2007.

page 149   *Buybacks like this usually came*   Laurie Kulikowski, "Buyback Seals CBOT Deal," TheStreet.com, May 11, 2007.

page 149   *When this tender offer was factored*   Ann Saphir, "New CME Offer Unlikely to Win Over CBOT Owners," *Crain's Chicago Business*, May 11, 2007.

page 149   *ICE's offer valued CBOT*   Ibid.

page 149   *ICE's offer valued CBOT*   "Before the Bell—CBOT Jumped on Sweetened CME Offer," *Reuters*, May 11, 2007.

page 149   *What they've done is readjust . . .*   Jesse Thomas, "Some CBOT Holders Say New CME Bid Not Enough to Earn Vote," *Dow Jones Newswires*, May 11, 2007.

page 149   *. . . As for me, this new*   Ann Saphir, "New CME Offer Unlikely to Win Over CBOT Owners," *Crain's Chicago Business*, May 11, 2007.

page 149   *He also couldn't help but add*   Ibid.

page 149   *. . . That's called fuzzy math . . .*   David Roeder, "Merc Bid Draws Backlash," *Chicago Sun-Times*, May 14, 2007.

page 149   *. . . That's called fuzzy math . . .*   Matthew Leising and Edgar Ortega, "Chicago Merc Agrees to Pay More for Board of Trade," *Bloomberg News*, May 11, 2007.

page 150   *His take on the Merc's tender offer*   Interview with Burt Gutterman, April 7, 2010; Roeder, "Merc Bid Draws Backlash."

page 150   *. . . The CME is and has been . . .*   John Lothian, "Thoughts on the CME's New Bid for the CBOT," *John Lothian Newsletter*, May 11, 2007.

page 150   *The problem for CBOT shareholders*   Ibid.

page 157   *On top of that statement*   Howard Packowitz, "CBOT Steps Up Efforts to Secure CME Merger Deal," *Dow Jones Newswires*, May 24, 2007.

page 157   *What's more, word broke that ICE*   Doug Cameron and Norma Cohen, "ICE Steps Up CBOT Takeover Bid," *Financial Times*, May 24, 2007.

page 158   *For an exchange that has championed*   Doug Cameron, "ICE Gears Up to Resume Battle for CBOT," *Financial Times*, May 25, 2007.

page 158   *The media jumped all over*   Robert Manor, "CBOT Reaffirms It Prefers Merc Bid," *Chicago Tribune*, May 29, 2007.

page 159   *ICE had refused these requests*   Doug Cameron, "CBOT Directors Asked ICE to Sweeten Bid," *Financial Times*, May 29, 2007.

Chapter 12   Fight for Your Right

page 161   *ICE and CBOE Enter Exclusive . . .*   "ICE and CBOE Enter Exclusive Agreement Regarding CBOE Exercise Rights as Part of ICE's Proposed Merger with CBOT; Agree in Principal on Commercial Partnership," ICE press release, May 30, 2007.

page 161   *He felt the Merc's proposal*   Christina Maria Paschyn, "Analysts Say CME Stock Will Soar," *Medill Reports Chicago*, January 24, 2007.

page 162   *. . . We believe this agreement enhances . . .*   "ICE and CBOE Enter Exclusive Agreement," ICE press release.

page 163   *This puts IntercontinentalExchange . . .*   Matthew Leising, "Intercontinental Gets CBOE Deal, Bolstering CBOT Bid," *Bloomberg News*, May 30, 2007.

page 163   *It certainly gives Mr. Sprecher . . .*   Ann Saphir, "ICE 'Winning Votes' with CBOT Members Over New Plan," *Crain's Chicago Business*, May 30, 2007.

page 163   *Serious questions were raised in my mind . . .*   John Lothian, "ICE–CBOE Deal: Sprecher Shows Leadership," *John Lothian Newsletter*, May 30, 2007.

page 164   *When the designated time arrived*   Jesse Thomas and Howard Packowitz, "ICE CEO Finds Support for Merger from CBOT Members," *Dow Jones Newswires*, June 1, 2007.

page 164   *Countless others were watching*   "ICE Urges CBOT Members to Support Its Offer," *Reuters*, May 31, 2007.

page 165   *CBOE seats were indeed trading*   Luke Jeffs, "CBOE Seat Hits $2.5m on ICE Accord," *Dow Jones Financial News*, June 1, 2007.

page 166   *It was hard not to feel sorry*   Daniel P. Collins, "ICE/CBOT Meeting: Jeff Sprecher Presents . . . ," *Futures Magazine*, June 2007.

page 166　*All right, thank you, sir,*　"ICE Hosts CBOT Member Meeting," Fair Disclosure Wire transcript, May 31, 2007.

page 167　*If you've got nothing . . .*　Interview with James von Moltke, March 8, 2010.

page 167　*The situation is just so rich . . .*　Interview with Chris Lown, March 9, 2010.

page 167　*He knew some of the men*　Interview with Jeff Sprecher, March 22, 2010.

page 168　*Our entire franchise would be*　CBOT member letter, June 5, 2007.

page 168　*I think it hurts CBOT members* . . .　Matt Leising, "Donohue Says Intercontinental's Plan Would Hurt CBOT," *Bloomberg News*, June 1, 2007.

page 168　*I think it hurts CBOT members* . . .　Jesse Thomas, "CME CEO: Confident Will Complete CBOT Merger Deal," *Dow Jones Newswires*, June 4, 2007.

page 168　*The CME team remained confident*　"Joint Mailing of Proxy Statement/Prospectus for Vote on Merger," Joint CME and CBOT press release, June 6, 2007.

page 168　*I am not going to say . . .*　Matthew Leising and Edgar Ortega, "Sprecher, Brodsky Say Further Talks on CBOE Deal Are Possible," *Bloomberg News*, June 8, 2007.

page 168　*For us to get a big position . . .*　Edgar Ortega, "NYSE May Need a Deal to Expand in U.S. Derivatives," *Bloomberg News*, June 6, 2007.

page 168　*Shares of all exchanges*　Gaston F. Ceron, "NYSE Signals Interest in Possible Futures Deal," *MarketWatch*, June 6, 2007.

page 170　*All we knew for sure*　"Statement of the Department of Justice Antitrust Division on Its Decision to Close Its Investigation of Chicago Mercantile Exchange Holding Inc.'s Acquisition of CBOT Holdings Inc.," Department of Justice press release, June 11, 2007.

page 170　*Finally, ICE had reserved*　"ICE Resubmits Merger Proposal to CBOT Board with Enhancements; Intends to File Proxy Statement to Oppose CME Acquisition of CBOT," ICE press release, June 12, 2007.

page 171　*Our offer, in our minds,*　Matthew Leising, "Intercontinental's Sprecher Won't Say Whether CBOT Bid Is Final," *Bloomberg News*, June 13, 2007.

page 171　*Full members would each gross*　Ann Saphir, "Taxman Cometh?" *Crain's Chicago Business*, June 25, 2007.

page 171　*Finally, they offered representation*　"CME and CBOT Revise Merger Agreement to Provide Increased Value to CBOT Shareholders," Joint CME and CBOT press release, June 14, 2007.

page 171   *Craig Donohue's interpretation was*   "CME Beefs Up CBOT Merger Terms for Second Time," *Reuters*, June 15, 2007.

page 171   *. . . It's not a simple question . . .*   "Ahead of the Bell: ICE/CBOT/CME: ICE's 'Enhanced' Offer for CBOT Does Not Overcome Intangible Shareholder Concerns," *Associated Press*, June 13, 2007.

page 172   *Russell Investment Group had never signed*   "ICE Announces Agreement to Acquire Exclusive License for Russell Index Futures Contracts," ICE press release, June 18, 2007.

page 172   *Russell Investment Group had never signed*   Howard Packowitz and Nicholas Hatcher, "ICE Inks Exclusive Rights for Russell Index Futures," *Dow Jones Newswires*, June 19, 2007.

page 172   *Sandler O'Neill analyst Richard*   Aaron Lucchetti, "ICE Hopes the Little Things Matter in CBOT Battle," *Wall Street Journal* Deal Journal, June 19, 2007.

page 172   *Further, the Merc planned to offer*   "CME and S&P Announce New E-mini Small Cap Stock Index Futures Contracts," CME press release, June 19, 2007.

page 173   *The letter ended, "DON'T SELL CBOT . . ."*   "ICE Urges CBOT Stockholders and Members to Reject Sale to CME," ICE press release, June 21, 2007.

page 173   *Later that day—thanks to*   Doug Cameron, "ICE Bid for CBOT Passes $12bn Mark," *Financial Times*, June 21, 2007.

page 174   *On June 22, they announced an agreement*   "ICE Announces Definitive Agreement to Acquire Winnipeg Commodity Exchange," ICE press release, June 22, 2007.

page 174   *The choice is clear: vote . . .*   "Chicago Mercantile Exchange Holdings Inc. Distributes Letter to CBOT Shareholders," Joint CME and CBOT press release, June 22, 2007.

Chapter 13   Down Under

page 178   *He found it, and summarized*   Ann Saphir, "Biggest CBOT Investor Votes Against Merc Deal," *Crain's Chicago Business*, June 27, 2007.

page 182   *But when you met Bernie,*   Interview with Will Vicars, April 8, 2010.

page 188   *No one could deny*   "ICE Sends Letter to CBOT Shareholders," *BusinessWeek*, July 3, 2007.

page 189   *As Ginger Szala, group publisher*   Ginger Szala, "Gold Fever," *Futures Magazine*, May 2007.

page 190   *He went on to declare*   Ann Saphir, "CBOT Will Nix Deal Without More Money: Investor," *Crain's Chicago Business*, July 5, 2007.

page 190 . . . *That creates a lot of confusion.* Ros Krasny and Christine Stebbins, "Plenty of Fireworks to Come in CBOT-CME Merger Push," *Reuters*, July 5, 2007.

Chapter 14 Take the Money and Run

page 192 *In fact, just seven months earlier* Ann Saphir, "Some Big CBOT Investors Oppose Merc Deal," *Crain's Chicago Business*, June 21, 2007.

page 194 *It was one of the rare* Robert Manor, "Merc's 11th-hour Bid Revealed as Desperation," *Chicago Tribune*, July 15, 2007.

page 196 *We have always supported this merger* "CME Sweetens Bid for CBOT Ahead of Vote," *Associated Press*, July 6, 2007.

page 196 *Now it was very close to* Aaron Lucchetti, "Chicago Merc Raises Bid for CBOT Owner," *The Wall Street Journal*, July 7–8, 2007.

page 196 *We believe there's a significant . . .* Ann Saphir, "Higher CME Bid Appears to Lock Up CBOT Vote," *Crain's Chicago Business*, July 6, 2007.

page 197 *The fact that they got . . .* Ibid; Ros Krasny, "CME Buy of CBOT Looks Likely as Shareholders Vote," *Reuters*, July 9, 2007.

page 198 *I think this is an extraordinary . . .* Ann Saphir, "Higher CME Bid Appears to Lock Up CBOT Vote," *Crain's Chicago Business*, July 6, 2007.

page 198 *Meanwhile, increasingly confident statements* Dan Wilchins, Jessica Hall, Christine Stebbins, and Sam Nelson, "CME Boosts Bid, Wins Support from Caledonia," *Reuters*, July 6, 2007.

page 198 *Janella replied that she was* Adam Satariano, "IntercontinentalExchange Won't Increase Bid for CBOT, WSJ Says," *Bloomberg News*, July 8, 2007.

page 198 *As the* Wall Street Journal *pointed out* Dana Cimilluca and Aaron Lucchetti, "For ICE, Victory or Defeat?" *Wall Street Journal* Deal Journal, July 6, 2007.

page 200 *The opulent, exclusive club* Union League Club of Chicago web site, www.ulcc.org/about/ (accessed July 7, 2010).

page 201 *In fact, July 9 would go down* Tim Halbach, "2007 Climate Summary for Chicago," *Climate Focal Point*, National Weather Service Chicago.

page 201 *After all, nearly everyone* David Roeder, "CBOT to Merc: I Do," *Chicago Sun-Times*, July 10, 2007.

page 202 *By 3:45 P.M., a press release* "CME and CBOT Shareholders Approve Merger: Companies Expect to Complete Historic Combination Within Days," Joint CME and CBOT press release, July 9, 2007.

page 202 *This is the greatest trade . . .* Ros Krasny, "CME Buy of CBOT Easily Approved by Shareholders," *Reuters*, July 9, 2007.

page 203   *He divulged that as the vote neared*   David Greising, "With the Battle Won, New Rivals Lining Up," *Chicago Tribune*, July 10, 2007.

page 203   *Terry described the 117 days*   Manor, "Merc's 11th-hour Bid."

page 204   *The future winners in our industry . . .*   "ICE Releases Open Letter to CBOT Holdings Members and Stockholders," ICE press release, July 9, 2007.

page 205   *With a tongue-in-cheek nod*   John Lothian, "Congratulations to the CME Group," *John Lothian Newsletter*, July 13, 2007.

page 206   *It's a special relationship . . .*   Christine Stebbins, "End of an Era as CBOT Merges with Chicago's Merc," *Reuters*, July 10, 2007.

page 206   *Another wheat trader, Jerome Israelov*   "Shareholders Approve Merc's Buyout of CBOT," *Associated Press* and *New York Times*, July 10, 2007.

Epilogue

page 209   *All of CBOT's electronic business*   CME Group press releases: "CBOT Agriculture and Equity Index Products Begin Trading on CME Globex," January 14, 2008, and "CME Group Completes Electronic Trading Integration as CBOT Interest Rate Products Begin Trading on CME Globex," January 28, 2008.

page 209   *By that point, CME Group*   Bloomberg News, "Nymex Shareholders Approve $8.3 Billion Takeover by CME," *New York Times*, August 19, 2008.

page 209   *Eager to avoid another Caledonia-type situation*   Isabelle Clary, "CME Made Deal with Nymex Shareholder," *Pensions & Investments*, March 21, 2008.

page 209   *One NYMEX member waged*   Ann Saphir, "CME's Bid Too Low for Some Nymex Owners," *Crain's Chicago Business*, March 24, 2008.

page 210   *The leader of the dissidents*   Zachery Kouwe, "NYMEX Nerve—Seat Owners Fume over Fat Exchange Bonuses," *New York Post*, January 18, 2006.

page 210   *Craig Donohue knew Bobby*   Heidi N. Moore, "CME-Nymex: Members Go in Like Lions, Out Like Lambs," *Wall Street Journal* Deal Journal, August 15, 2008.

page 210   *With the addition of NYMEX's metals*   Tim Cave, "NYSE Euronext Adds to Clearing Venture Team," *Financial News*, May 28, 2010.

page 210   *Yet the hedge fund was allowed*   United States Senate Permanent Subcommittee on Investigations Staff Report, "Excessive Speculation in the Natural Gas Market."

page 210   *Eventually NYMEX turned up*   Mark Jickling, "The Enron Loophole,"
CRS Report for Congress, July 7, 2008.

page 210   *This controversial exemption*   James Ridgeway, "Phil Gramm's Enron
Favor," *Village Voice*, January 15, 2002.

page 211   *ICE, however, did not*   Testimony of Jeffrey C. Sprecher Before the
Senate Permanent Subcommittee on Investigations, Committee on Home-
land Security and Governmental Affairs, July 9, 2007. Asjylyn Loder,
"CFTC Shuts 'Enron Loophole' for Gas, Limits ICE Swaps," Bloomberg
.com, July 27, 2009. Chris Baltimore, "ICE Agrees to Position Limits on
WTI Contract: CFTC," *Reuters*, June 17, 2008.

page 211   *In 2008, as oil prices skyrocketed to $147*   Garry   White,   "Will   Oil
Prices Recover After Tanking in 2008?" Telegraph.co.uk, December 29, 2008.

page 211   *Several reports ended up concluding*   Ibid. Daniel P. Collins, "Speculative
Position Limits: How Hard Will They Be?" *Futures Magazine*, March 4, 2010.

page 211   *Data also proved that*   Collins, "Speculative Position Limits."

page 212   *In the fall of 2008, ailing insurance company*   Hugh Son, "AIG's Trustees
Shun 'Shadow Board,'" Seek Directors," Bloomberg.com, May 13, 2009.

page 212   *Now the U.S. government*   2002 Berkshire Hathaway shareholder letter, p. 15.

page 212   *The prevailing solution*   Peter A. McKay, "Financial Regulation: The
Faces of the Affected," *Wall Street Journal*, June 7, 2010.

page 212   *He worked with his Morgan Stanley*   Melinda Peer, "ICE Keeps Cool
with Creditex Acquisition," Forbes.com, June 3, 2008.

page 212   *The Clearing Corporation's infrastructure*   "IntercontinentalExchange, The
Clearing Corporation and Nine Major Dealers Announce New Developments
in Global CDS Clearing Solution," ICE press release, October 30, 2008.

page 213   *By the end of April 2010, the ICE subsidiary*   "The   Brighter   Side,"
Economist, April 29, 2010.

page 213   *In addition to pursuing over-the-counter*   Bank for International Settlements,
"OTC Derivatives Market Activity in the Second Half of 2009," May 2010.

page 213   *Since July 2007, in addition to integrating CBOT and NYMEX*   "CME
Group and Dow Jones & Company Launch Joint Venture of Dow Jones
Indexes Business," CME Group press release, March 18, 2010.

page 213   *At the end of July 2009, the Delaware Court*   Ann   Saphir,   "CME-
CBOE Reach $1B Deal," *Crain's Chicago Business*, June 2, 2008. CBOE
proxy statement, April 27, 2010.

page 214   *Its latest triumph was the $600 million purchase*   Steve   Goldstein,   "ICE
Buying Climate Exchange for Over $600 million," *MarketWatch*, April 30, 2010.

page 214   *The first quarter of 2010 was ICE's strongest to date*   Jacob Bunge, "ICE Earnings Jump 40%, Sees a Future in Clearing," *Wall Street Journal*, May 6, 2010; data supplied by ICE.

page 216   *The brokerage had already begun to struggle*   Laura Mandaro, "MF Global Tries to Calm Market After Shares Plunge," *MarketWatch*, March 17, 2008.

page 216   *The firm's share price had dropped*   Tom Bawden, "MF Global Chief Kevin Davis Replaced," *Times Online*, October 29, 2008.

page 216   *While he's very busy overseeing*   "NYSE Euronext to Purchase CME Group Metals Complex," Joint CME Group and NYSE Euronext press release, March 14, 2008.

Glossary

binary option A type of option in which the payoff is structured to be either a fixed amount or nothing at all.

BOTCC The Board of Trade Clearing Corporation. Pronounced "bot-see." The first independent futures clearing house in the United States, established by CBOT members in 1925. Now renamed The Clearing Corporation (CCorp).

cash/spot market A financial market in which financial instruments or actual physical commodities are bought and delivered immediately (as opposed to a futures or options market, where delivery is delayed, or might not ever happen). For example, a farmer sells grain directly to his local grain elevator in the cash market.

CBOE Chicago Board Options Exchange. Pronounced C.B.O.E or "see bo." The world's first and largest options exchange, which spun off from CBOT in 1973.

CBOT Chicago Board of Trade. Pronounced C.B.O.T. or "see bot." The world's first futures exchange, founded in 1848.

CCL Common Clearing Link. A 2004 (pre-merger) arrangement between CME and CBOT that established CME Clearing as CBOT's clearing house, instead of BOTCC.

CFTC Commodity Futures Trading Commission. An independent government agency that regulates the commodity and financial futures and options markets in the United States.

clearing house An entity that clears and settles an exchange's transactions. It stands in between each trade, acting as a buyer to every seller and a seller to every buyer in order to virtually eliminate counterparty credit risk. Clearing houses are responsible for monitoring risk, collecting and maintaining margin funds, reporting data, and handling any defaults.

CME Chicago Mercantile Exchange, or *the Merc*. Pronounced C.M.E. Originally founded as the Chicago Butter and Egg Board in 1898.

convergence The movement of the price of a futures contract toward the price of the underlying commodity in the cash market; this happens as a contract nears its expiration date.

derivatives Financial instruments, such as futures and options, whose values are based upon their underlying assets.

ERP Exercise right privilege. Pronounced E.R.P. or "urp." Special rights given to full CBOT members that allowed them to trade at CBOE. CBOT members believed holding an ERP also entitled them to partial ownership of CBOE, but CBOE members disagreed. CBOT brought a lawsuit against CBOE over this issue in the summer of 2006.

FCM Futures commission merchant. An individual or organization granted clearance by the National Futures Association and CFTC to handle futures contract orders, as well as extend credit to customers. Analogous to a broker.

FIA Futures Industry Association. A Washington, D.C.-based trade association largely composed of FCMs.

FIRDster A member of the Financial Instruments Research and Development group at CBOT, led by Gene Mueller and ultimately managed by Julie Winkler.

futures contract A legally binding agreement to buy or sell a certain asset for a specific price at a predetermined date in the future; traded through an exchange.

hedger A market participant who enters into a futures contract that is equal to, but opposite, his position in the cash (or spot) market in order to protect against losses from unfavorable price fluctuations.

ICE IntercontinentalExchange, based in Atlanta; established in 2000.

margin Also called a *performance bond*. A deposit, required to trade, that is based on a percentage of the notional value of a futures contract. Exchanges set the margin levels for each contract; additional margins are sometimes required by the clearing house and the customer's broker. Margin levels usually range from 2 to 10 percent of a contract's notional value.

marking-to-market The process a clearing house undertakes to zero out customer gains or losses from every contract at the end of each business day (sometimes more than once per day); the amount transferred to or from traders' margin accounts is based on present market values. Marking-to-market enables clearing houses to keep close, frequent tabs on the margin levels of all customer accounts, thereby heading off defaults.

member An individual or company (a *member firm*) that has complied with an exchange's membership requirements in order to receive fee discounts. In most cases, derivatives exchanges were owned and governed by their members prior to going public.

National Futures Association The self-regulatory organization for the U.S. futures industry.

notional value   The underlying value of a derivatives contract, which is never the amount that actually exchanges hands. If Wheat contracts are trading at $6 per bushel and a contract represents 5,000 bushels, then its notional value is $6 × 5,000, or $30,000. However, only a small percentage of that amount will be required for a trader's margin deposit and subsequently added to or subtracted from in the daily marking-to-market process.

NYMEX   New York Mercantile Exchange.

NYSE   New York Stock Exchange. Merged with Euronext in 2007 to form NYSE Euronext.

open outcry   A form of trading involving shouting out bids and offers; takes place in the trading pits on the trading floor of an exchange, rather than through an electronic trading platform.

options contract   A contract that gives its owner the right to either buy or sell a certain asset at a specified price before a designated date. Unlike a futures contract, an options contract does not represent an obligation to buy or sell an asset in the future; it just gives its owner the option to do so.

OTC   Over-the-counter. Refers to trades handled directly between two parties and, until recently, completely outside of exchanges.

pit   An area of the trading floor that is designated for the trading of a specific futures or options contract.

position limit   The maximum number of speculative futures contracts a trader or trading firm is allowed to hold.

price limit   The maximum daily price fluctuation allowed on a given futures contract during any one session.

speculator   A market participant who enters into a futures contract because he thinks he can profit from correctly anticipating price movements, and is willing to take on the financial risk of being wrong.

underlying asset   Also called *the underlying*. The commodity, financial instrument, cash index, or event upon which a contract's value is based.

References

Bronstein, Arlene Michlin. 2008. *My word is my bond: Voices from inside the Chicago Board of Trade.* Hoboken, NJ: John Wiley & Sons.

Collins, Julie, and Mark Melin. 2006. *The Chicago Board of Trade handbook of futures & options.* New York: McGraw-Hill.

Durbin, Michael. 2006. *All about derivatives: The easy way to get started.* New York: McGraw-Hill.

Else, Jon. 2007. *Open outcry* (documentary). California: Direct Cinema Limited.

Greising, David, and Laurie Morse. 1991. *Brokers, bagmen, and moles: Fraud and corruption in the Chicago futures markets.* New York: John Wiley & Sons.

Hull, John C. 2002. *Fundamentals of futures and options markets.* 4th ed. New Jersey: Prentice Hall.

Jaeger, Robert A. 2003. *All about hedge funds: The easy way to get started.* New York: McGraw-Hill.

Keegan, Edward. 2005. *The Chicago Board of Trade building: A building book from the Chicago Architecture Foundation.* California: Pomegranate.

Kilpatrick, Andrew. 2010. *Of permanent value: The story of Warren Buffett; A trilogy.* Alabama: Andy Kilpatrick Publishing Empire.

Lofton, Todd. 2005. *Getting started in futures.* 5th ed. Hoboken, NJ: John Wiley & Sons.

Melamed, Leo, with Bob Tamarkin. 1996. *Escape to the futures.* New York: John Wiley & Sons.

Melamed, Leo. 2009. *For crying out loud: From open outcry to the electronic screen.* Hoboken, NJ: John Wiley & Sons.

Partnoy, Frank. 1999. *F.I.A.S.C.O.: The inside story of a Wall Street trader.* New York: Penguin Books.

Tamarkin, Bob. 1993. *The Merc: The emergence of a global financial powerhouse.* New York: HarperBusiness.

Acknowledgments

By the time I left CME Group in August 2007, I knew I wanted to write a book about the bidding war for CBOT, but struggled with how best to tell the story. My agent, Scott Hoffman at Folio Literary Management, saw the potential for my project and helped me nail down the right content, tone, and narrative structure. I thank him for his sage advice and endless patience during this process. Along those same lines, I must also thank Debby Englander at John Wiley & Sons. As a naïve first-time author, I figured I'd piece this book together from my extensive notes and the teetering stacks of newspaper articles I'd saved for the better part of four years. Debby gently pushed me to tackle the manuscript like a journalist would, and succeeded in getting me over my fear of calling my former co-workers and saying, "Uh, guess what I've been up to . . . wanna chat?"

I truly believed that no one would cooperate, especially since the first half of 2010—when I conducted my interviews—wasn't exactly a serene period in the history of financial markets. The fact that nearly every person I reached out to made time in his or her ridiculously busy schedule to share memories and thoughts with me—on top of agreeing to be on the record—speaks volumes about the passion and pride that exists in the futures industry. And rightly so.

I am forever grateful and indebted to Bernie Dan, Jeff Sprecher, Charlie Carey, Kelly Loeffler, James von Moltke, John Lothian, and Will Vicars (a true international man of intrigue with whom I'd like to switch lives for a day . . . or a month). I thank each of them for their candidness, their enthusiasm for this project, the multiple hours they spent talking to me, and the countless e-mails they replied to. I don't want to imagine how this book would've turned out if they hadn't been involved.

I would also like to thank Terry Duffy, Bill Brodsky, William M. Farrow III, Chris Lown, Burt Gutterman, Chris Hehmeyer, Ray Cahnman, and Russell Wasendorf Sr. for sharing their unique vantage points. Richard Repetto at Sandler O'Neill & Partners and Chris Allen at Ticonderoga Securities provided especially helpful perspectives on the CME/ICE bidding war, and I greatly enjoyed talking to them both. It was also loads of fun to chat with Steve Fanady, who never failed to respond to one of my urgent e-mails or calls with superhero speed.

For any scene in which I had been physically present, I relied on the comprehensive notes I took each night after I returned home from 141 W. Jackson in order to reconstruct conversations and meetings. Beyond dialogue, however, there were several descriptive and situational details I strove to confirm, and the wonderful Julie Winkler, Fred Sturm, Ted Doukas, and Maria Gemskie assisted me in those instances. Another round of thanks goes to Julie—along with Dave Lehman and Jonathan Kronstein—for ensuring that I explained some of the book's tougher concepts correctly.

Others I spoke to or exchanged e-mails with in order to check facts or validate details, and whose help I appreciate tremendously, include Phupinder Gill, Carol Kennedy, Steve Munger, Tom Hammond, Will Acworth, Kevin Lennon, Bob Ray, Dean Payton, Geoffrey Price, Chris Malo, Dennis Flynn, Barb Lorenzen, Janella Kaczanko, Franco Campione, David Mitchell, Allan Schoenberg, Joyce Blau, Julie Gish, Andy Kilpatrick, Mary Porter, and Peter A. McKay. Equally important to the process were the following people, who either put me in touch with those I was hoping to interview, or otherwise took on the daunting task of scheduling meetings: Ellen Paparelli, Charlene Roberts, Sue Reed, Sharon Brazeal, Diana Mauceri, Pat Campbell, and Mike Brodsky. Finally, there were just a few folks who preferred to speak "on background"—meaning that I could use what they said as long as I did so without attribution. They know who they are, and I tip my proverbial hat to them as well.

I heard a lot of amazing (and, more often than not, hilarious) anecdotes while conducting interviews, and regret that I wasn't able to fit all of them in. On that note, there were, of course, dozens of people at CME, CBOT, and ICE—and many other firms—whose names weren't mentioned across these 240-odd pages, but who nonetheless played critical roles in the various events and company histories I covered. I did not leave anyone out intentionally; my belief was that the best book *I* could write was one told through the recollections of those I worked alongside day in and day out—and those who had the most direct influence over what transpired. That being said, I'd still like to thank everyone I met during my time at CBOT. What a remarkable group of people; I am privileged to have been among their ranks.

Supplementing my firsthand account, and my interviews and e-mail volleys with those already mentioned was the top-notch reporting from journalists who follow the exchanges. Aaron Lucchetti at the *Wall Street Journal* and Ann Saphir—formerly of *Crain's Chicago Business* and now at Reuters—were particularly awe-inspiring in their coverage of the bidding war and I bow down before them. Others whose articles I found myself reading and citing most often include David Roeder at the *Chicago Sun-Times*, Matthew Leising and Edgar Ortega at Bloomberg News, Ros Krasny at Reuters, Susan Diesenhouse and Robert Manor at the *Chicago Tribune*, Jeremy Grant at *Financial Times*, Daniel P. Collins at *Futures* magazine, Jesse Thomas and Howard Packowitz at Dow Jones Newswires, and Doug Cameron at Dow Jones Newswires (formerly of *Financial Times*).

After I finished my manuscript, I began working with Kelly O'Connor, Adrianna Johnson, Mary Daniello, and Sharon Polese at John Wiley & Sons. I thank Kelly and Mary for making the editing process as fun and stress-free as possible, and applaud Adrianna, Sharon, and their respective teams for their wonderful marketing ideas. For all different types of advice—legal, procedural, writerly, and otherwise—I am grateful to Min Lee, Chris Bennett, Emily B. Kirsch, Harvard Business School professor emeritus Richard Tedlow, Claire Zulkey, Annie Logue, Jonathan Eig, Zibby Right, Peggy Garry at Folio, and Dr. Michele Miner. I am also incredibly honored that Rick Santelli, Jim Rogers, Harvard Business School professor Max Bazerman, Harvard Business School and Harvard Law School professor Guhan Subramanian, University of Chicago professor Steven Kaplan, Craig Bouchard, Pete Briger, and Harris Brumfield all took the time to read an early draft of my manuscript and provide supportive endorsements.

Now it's time to talk about my magnificent friends, who are still my friends despite my dropping off the face of the earth for the past year. I owe a lot to my army of proposal-critiquers who spent hours giving me their honest feedback, and in turn helped me land representation. They are Debra Yurenka, Michelle Kraemer, Kristina and Emmet Gaffney, Mark Graham, Jennifer and Bill Barker, Jason Ciaglo, and Mikie Benedict. A special thanks to Jason Perlioni, who not only provided thoughtful suggestions early on, but also put me in touch with several key people and pointed me in the direction of much-needed articles, transcripts, and reports. Pam O'Neal, my best friend since birth, is due a never-ending supply of frozen mango margaritas for both reviewing my proposal and helping to keep me sane from that point forward. Ah, who am I kidding? Pam's kept me sane my entire life. Susie Grabowski, a dear friend since 1982, also deserves a huge thank-you for the conversation that sparked a fire within me and made me realize it was time for a career change.

Jason Chernoff is another great friend who read chapter drafts; served as a living, breathing *Chicago Manual of Style*; came up with the idea for the chapter titles; and didn't get *too* annoyed at my many "How does THIS sound?" e-mails. I'm hoping he'll accept large amounts of Belgian beer for his troubles.

I'm also enormously indebted to Craig Grabiner. Craig worked with me at JPMorgan, joined CBOT seven months before I did, and then helped fast-track my interviews there. So this book literally would not have been written if it weren't for him. Besides helping me get my foot in the door at the exchange, he has never wavered in his support for all of my writing endeavors and can always be counted on to lift my spirits.

I also must recognize Cory Hansen, who braved the heat (and Loop traffic) in order to shoot my cover-flap and web site photographs, in addition to graciously taking on the challenge of creating my "book trailer" video. He is one talented—and extremely, extremely patient—guy.

An underground hatch stocked with Dharma Beer is being constructed for Andy Page at DarkUFO/Spoiler TV, and a super-size popcorn bucket brimming with gratitude is being readied for both Elizabeth Arnold and Elizabeth Powers-Charest at Redbox. These three have given my TV and movie-centric musings enviable exposure over the past few years; most writers can only dream of such opportunities. I would be remiss if I didn't also mention my Redbox co-blogger Locke Peterseim, film critic extraordinaire, who picked up my slack as I neared my manuscript deadline, and whose way with the written word constantly blows my mind. While we're on the subject of my blog-based work, I must give a shout-out to everyone who has ever sent me a comment or e-mail with positive things to say about my writing. Such feedback had a profound effect on me, because it came from people who took the time to share their thoughts despite the fact that we've never met. I would've given up on this career by now if it weren't for their encouragement.

Three of my writer heroes provided much inspiration for this particular project, so I'd also like to thank Michael Lewis, whose *Liar's Poker* is the be-all and end-all in financial services–based nonfiction narratives; and Damon Lindelof and Carlton Cuse of the TV series *Lost*, whose work motivated me to start writing again for the first time in years. "Mahalo" to Terry O'Quinn as well, for bringing to life one of the best characters of all time, John Locke. I ask my fellow fans of the show, was my tuning in on September 22, 2004, coincidence or fate?

And now a word about my phenomenal relatives. I'm fortunate to have been born into a very large and very close extended family. My grandparents, aunts, uncles, and cousins—and, for the past decade, my in-laws—have had a positive influence on every aspect of my life, and I hope I've made them proud. My aunt Sue Jones in particular has always been my biggest cheerleader, and my grandma Geraldine Roesner is my favorite person on the planet—and not just because she seems to get a kick out of everything I do. My brother Nick Olson and sister-in-law Jill Boezwinkle have been indispensable during this process and I'll never be able to repay them (but I will try). My parents, Nels and Kathy Olson, were the only ones besides my husband to have read my manuscript from beginning to end before I turned it in, and I'm beyond thankful for their time and support. I know how lucky and blessed I am to have parents who've always been confident that I would achieve any goal I set for myself. But really, where would I be if I didn't have my mom's "safety rules" and my dad's common sense to fall back on?

Finally, I am beholden to my black Lab Shaddy for ensuring I got at least 10 minutes of fresh air each day, and to my husband Dustin Weinberger, for more than I could ever express in writing. He transcribed nearly all of my interviews, read and provided feedback on the entire book several times over, leveled with me when I wanted to take the easy way out of certain sections, and provided moral support 24/7. He didn't even say anything about the fact that our kitchen table (a.k.a. my desk) disappeared long ago under mounds of printouts, or that the rest of our condo looks like a whirling dervish took up residence. And so I have no choice but to admit once and for all that he is more than deserving of that Eddie Van Halen guitar replica he convinced me he "needed."

E. S. O.

About the Author

Erika S. Olson earned her BBA from the University of Michigan Ross School of Business and her MBA from Harvard Business School. She spent more than 10 years working in and consulting to the financial services industry before embarking on a freelance writing career at the close of the CME/CBOT merger. Erika lives in Chicago with her husband and their black Lab, and enjoys traveling whenever she gets the chance. Though she has been fortunate enough to visit all seven continents, she still considers the Windy City her favorite place on earth—and the trading floor at 141 W. Jackson remains one of the most breathtaking spectacles she's ever seen.

Index